MUSLIM COMICS AND WARSCAPE WITNESSING

STUDIES IN COMICS AND CARTOONS
Jared Gardner, Charles Hatfield, and Rebecca Wanzo, Series Editors

MUSLIM COMICS AND WARSCAPE WITNESSING

Esra Mirze Santesso

THE OHIO STATE UNIVERSITY PRESS
COLUMBUS

Copyright © 2023 by The Ohio State University.
All rights reserved.

The various characters, logos, and other trademarks appearing in this book are the property of their respective owners and are presented here strictly for scholarly analysis. No infringement is intended or should be implied.

Library of Congress Cataloging-in-Publication data available online at https://catalog.loc.gov
LCCN: 2023017338
Identifiers: ISBN 978-0-8142-1541-8 (hardback); ISBN 978-0-8142-5884-2 (paperback); ISBN 978-0-8142-8312-7 (ebook)

Cover design by Sarah Flood-Baumann
Text composition by Stuart Rodriguez
Type set in Palatino

CONTENTS

List of Illustrations		vii
Preface	Muslims in Comics	ix
Acknowledgments		xv
INTRODUCTION	Defining Muslim Comics and Warscapes	1
CHAPTER 1	The Politics and Aesthetics of Muslim Comics	23
CHAPTER 2	Reluctant Witnesses in Prison Camp Narratives	62
CHAPTER 3	Vulnerability, Resistance, and False Witnesses	90
CHAPTER 4	*Shaheed* and Border Witnesses	115
CHAPTER 5	Surrogate Witnesses and Memory	144
CONCLUSION	The Future of Muslim Comics	172
Works Cited		179
Index		193

ILLUSTRATIONS

FIGURE 0.1	Opening page of Malik Sajad's *Munnu*	2
FIGURE 0.2	Diagram of the family's home in Zeina Abirached's *A Game for Swallows*	7
FIGURE 0.3	The making of za'atar in Leila Abdelrazaq's *Baddawi*	10
FIGURE 1.1	Joker's speech in *Batman: A Death in the Family*	29
FIGURE 1.2	The cover of *Kismet*	31
FIGURE 1.3	Dodola lying on a couch in Craig Thompson's *Habibi*	33
FIGURE 1.4	*New X-Men* #133 featuring Dust on the cover	42
FIGURE 1.5	Mugshots of terrorists in Toufic El Rassi's *Arab in America*	53
FIGURE 1.6	A panel from Soufeina Hamed's comics	59
FIGURE 1.7	A panel from Norédine Allam's *Muslim Show*	59
FIGURE 2.1	Two characters walking among the cages in Jay Cantor, James Romberger, and Jose Villarrubia's *Aaron & Ahmed*	72
FIGURE 2.2	Illustration of Moazzam Begg in Sarah Mirk's *Guantanamo Voices*	82
FIGURE 2.3	Mohammed explains the methods of torture in Jérôme Tubiana and Alexandre Franc's *Guantánamo Kid*	86

FIGURE 3.1	Marjane Satrapi's *Persepolis* shows a family member being tortured	94
FIGURE 3.2	Two-page illustration of the protestors in Amir and Khalil's *Zahra's Paradise*	98
FIGURE 3.3	A symbolic representation of Mana's guilt in Mana Neyestani's *An Iranian Metamorphosis*	102
FIGURE 3.4	The punitive machinery created by Khomeini and Khamenei appears as all-consuming in Amir and Khalil's *Zahra's Paradise*	105
FIGURE 3.5	Neyestani re-creates Leonardo da Vinci's *The Last Supper* in Mana Neyestani's *An Iranian Metamorphosis*	112
FIGURE 4.1	Mushtaq praying in Naseer Ahmed and Saurabh Singh's *Kashmir Pending*	120
FIGURE 4.2	The training camp in Naseer Ahmed and Saurabh Singh's *Kashmir Pending*	129
FIGURE 4.3	An illustration of Mustafa's funeral in Malik Sajad's *Munnu*	131
FIGURE 5.1	"The Cluster Bombs" in Leila Abdelrazaq's *Baddawi*	153
FIGURE 5.2	Ahmad's nightmare in Leila Abdelrazaq's *Baddawi*	156
FIGURE 5.3	A Palestinian boy with a weapon in Ari Folman's *Waltz with Bashir*	161
FIGURE 5.4	Soldiers looking with binoculars in Ari Folman's *Waltz with Bashir*	162
FIGURE 6.1	Illustrator Matt Stefani's drawing of Kamala Khan punching President Trump	175
FIGURE 6.2	Billboards in Iran reading "Zahra for President—Iran 2013"	178

PREFACE

Muslims in Comics

When I assigned Marjane Satrapi's *Persepolis* in my upper-division course on literature and human rights in 2015, I suspected it would be an atypical read for my students, many of whom were not at all familiar with the graphic memoir medium. I was curious about how they would react to reading comics in a literature course that focused on human rights issues—their implementation and violation—across the globe. I was convinced of the benefits of adding a graphic novel. I reasoned that broadening the scope of the reading material would push students to read and analyze differently: Not only would they make connections between different modes of aesthetic and political expression, but they would also develop new skills to interrogate the graphic form's engagement with the complex (and sometimes agonistic) relationship between text and image. I was thinking of what Edward Said stated in his foreword to Joe Sacco's *Palestine*: "I felt that comics freed me to think and imagine and see differently" ("Homage" ii). The visual elements of *Persepolis* would certainly enhance the students' grasp of the Iranian revolution, the glorification of martyrdom during the Iran-Iraq War, and the intensity of Marjane's disorientation abroad. The narrative voice, which imbricates Iranian and female perspectives, would also contribute to a consideration of Muslim female subjectivity. What does it actually mean, for example, to force the Islamic veil on Iranian women, pragmatically speaking? How does this ideological imposition use a visual aesthetic to convey a different type of gender identity? How does the "revolutionary guard" become a state apparatus to ensure "modesty"? And in what way does the street scene change optically as the state regulates and maintains control over the way women are seen? These questions were integral to understanding the "look and feel" of a changing, complex, and internally divided nation that has regularly been stereotyped and vilified as an antithesis to America.

An equally important goal for me was to situate *Persepolis* vis-à-vis the centuries-old Islamic doctrine that banned representational art. Painting, especially Western portraiture, was forbidden in early Muslim societies: The Qur'an explicitly prohibits lifelike illustrations as a gateway to idolatry and blasphemy.[1] In the Islamic tradition, it is especially important to enforce aniconism, the proscription of images depicting God and the Prophet. Across the centuries, these strict measures boosted other forms of visual arts—such as miniature, gilding, calligraphy, and ornamentation, which operated according to completely different sets of conventions that emphasize the symbolic value of the object as opposed to its mimetic depiction on paper. In stark contrast to the "crudeness" of Western art, with its emphasis on originality and verisimilitude, Islamic art aimed at apprehending the non-literal meaning of objects by attempting to emulate (not replicate) Allah's vision. Miniature artists, for example, often adopted an elevated viewpoint—as if looking down from a minaret—and worked collaboratively to illustrate objects based on their personal strengths: One master might be good at drawing coins, while another might have a reputation for sketching horses. Masters refrained from leaving recognizable signs of their individuality in their work: By eliminating personal style and denying ownership of a work, they saw themselves as triumphing over vanity and hubris. In Orhan Pamuk's *My Name Is Red*, which explores the attitudes of miniaturist artists opening up to the West, the head illustrator insists on the anonymized norms and values of the Islamic tradition, stating that "where there is true art and genuine virtuosity the artist can paint an incomparable masterpiece without leaving even a trace of his identity" (19).

Pushing the boundaries of convention is still viewed as taboo in some Muslim societies—so much so that these apprehensions about the medium have occasionally fed into full-blown iconophobia, co-opted by radical extremism. My students quickly became aware that comics were not a "safe"

---

1. Martin Lund and A. David Lewis rightly assert that "it cannot be said flatly that 'Islam forbids illustration,' nor can it be said that comics and Islam are inherently at cross-purposes. Muslims in comics, in reality, prove to be a complicated phenomenon" (2).

or less-than-serious option for political commentary or literary production: The Mohammed cartoon crisis and the *Charlie Hebdo* attacks had shown them that comics were not an area that religious radicals are willing to ignore simply because it originated in non-Muslim societies. Those attacks shone a new light on cultural fissures often (falsely) attributed to the demarcation between East and West. For Islamic extremists, the *Charlie Hebdo* cartoonists revealed the West's insensitivity or apathy to the issue of introducing religious elements into the marketplace and their lack of interest in showing tolerance and restraint in an environment saturated with Islamophobic attitudes. For artists and publishers, of course, that very indiscretion is a gesture made in support of free expression. The trial of fourteen *Charlie Hebdo* suspects began as I was drafting this preface; the magazine republished the controversial images to reiterate their commitment to artistic freedom. The tense climate illustrates the extent of the risks taken by visual artists from Muslim backgrounds. Marjane Satrapi, for example, decided not only to narrativize her life as comics but, more importantly, to depict God visually as a soothing imaginary friend for her younger self. Of course, Satrapi's own background is not purely Muslim: Her immediate environment was largely secular and partly Zoroastrian; still, her decision is testament to her courage as a cartoonist, her commitment to pushing back against the naturalization of iconophobia, and her willingness to stand up against extremist versions of Islam. Framing *Persepolis* from this perspective allowed my students to read Satrapi's work as an example of a potential new Muslim aesthetics as well as a symptom of the Muslim artist's willingness to be culturally and politically subversive.

In many ways, student reception of *Persepolis* as a graphic novel was uncontroversial: They recognized it as an ambitious work of literature that participated in a vital international dialogue about religion, gender equality, war, and violence. Including a graphic text in a "serious" course felt natural to them, and at the end of the course they expressed their eagerness to read more comics, to continue to engage with the visual-verbal forms of storytelling, and to meditate further on the role of the cartoonist as a witness to injustices. But they *were* surprised to encounter a graphic novel that depicted a Muslim society and Muslim characters in a sensitive and thoughtful way. Generally, they associated Muslim characters in comic books with stereotyped villains. And they were not entirely wrong. As I started to trace the history of Muslim characters in Western comics, it became apparent that more often than not, Muslims were misrepresented, belittled, and vilified; it was virtually impossible to find a relatable, fully rounded, nonextremist Muslim character in Western comics—a sentiment voiced by many comics scholars before me. As Leonard Rifas explains, since cartoonists rely on "simplification, generalization, distortion, and exaggeration" to create recognizable types, illustrations can devolve into caricatures, perpetuating stereotypes ("Race and Comix" 33). Muslim characters have obviously suffered from this kind of pigeonholing. Deep-seated stereotypes about Arabs and Muslims that predate 9/11 add additional challenges to the representation of the Muslim Other. By the 1960s and 1970s, in the wake of the Suez Canal crisis and the oil embargo, Arabs and Muslims generally had become easy picks for villains. The decline of Arab-American relations during the Six Day War helped inspire the appearance of the Arab villain Ra's al Ghul in *Batman*.[2] Even Captain America, despite his propagation of a certain type of tolerant Americanness based on racial diversity, expressed unease at the moral and ideological axis of the Muslim (as evidenced in *Captain America* #1 issues 2–6). Fighting against Faysal al-Tariq, a terrorist responsible for planting bombs in a small town called Centerville, Captain America questions whether Muslims can assimilate successfully into American culture. Jason Dittmer argues that

> while Islam is never explicitly mentioned, the references in the text are quite clear in their intended connotation for the reader. The obvious interpretation of this text draws on Huntington's (1993) "clash of civilizations" thesis. In this geopolitical narrative, culture and religion serve as the fundamental schism in world politics, and the current geopolitical situation derives from secular modernity reaping the whirlwind of religious revival. [. . .] Islam, in particular, is given as an example of a civilization innately tied to religious violence. (639)

Indeed, Jack G. Shaheen's comprehensive study of Arab/Muslim characters in the second part of the twentieth century reveals that Muslim visibility is limited to three categories: "the repulsive terrorist, the sinister sheikh or the rapacious bandit" ("Arab Images" 123).[3] There is no question that racism

---

2. It is easy to read the "Arabness" of Ra's al Ghul, the leader of the League of Assassins: Cast as a terrorist, this dark-skinned villain with bushy eyebrows and a carefully trimmed beard is accompanied by ancient weapons associated with the Middle Eastern region. His acquired supernatural powers (transferring his soul to other bodies, levitation, etc.) also hint at black magic, reinforcing his malicious and immoral inclinations. Of course, while using these elements may not seem to be racist in themselves, the repetition of these tropes as established truths perpetuates racist stereotypes.

3. It is worth taking a moment here to see how this conflation of race and religion leads to misidentifications. As I discuss in chapter 1, erroneously identifying Islam as an ethnicity has been a tactic that weaponized identity politics.

in comics coupled with rising national antipathy to the Muslim world has had an impact on the creation of hyperbolic representations of the religious Other.

But what about comics written by Muslim authors or originating from Islamic societies themselves? Could these perhaps assuage the lopsided representations of Muslims? When students asked me to recommend more graphic novels that follow in Satrapi's footsteps, I was taken aback. Somehow, I suddenly realized, I had been thinking of Satrapi's graphic memoir as an anomaly. Growing up in Turkey, the comic books I read as a child were all Western works in translation, mostly featuring cowboys from the American West (*Tom Braks*, *Tom Miks*, and *Red Kit*, a.k.a. *Lucky Luke*)—and I realized now, as an adult, that I had never truly seen comics as a part of the mainstream literary tradition, certainly within Turkey. This was partly because comics were a Western import (with almost no locally produced works) and partly because they belonged, more or less, to the pulp tradition: Comic books were not sold in bookstores but at newspaper stands; they were considered to be purely entertainment and not serious productions; they were not aimed at adults but at children. By and large, I was under the impression that the Middle East had still not embraced the gentrification of comics in the way the West had.

I was wrong. A quick investigation showed that Middle Eastern, Muslim comics for adults had become widely popular and highly respected in the region. As the comics industry in the West was starting to question its racial politics and trying to diversify its characters, an unprecedented number of Muslim comics were entering the mainstream. From the autobiographical writings of Toufic El Rassi's *Arab in America* to Malik Sajad's *Munnu: A Boy from Kashmir*, from Hamid Sulaiman's *Freedom Hospital: A Syrian Story* to Özge Samanci's *Dare to Disappoint: Growing up in Turkey*, from Riad Sattouf's *The Arab of the Future* to Naif Al-Mutawa's *The 99*, it was clear that Muslim protagonists were slowly filling the pages of comic books. European examples of racially and religiously diverse comics—including the portrayals of African immigrants in French *bandes dessinées* (e.g., Jerome Ruillier's *The Strange*) or the Syrian refugees in recent German publications (e.g., Ali Fitzgerald's *Drawn to Berlin*)—were quick to follow suit. Even Marvel has recently joined in this trend by introducing its first Muslim headliner, Kamala Khan, a sixteen-year-old Pakistani American from Jersey City, as the new reincarnation of Ms. Marvel.

Many Muslim cartoonists recognize Satrapi as a pioneer, one who enabled their own careers in sequential arts. For Mana Neyestani, the author of *An Iranian Metamorphosis*, Satrapi's achievement was inspiring:

> Satrapi is the one who paved the way for graphic novelists today who are not European or American. After her book, *Persepolis,* received so much international attention, publishers began to pay attention to other work by Iranian and Arab cartoonists. Really, I have to say that if *An Iranian Metamorphosis* gets translated into other languages and cultures, it is because of Satrapi's work and success in the 1990s. (Karim 40)

Amir, the creator of *Zahra's Paradise,* echoes the sentiments, describing Satrapi as someone who "gave my generation a voice. And it was as if a great deal of the trauma in which our life stories had been frozen were finally melting away" (Gallaher). Of course, this new wave of comics with multifaceted Muslim characters is not unique to Iran but is spread over a wide geography in the Middle East. However, they widely share Satrapi's investment in challenging long-standing negative and simplistic perceptions of the religious Other. In these comics, Muslims are no longer reduced to a mouthpiece for radicalism, a token sidekick, or a jester providing comic relief; rather, they are taking center stage as thoughtful, active agents with various political alignments and creative impulses. These are bold, emphatic, and forward-thinking narratives, focusing on a range of challenges faced by Muslim subjects in their communities. Like Satrapi, they aim to give Muslims the license to narrate their own stories.

As I began to read more comics emerging from the Muslim world, the questions multiplied: Why has the graphic form become such a popular and useful medium for the articulation of Muslim subjectivities—inside and outside Muslim homelands? Why are Muslim authors/artists choosing this particular form to explore Muslim subjectivity—especially given Islam's history of aniconism? How do these authors hope to present a vision of Muslim life within the comic book form, a category imported from the West? Who is their target audience? Do they embrace the same aesthetic principles (shape, color, shading, framing) established by their Western counterparts, or do they advocate for innovative techniques to set themselves apart? This book aims to answer some of these questions by bringing together a variety of graphic productions engaged with the representation of Muslim life, penned by Muslims and non-Muslims alike. Together, they enunciate the emergence of a new movement that we can recognize as "Muslim Comics."

ACKNOWLEDGMENTS

A few years ago, I visited my colleague Chris Pizzino's class on comics. As he discussed Marjane Satrapi's *Persepolis* with his students, I found his enthusiasm for the medium infectious. When I came home that night, I carried that passion and curiosity with me; as I relayed my observations to my husband, Aaron, he said: "There's your next book project!" So my first thanks goes to Chris: He has been an incredible friend and a mentor during this process. His kindness and generosity opened my eyes to a new field of study. And, of course, many thanks to Aaron for not only cheering me on with this project, but reading multiple drafts, giving me invaluable advice, editing my work, and baking delicious scones and cakes during the COVID lockdown to keep me going. He has always been my anchor amid a world of uncertainties.

I was grateful to receive funding from a number of institutions for this project. I would like to thank the National Endowment for the Humanities, the Willson Center for Humanities at the University of Georgia, and UGA's Office of Institutional Diversity for their generous support. I would also like to thank two of my professional organizations, the British and Postcolonial Studies Association in the US and the Postcolonial Studies Association in the UK, for providing a stimulating environment in which I could present my work and receive valuable feedback. This book would not be where it is without Asha Sen, Lopa Basu, Nasra Smith, Joe Pellegrino, Dustin Anderson, and Hans-Georg Erney. I have been lucky to know Claire Chambers and Alberto Fernandez Carbajal on the other side of the Atlantic; they have been great colleagues and friends over the years. Two other professional organizations have been instrumental in shaping this project: I am proud to be a member of the Muslim Women's Popular Fiction Network with an incredible group of women (Amy Burge, Aroosa Kanwal, Şima İmsir, and Lucinda Newns), all of whom worked tirelessly to secure funding from the Arts and Humanities Research Center in the UK. I extend my thanks to the members of UGA's Postcolonial Collective—Aruni Kashyap, Alex Fyfe, and Jamie McClung—who have been generous teammates. A special thanks to Alex for assisting me with various projects and endeavors. I look forward to many more events and discussions together.

That brings me to another group of confidants who became my biggest support group during COVID: Maggie Zurawski, Aruni Kashyap, Channette Romero, LeAnne Howe, and Andrew Zawacki. The night Maggie and I performed at Flicker in Athens with our band, Ottoman Slap, now allows me to say: "I performed in the same city as REM." Aruni has connected me with a larger group of scholars and reignited my passion for Bollywood films. Thank you, LeAnne and Channette, for giving us many occasions to celebrate—from acclaimed documentaries to wedding cheer! And Andrew, whose memes brought smiles on rage-inducing days during the shutdown. You all have my undying gratitude.

There are more colleagues at the Department of English at UGA whose presence has been a blessing. John Lowe, Barbara McCaskill, Isiah Lavender, and Susan Rosenbaum have helped me feel part of a community: exquisite culinary experiences at John's charming home, long phone conversations with Barbara, commiserations with Isiah over the travails of being soccer parents, and lovely lunches with Susan—they are all proof of my good fortune at UGA. To this list, I add Aidan Wasley, Adam Parkes, Eric Morales-Franceschini, Becky Hallman Martini, Michelle Ballif, Simon Gatrell, Elisa Henken, and David Diamond, among others. My graduate students (Zach Bordas, Travis Dular, Morgan Richards Dietz, Sayantika Mandal, Meltem Safak, and Asmah Mir) have helped me expand my horizons in many ways. I am indebted to my research assistant, Safeer Hussain. Also, a big shout-out to Brennan Murphy, who will be a field-shaping comics scholar, I am certain.

Outside the department, what started casually with Zoom meetings with the "Gang of Eight" ended with constructive efforts to strengthen shared governance at the university. I especially want to thank Elizabeth St. Pierre and Barbara Biesecker for their leadership and friendship and Gerald Maa at the *Georgia Review* for bringing wonderful speakers to campus.

Aliyah Khan at the University of Michigan has been instrumental in helping me develop my chapters over the years; her idea to host a symposium and a workshop in Michigan with Chris Gavaler and Karla Mallette helped enhance the argumentative arc of chapter 4. I am indebted to Amit Baishya at the University of Oklahoma for his brilliant essay on *Munnu* as well as his assistance in helping me locate primary sources. I extend my thanks to Kanika Batra at Texas Tech University and Moustafa Bayoumi at Brooklyn College for their generous support over the years. I had the great pleasure of sharing a Zoom conversation with Ozge Samanci, Leila Abdelrazaq, and Aliyah. Many thanks to the speakers for sharing their creative insights with me and my students. Their brilliant work is the engine behind this project.

Special thanks to Malik Sajad for the original cover art; connecting with him and discussing possibilities for the cover of the book was a treat. I am humbled by his interpretation of my work and his vision for the book. Thank you for sharing your art with me.

It was a pleasure to meet and chat with Hillary Chute during her visit to UGA. Her superb work, especially *Disaster Drawn*, has been a beacon. I also extend my thanks to Leonard Rifas, who generously shared his thoughts with me on Muslims in comics over a series of emails.

Athens is a great community: I want to thank Genaro Angeles at Tennis for Life for being an excellent (and a very patient) coach. I would also like to thank Liz Doerr, an avid reader and a critic, and Serena Scibelli and Madeline Bates at the Athens Commission for Culture and Arts. I extend my thanks to the Edwardses and the Davenports for their friendship over the years; it takes a village!

I was lucky to meet Ana Maria Jimenez-Moreno at The Ohio State University Press booth at MLA; she has given tremendous guidance and gentle pushes from time to time to make sure that the project was progressing. I also thank the series editors, Jared Gardner, Charles Hatfield, and Rebecca Wanzo, for their feedback and suggestions. Their exemplary work continues to shape my thinking. It was my privilege to work with an excellent team at OSU; I extend my thanks to Elizabeth Zaleski, Olivia Sergent, Samara Rafert, Rebecca Bostock, Stuart Rodriguez, and Sarah Flood-Baumann.

To my Turks (Kadri, Nilgun, Omer, Bahar, Nili, Nedim, Murat, Asli, Ipek, Hakan, and the youngest member of the clan, Lavin) and my Canadians (Frank, Deirdre, Rachel, Nathan, Fumika, and new arrival Gemma): You make my life rich.

Finally, to my Kaya: True to your name, you have been a rock in our little family. I admire all the stories, poems, and comics you created on your own and shared with us. I am always inspired by your discipline as an athlete—an inspiring teammate on the soccer field and a formidable force on the tennis courts. May the creative spark continue to guide your endeavors!

INTRODUCTION

Defining Muslim Comics and Warscapes

> Cultivated countryside is land already exhausted by humanity to the point where the humanization of the countryside has served as model and name for all the more specifically human ways of life: the *culture*. To walk then, through an orchard, sown field, or stubble field, through an olive grove laid out in diagonal rows or a methodically planned grove of pin oaks, is to follow man travelling within himself. The battlefield is similar. [...] When it is used for battle the field converts a piece of the planet into a geometric area where only strategic conditions are important.
>
> —Jose Ortega y Gasset, *Meditations on Hunting*[1]

Malik Sajad's graphic novel *Munnu: A Boy from Kashmir* begins with a chapter titled "Family Photo" (see figure 0.1). On the opening page, a hand-drawn "photo" features the young Sajad (known then as "Munnu," or "the youngest") with his siblings—all depicted as hanguls, an endangered species of deer native to the region—posing for the camera against a backdrop of the Kashmiri countryside. The photograph is eventually revealed to be a picture taken as part of the family's Eid celebrations marking the end of Ramadan. The snapshot of the siblings overlaps on the page with a larger depiction of Sajad's hometown, Srinagar. At first glance, the town appears picturesque: rolling fields around the banks of the Jhelum River are divided into various neighborhoods; numerous buildings, bridges, barns, and towers give the impression of a prosperous, serene locale. A central element of the panorama is the naturalized presence of Islam: Mosques with minarets appear as part of the quaint landscape; Eidgah, an open space reserved for religious rituals and instruction frequented by Munnu emerges from the

---

[1]. For a more complete poetic realization of this abundance of human meaning in "field," see Ponge.

FIGURE 0.1. *Munnu*'s first page features a family picture with a landscape.

edge of the city. These markers signal that Islam is not merely knitted into the local cultural fabric but into the countryside itself.

To orient his readers with the geography of his story, Sajad includes an inset with a basic map showing Srinagar at the center of Kashmir, surrounded by China, India, and Pakistan—each nation having its own political ambitions in the region. This introduces the second theme of the narrative: the looming sense of violence in the region. Indeed, a closer examination of the panel reveals that the many towers scattered across the landscape do not consist only of minarets but also military watchtowers built by the occupying Indian army. The effect of the illustration shifts dramatically: The countryside no longer conveys calm and tranquility; now, it resembles a warscape, a term used by Carolyn Nordstrom and many others since to refer to the lifeworld of those in simmering, dormant, or incipient conflict zones, a "tortured geography" in which daily life is dominated by military activity and ever-present violence (Gregory 405). In this illustration, the seamless interweaving of civil life with military activity suggests that the "community has incorporated the army's potentially violent behavior and presence" into everyday existence (Nayar, *Human Rights* 159). Within this particular warscape, Islam has ceased to be a private spiritual practice confined to the household and has instead become a public, ethnicized, politicized, and indeed militarized marker of difference. Munnu's family photograph for Eid, it turns out, is something more than a personal memento: It acts as a political-military document, in the sense that it identifies those in it as part of the majority Muslim population, not the Hindu-dominated military force. This blurring of the personal and the political, the domestic sphere and the warscape, is central to the existence of the inhabitants in the region as they attempt to create a peaceful future while retaining their Kashmiri identity. Sajad's desire to establish his roots only makes sense in the context of these maps and illustrations of warscape environments; understanding his personal journey as a budding political cartoonist as he "travel[s] within himself" requires situating him in this warscape, which is in constant flux while symbolizing permanent danger.

MUSLIM COMICS AND WARSCAPE WITNESSING focuses on contemporary graphic narratives, primarily but not exclusively set in Muslim nations, offering new approaches to representing local and global Muslim identities. The book revolves around two key concepts, reflected in the title, both of which require some initial unpacking. The first is Muslim identity. "Muslim" is a complicated signifier; it has come to designate a "socially constructed racial category used to simplify and define a diverse number of racial and ethnic groups with an Islamic association" (Islam 430). Bringing forth the plurality and underscoring the heterogeneity of this faith group is one of the goals of this book. The flattened, stereotyped image of the Muslim has long dominated Western comics; increasingly exhausted by reductionist depictions, Muslim artists/authors are depicting a vast number of "Muslim identities" across multiple nations, ethnicities, races, and linguistic groups, as well as religious subtraditions. It would be naive to assume that the type of religion promoted by the theocratic state in Iran (as we see in Amir and Khalil's *Zahra's Paradise*) is somehow identical to the creed practiced in a Palestinian refugee camp in Lebanon (as featured in Leila Abdelrazaq's *Baddawi*). At the same time, Muslim comics artists are increasingly exploring the transnational, transcultural aspects of Islam, especially in the context of the global *ummah*—Muslims bound together worldwide under shared practices and rituals. Hence, while these artists resist the Western habit of lumping all Muslims into one oppositional group, they are equally determined to recognize and analyze the connections between diverse Muslim communities in a global framework.

Considering the plethora of potential religious subjectivities and communities included under the umbrella of Islam, when I use the term "Muslim" in this book, I mean nothing more than an identity defined by an attachment to basic Islamic tenets—regardless of how loose such an attachment may be. My emphasis on religious identity is a gesture toward a postsecular examination of subject constitution—an important and urgent academic inquiry into the revitalization of religion with all its political and ideological implications. Postsecularism—which requires "a re-engagement with, but not necessarily a re-affirmation of certain kinds of religious thought and discourse"—allows us to examine the variety of loyalties that situate the Muslim in relation to complex local, national, and global networks (Kaufmann 69).[2] In addition to the discussion of Muslim identity, I will be referring to a group of contemporary graphic narratives as "Muslim Comics." A more detailed explanation of what the term "Muslim Comics" means and how it can be useful will follow in the next chapter. For now, it should suffice to say that the category of Muslim Comics describes any graphic narrative

---

2. Religion's role in identity formation has been brought to the center by recent academics invested in postsecular inquiry. Talal Asad and Saba Mahmood, among others, have started to push back against the secular/religious binary to promote instead the codependence of the two terms, paving the way toward a more complex understanding of identity that includes the material basis of existence with spiritual codes that shape individual agency. Asad makes the following case:

> I believe we must try to unpack the various assumptions on which secularism—a modern doctrine of the world in the world—is based. For it is precisely the process by which these conceptual binaries are established or subverted that tells us how people live the secular—how they vindicate the essential freedom and responsibility of the sovereign self in opposition to the constraints of that self by religious discourses. (15–16)

that features three-dimensional Muslim characters and foregrounds Muslim experiences in relation to various power structures inside and outside the Muslim homeland.

The other central concept of the book is one I have already touched upon: warscape—what I and other critics define as a civilian-occupied environment marked by prolonged "disruptions and instabilities" generated by political uncertainty and military involvement (Hoffman and Lubkemann 316). For many in the West, Islam has come to be associated at least in part with struggle, tension, and unrest. I do not intend to engage too closely with sensationalist and often xenophobic rhetoric about the "aggressive roots of Islam" or the ostensibly natural connection between Islam and terrorism.[3] Instead, I want to reframe this conversation by considering the varying effects of violence *on* Muslim subjects around the globe. "Warscape" helps me shift the focus from the Muslim perpetrator to the disaffected Muslim. As a term, "warscape" alludes to topographies of violence that do not necessarily designate an active warzone: As opposed to the conventional rules of battlefield engagement, where "regular armed forces" with "a fixed distinctive sign recognizable at a distance" attack each other, a warscape refers to a civilian space in which different factions are participating in asymmetrical struggles, transforming a familiar, everyday terrain into a defamiliarized, politicized, and sometimes (but not always) overtly militarized space (Butler, "Guantanamo Limbo"). As will become evident in the ensuing chapters, war itself is not necessarily a precondition of a warscape; indeed, the use of "warscape" as a category underscores the prolonged effects of violence as opposed to the finality denoted by "war." Just as importantly, "warscape" indicates a territory marked by *anticipation* of violence, especially in the context of unconventional and volatile forms of hostile engagement (contested borders, civil unrest, racial and cultural tensions). In this regard, the warscape becomes an uncanny site, where individuals feel "out of place in their homes" due to sporadic, ongoing, and unpredictable violence. From the university campuses and public squares of Iran to the checkpoints of Palestine, from the shattered cities of Syria to the border territory of Kashmir, warscape is an ominous and oppressive space that represents a "crisis of transition" (Ndebele 8). I am interested in exploring how this unstable space initiates a drawn-out process of becoming for those trapped inside it.

---

3. The vast number of discussions about fierce Muslims in the battlefield throughout the centuries reinforced Islam's violent roots; from the vicious Mohammedan warrior in numerous examples of *chanson de geste* in the Middle Ages to the bloodthirsty jihadi attacking present-day targets in the West, the Muslim militant came to represent a significant threat to Western democracy and values.

How do comics show Muslims reacting to violent attacks unleashed on (and sometimes from within) their communities? How does the anticipation of violence change the everyday habits of Muslims in their communities? How does one turn vulnerability into resistance? How does a warscape help create and sustain communal myths about the Muslim martyr (*shaheed*) or the abject figure known as the "Muselmann"?

A warscape designates an interrupted and contested space; warscape existence, on the other hand, refers to a disrupted identity caused by reconfigured space. The ultimate feature of a warscape, besides the threat of violence, is the mitigation and mutation of day-to-day habits, rituals, and interactions of civilians. As the selected comics illustrate, warscape restructures everyday life via its altered geography. Zeina Abirached's comic *A Game for Swallows: To Die, to Leave, to Return* is a good example of warscape existence that reveals the challenges of navigating everyday life amid the ongoing threat of violence. Reflecting back on her childhood in Beirut during the Lebanese civil war, young Zeina recalls "the green line" between East Beirut (Christian) and West Beirut (Muslim). On a full-page spread, she inserts several diagrams of the neighborhood with a dotted line between her and her grandmother's house to show how people used various tactics to avoid being targeted by snipers: "People had perfected a way of moving between buildings," she writes as she draws a meandering line with specific instructions indicating where to "walk, run, jump, hug the wall, bend over, etc." (17). She adds: "Crossing the handful of streets between us meant following complicated and perilous choreography" (17). The exact instructions reveal the stipulations imposed by a warscape—visiting a grandmother, in this case, requires a spatial reorientation and new physical behaviors to accommodate shifting topographical and urban conditions. This adjustment does not only apply to public space; the damaging effects of the warscape are felt equally in the domestic space—since the private domain cannot be insulated from the political one. To avoid stray bullets and shrapnel, Zeina's family confines its domestic activities to the inner parts of their home; as time goes by, the useable space in the family apartment keeps "shrinking" until it is "just a tiny square: the foyer" (36). Abirached visually explains this retreat into the interior with a diagram of the apartment, indicating the movement of the family with directional arrows as they close off one room after another (see figure 0.2). For Abirached, the remapping of her altered environment—the visual and cognitive rearranging of space—is a crucial step toward acclimatizing herself to her warscape existence. Warscape essentially changes one's *perception* of space; warscape existence regulates one's *participation* in everyday life.

DEFINING MUSLIM COMICS AND WARSCAPES • 7

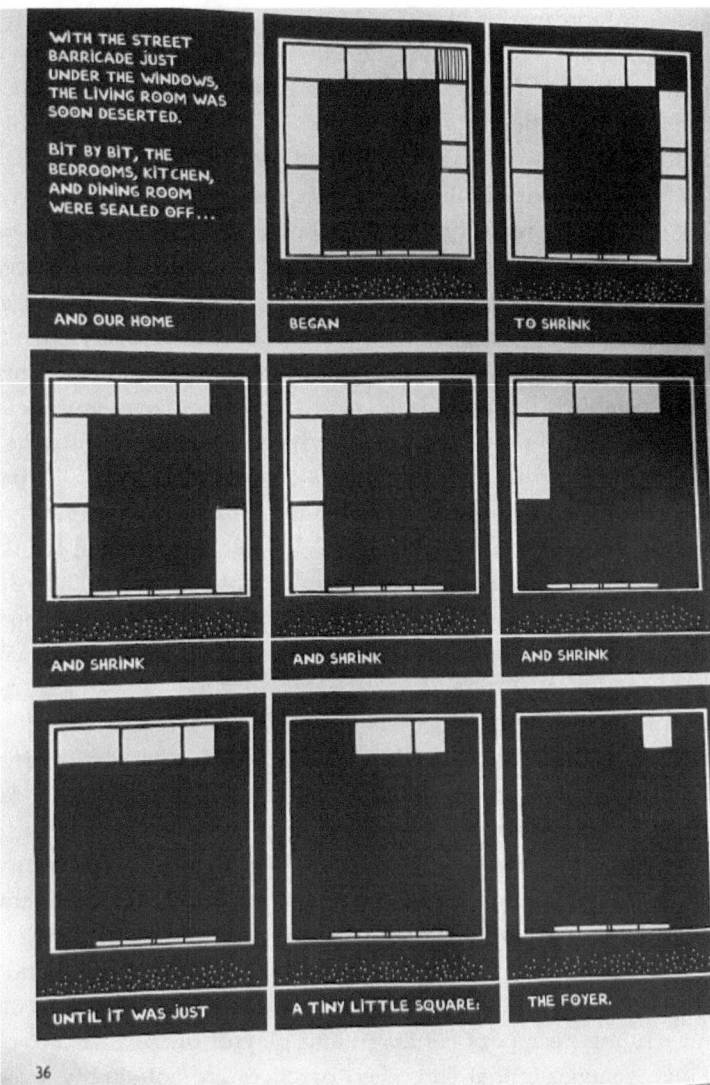

FIGURE 0.2. Abirached's home keeps shrinking.

The term "everyday life" can be ambiguous: Mike Featherstone characterizes it as "a residual category into which can be jettisoned all the irritating bits and pieces which do not fit into orderly thought" (160). Still, it remains a valuable concept through which we may study subjectivity in relation to the cultural and social structures embedded in specific places "produced and reproduced through human intention and action" (Ortner 158). Certainly, studying the everyday routines and habits (as opposed to the heroic and extraordinary actions) of Muslim communities, especially those in warscapes, greatly complicates the way we might understand the nature of religious existence. Like any other faith-based subjectivity, Muslim identity depends on a "reflexive re-enactment of a proscribed series of roles and expectations" expressed through embodied practices—from dress to prayer, from fasting to performing ablutions, from greeting gestures to funeral rites (Bennett 3). Within a warscape, these embodied practices regularly become disciplinary gauges, a way of distinguishing "acceptable from unacceptable beliefs and practices, desirable from denigrated identities and statuses, and worthy from unworthy ideals and values" (McGuire 6). Everyday religious rituals, in other words, come to serve political and pragmatic purposes: They help establish the boundaries and customs citizens must follow to enter into specific communities and survive their environment. The abandoned homes of Pandits in *Munnu* illustrate the escalating hostility between religious groups after the Indian occupation: "Back then we hardly cared who was Pandit and who was Muslim. [. . .] But [the Pandits] felt isolated after the armed struggle against the Indian occupation erupted" (Sajad 280). With the emergence of warscape, imaginary borders between neighborhoods become typical to keep religious communities apart, splitting the Kashmiris into rigid identity categories.

By depicting the little particulars of everyday existence in Muslim communities, especially those located in warscapes, Muslim comics artists are able to draw attention to the complex realities of a detailed, fully realized Muslim life. We may recall the opening pages of Marjane Satrapi's *Persepolis*, showing young Marjane introducing herself and her friends wearing the veil—a new requirement after the revolution and a sign of the transformation of the nation into a theocratic regime. On the same page, a panel depicts the students at school with their veils turned into playground props (jump ropes, horse reins, blindfolds), revealing the girls' reaction to the government's ruling—a mix of contempt and playful pragmatism. The image is striking: It suggests that embodied practices are not simply a result of personal decisions but often grow out of political and cultural pressures outside the individual's control. And the sight of girls recasting a controversial emblem of oppression into toys makes the larger point that mandated religious practices, without internalization, can only lead to hollow performances of conformity across pious and impious bodies alike. This scene, then, is a perfect illustration of the way everyday life is shaped by politicized religion, but also how religious rituals are subject to the practices of everyday life.

The emphasis on everyday life, however, does not mean that Muslim Comics are intended as encyclopedias or introductory guidebooks to Muslim life. While the artists may take the role of translators from time to time to explain cultural idiosyncrasies for outsiders, the focus remains on individual characters and larger story lines. The intersections between the individual chronicle and collective memory thus operate as reminders of a shared consciousness. In *Baddawi*, for example, Abdelrazaq includes a section on za'atar—a mixture of herbs and spices commonly used in Middle Eastern cuisine. Abdelrazaq describes the process of making za'atar (see figure 0.3): "First, we need to lay the herbs out on the roof to dry. Then we take the dried herbs inside to pound them! Roast the sesame seeds in a dry pan. Finally mix everything together and add salt. And that's how you make za'atar" (33). But her recipe includes more than step-by-step directions; it shows za'atar's cultural significance for the Palestinian community specifically. Picking, roasting, and jarring the herbs becomes a symbol of the preservation of culture under threat. In this series of panels, the lines that emanate from the roasting pan to signify its inviting smell pass through to other panels and merge with the dialogue bubbles. In this way, sensory memory is transcribed into public knowledge through text and image. As Abdelrazaq uses her narrative as a cultural repository to preserve generational knowledge, she moves from the material to the emotional, capturing the symbolic value of this mixed spice: "Next time you gather thyme for the za'atar, it will be in Palestine" (34). The spice is enmeshed with the idea of home and acts as a reminder of the Palestinian right of return.

At first glance, the relationship between warscape and everyday life may seem somewhat contradictory; war, after all, is more closely linked to trauma and extreme disruption than to regular, everyday existence. Yet warscape imagines disruptive trauma not as a moment of crisis but as an uncanny and ongoing process—the transformation of "shocking things" into normal events, passing "from horror into banality," as Hillary Chute puts it—with prolonged effects in both the domestic and national spheres (*Disaster Drawn* 30). My focus on everyday life serves two purposes: First, I show how artists use the daily routines of the Muslim to encourage the reader to reflect on the difference between the familiar and the unknown. To go back to the previous examples: The reader might be familiar with za'atar as a Middle Eastern spice, but its deeper connotations for a Palestinian may be unknown. Similarly, the reader might be informed about the practice of veiling as described in *Persepolis* but may not be aware of the numerous reasons why a woman chooses to veil herself (to affirm her modesty, to protect herself, to conform

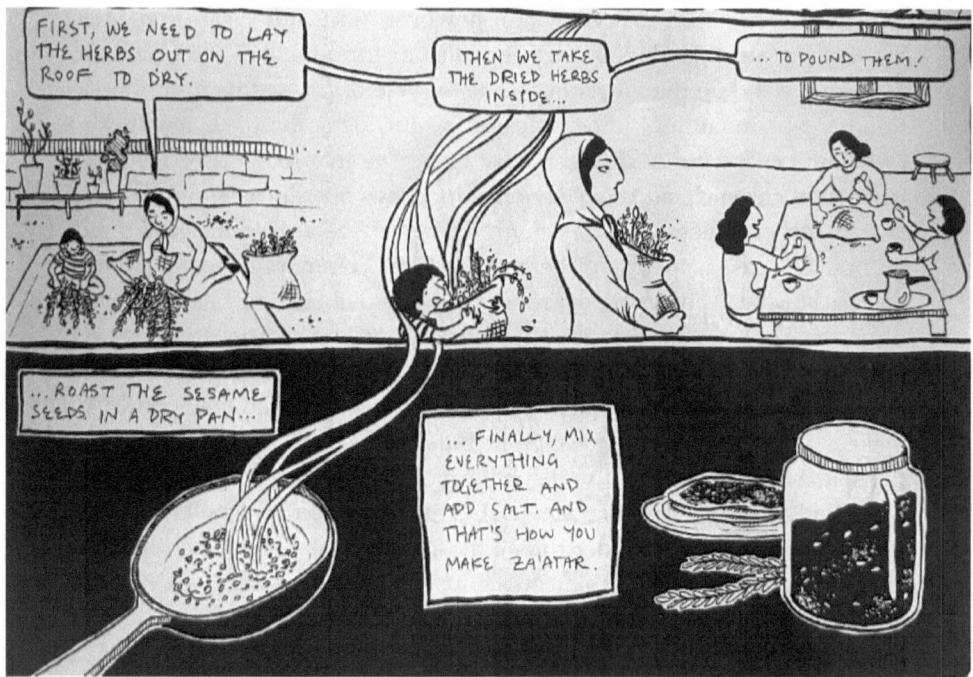

FIGURE 0.3. Ahmad and his mother gather herbs to make za'atar.

with patriarchy, to highlight her difference as a diasporic subject, etc.). Both za'atar and the veil, in other words, can allude to a familiar, everyday habit but may also be associated with a traumatic new reality (regime change, displacement, exile, etc.). Second, capturing the small realities of everyday life enhances the pluralization of the Muslim Comics character. Traditionally, trauma has been the one consistent trope in exploring Muslim subjectivity in comics (and perhaps in Western cultural productions generally): The Muslim either inflicts trauma (e.g., as a terrorist, autocrat) or is the victim of trauma (e.g., manhunt, honor killing). Both options imply a certain flattening of affect or behavior, and both fail to push beyond a myopic understanding of the subject defined by a harrowing moment without addressing what precedes or follows it. As Sajad's teacher reminds him, "history is nothing but documented everyday events" (Sajad 178). The emphasis on everyday life allows us to move beyond hasty representations of trauma and adopt a broader gaze that helps complicate the portrayals of the Other. Michael E. Gardiner argues that everyday life is "where we develop our manifold capacities, both in an individual and collective sense, and become fully integrated and truly *human* persons" (2). The idea of growing into a "human"—

that is, acquiring awareness and agency as well as gaining recognition—is particularly important at a time in which discussions about this faith group have been taken over by extreme voices, rendering it almost impossible to imagine the "everydayness" of Muslims.

THUS FAR, I have been speaking of the relationship between Islam and warscape, and how a transition into warscape existence can reshape physical, social, and cultural space and rearrange communal rituals and interactions. This transition, and the new everyday existence that ensues, is the focus of the comics I will be examining in this book. The protagonists are neither heroes nor villains; they are individuals with moral complexities who find themselves having to cope with warscape realities on a daily basis. But what about the medium itself? What do comics do specifically as a multimodal form to convey Muslim experiences? How do visual aesthetics and visual politics work in Muslim Comics? Are there common tactics in envisaging warscape aesthetically to capture the effects of violence on Muslim communities? What do comics do in terms of imagining Muslim existence that other media cannot?

Comics studies has developed into a distinct and vital field of academic inquiry in the last few decades: Abundant critical attention is now paid to what are widely seen as aesthetically ambitious and politically informed multimodal "storyworlds" (Aldama 2).[4] While "the problem of status" initially impeded the growth of comics as an academic field, its "natural development from pulp infancy to literary adulthood" is now regarded as essentially complete—due to efforts of scholars such as Leonard Rifas, Frederick Luis Aldama, and Hillary Chute, to name a few (Pizzino, *Arresting Development* 3). Doubts about the academic and intellectual validity of the medium were largely vanquished once the "graphic novel" began to flourish in the mid-1980s, and comics as a whole gentrified. The cultural reputation of the medium initially lagged somewhat in the Middle East, but there, too, comics have now assumed a position of serious critical importance, as I will discuss in later chapters. In this book, I focus especially on "graphic narratives," a term I use to refer to a subgroup of comics that displays a

---

4. Much has been written about the definition of comics, and I do not wish to revisit the debate. For my own purposes, I start with Greg Hayman and Henry John Pratt's characterization of comics as "pictorial narratives" and add Will Eisner's description of the medium as "sequential art" to arrive at McCloud's working definition as "juxtaposed pictorial and other images in deliberate sequence, intended to convey information and/or produce an aesthetic response in the reader" (20).

thematically cohesive, extended account with an interest in "building up tension, generating atmosphere, [and] developing characters" (Sabin qtd. in Hescher, *Reading* 32). For my purposes, "graphic narrative" is narrow enough to emphasize the self-contained and character-focused composition of the books selected for this project and broad enough to include a range of sequential categories and genres—including graphic novel, autobiography, travelogue, comics journalism, and web comics.

The term "graphic narrative" may appear to prioritize text over image—a concern that a number of comics scholars have been vocal about. David Kunzle, for one, insists upon the "preponderance of image over text" in comics (2); Aaron Meskin worries about the impact of categorizing comics as "literature," not least because it might privilege textual elements over pictorial ones. Other critics have pushed back against the consideration of comics as part of the literary critical enterprise: Bart Beaty makes the case that the examination of the graphic narrative through a literary lens creates "a sort of confirmation bias" driven by "the study of literature, into which [comics studies] has been rapidly subsumed. [. . .] As a result, the methodological, theoretical, and political potential of comics studies is blunted" (186). Eileen John and Dominic McIver Lopes follow a similar logic as they assert that "a comic book that [. . .] has aesthetic merit may be a work of art but not a work of literature" (43). Yet I remain suspicious of criticism that disavows the presence of rhetoric, or narrative, or "literature" in comics entirely. It seems obvious that any study of comics necessitates a serious and extended consideration of what lies beyond the textual; attention to rhetoric must clearly be combined with analysis of graphical and pictorial elements. But I see no drawbacks in employing some of the tools made available by literary scholarship to comment on another discipline—just as scholars have done with film, theater, art, performance, and other fields. This is not to say these academic areas do not deserve their own, independent critical vocabulary, but the fact that they have an ongoing and central interest in storytelling via print points to a natural alliance with literary studies. As Jared Gardner observes, "once two panels are put together, narrative is inevitable" ("Same Difference" 136–37). Therefore, while I agree that studying comics requires a different approach, and a specific attention to visual-verbal blending, it seems unproductive to argue about whether image or text has supremacy over the meaning-making process. Such an approach indeed seems to miss the point entirely by dismissing the cross-discursivity of comics.

The compound nature of comics remains at the heart of this project as I investigate how visual arguments support, augment, and sometimes even contradict rhetorical claims. As Martha Kuhlman argues, the graphic narrative is an idea [. . .] translated through the medium of the hand and graphically rendered as an expression of lived experience in a way that cannot be conveyed by prose alone. Even when the writer, the artist, and the subject of the story are separate individuals, the form of comics—the quality of the line, the sequence of panels, the page layout—introduces elements of interpretation and reception that are markedly different from prose. (125)

Documenting "lived experience" in Muslim Comics—whether in the form of life writing, autobiography, memoir, or even fiction—is a way of capturing the interplay of visual and verbal cues that shed light on the changing structure of everyday life in response to violence. In *Persepolis*, after the bombing of Tehran during the Iran-Iraq war, Marjane finds the next-door apartment reduced to rubble. She sees a bracelet and explains its significance ("It was Neda's. Her aunt had given it to her for her fourteenth birthday" [Satrapi 142]) and then realizes that it confirms the death of her friend and her family; Marji's reaction to it is an inaudible scream, represented by a completely blacked-out panel. These two registers—the objective history of what was lost, conveyed through text, and the subjective reaction to loss, conveyed through symbolic and abstract visuals—work in tandem to communicate how violence is inscribed on everyday life in a warscape.

Finally, this book follows the lead of comics studies in not only investigating the various layers of semiotic coding present in graphic texts but also reflecting on the "changing nature of reading" itself (Tabachnick 2). The comics reader is an involved one; as Charles Hatfield argues, "the reader's responsibility for negotiating meaning can never be forgotten, for the breakdown of comics into discrete visual quanta continually foregrounds the reader's involvement" (xiv). The reader's unique participation in the meaning-making process in comics has often been attributed to the presence of "gutters," the empty space between the panels, seen by some as "sites of elision and erasure" (Postema 50). The gaps between the frames force the reader to rely on the power of inference to move from one panel to the next, filling in informational voids in order to complete the storyline, in a process Scott McCloud refers to as "closure." That is not to say, however, that the comics reader has infinite freedom; Pizzino asserts that "gutters separating panels do not give a reader's imagination free play to construct what is not shown" ("Gutter" 124). Indeed, recent discussions of gutters have tended to emphasize that meaning is not dependent on imagination but on the consistency of visual signs. According to Kate Polak, for example, "it is not so much that the collaboration occurs 'in' the gutter in the initial reading process but that the gutter provides an essential space whereby we are cued to a creative investment" (12).

The reconsideration of the gutter not as a blank space but a series of relational intervals shifts the reader's focus from "absence" to "presence" and points to a far more complex relationship between delivery and reception. This collaborative rapport between the creator and the reader takes on extra significance when considering the revisionist nature of Muslim Comics: What happens when a Muslim author creates a narrative about Muslim warscapes, and the reader is potentially not a part of the Muslim world? What happens when Muslim Comics promote a new set of symbols and visual codes that directly challenge the stereotypes internalized by the non-Muslim reader? What kind of interpretive tools should the reader be employing when he or she does not inhabit a warscape personally, or has never even set foot in one? For the non-Muslim reader, external framing (the reader's role in constructing meaning) can become fraught with tensions; for this reason, establishing a temporary creative alliance between the reader and the artist is instrumental in launching a readerly ethics of recognition, an interpretive practice that strengthens the empathetic affect/effect of the narrative, and paves the way for a mutual understanding between Muslims and non-Muslims. For James Phelan, there is a direct correlation between "the reader's cognitive understanding, emotional response, and ethical positioning" (22) underlining the "multifarious relations among the narrative texts and our responses to them" (60). In this context, "closure" in Muslim Comics becomes not just a matter of imagining actions unrepresented on the page but an act of translation, where non-Muslim Western readers attempt—sensitively, empathetically—to decipher the reality of everyday life in a Muslim, non-Western society.

Muslim Comics plainly appeal to a bifurcated audience: They are not only intended for non-Muslims but can also be transformative for the Muslim reader—directly or indirectly affected by warscapes. That is to say, we cannot underestimate the local political ambitions of these new comics as they appeal to their immediate communities. In their desire to display the inner struggles of nation-building practices in Muslim homelands, they utilize a subversive grammar that has not traditionally been part of civil discourse in authoritarian states. By focusing on the day-to-day realities of aggrieved populations under repressive regimes and military occupations, they emerge as political voices representing disenfranchised groups. When Amir and Khalil started working on *Zahra's Paradise* as a web series to chronicle the unlawful detainment, torture, and killing of protestors in Iran, they were concerned about the personal ramifications of their artistic dissent. Their fear of backlash forced them to remain anonymous:

Are we scared for our personal safety and that of our loved ones? Is that why we're hiding our true identities? Honestly, yes. And nobody should be surprised. The Iranian government has consistently shown its ruthlessness against those who dare to denounce it. The important thing is that, thanks to our anonymity, we have been entirely free to speak the truth without self-censoring in the least. ("Zahra's Paradise")

Despite their distance, both creators were fully aware of the potential political fallout of their artistic endeavor. Still, rather than censoring themselves, they continued to provide pointed political commentary for Iranians on the creep of theocratic autocracy and the various civil rights violations committed by the state. Their public critique, masked behind comics, was first and foremost an effort to inform and mobilize readers in Iran itself.

At the same time, these comics are almost always necessarily interested in attracting wider attention, in recruiting ideological and cultural allies (or at least procuring empathy) from all over the world. Many of these comics are written originally in English and with an eye to future translation into other languages. Their observations extend beyond national borders: They engage with Western-associated norms and concepts (secularism, multiculturalism, democracy, etc.) and ask about the future of such ideas in an increasingly ultranationalist world. To go back again to Amir: "No one seemed to notice or care about the tragedy taking place in Iran. At a certain point you start to question not only yourself, and your countrymen, but also the world. You wonder what is the point of knowledge if it does not get translated into action?" ("Zahra's Paradise"). In this way, Muslim Comics perform a kind of double critique by oscillating between the local and the global: If confronting real and serious challenges faced by Muslim homelands marks these graphic narratives as locally subversive, their interrogation of large-scale power mechanisms in general positions them as globally interventionist. It is clear that this new enthusiasm for transcultural outreach and inclusivity is not merely an attempt to educate and inform the comics readers around them, nor even to cultivate a new fan base across the international Western market, but to enter fully and confidently, as equals, into a global political and social debate.

THE ABILITY to move between Muslim and non-Muslim audiences, and indeed the very accessibility and international comprehensibility of comics as a medium leads us to a third and final element of Muslim Comics depicting warscapes: witnessing. Chute attests to the synergy between the form and content of comics, arguing that comics have "a peculiar connection to expressing trauma" and that it is natural that "acts of witnessing and testimony are created and find shape in this form" (*Disaster Drawn* 33). Witnessing in comics—through visualization and narration—offers a way to change vulnerability into resistance. Judith Herman observes that "in order to escape accountability for his crimes, the perpetrator does everything in his power to promote forgetting. Secrecy and silence are the perpetrator's first defense" (8). Muslim Comics set in warscapes defy that silence and undo that forgetting. Henry Giroux's *The Violence of Organized Forgetting: Thinking beyond America's Disimagination Machine* warns against collective amnesia brought about by neoliberal pedagogy, which "undermin[es] our capacity to bear witness"; he underscores the importance of engaging critically with political and cultural apparatuses to develop "agency, ethics, and collective resistance" (12). Muslim Comics adhere to this tenet by refusing to participate in "organized forgetting"; if the idea of a warscape signifies everyday life rendered unstable, permanently in flux, then witnessing in Muslim Comics reflects a desire to restore stability and certainty by creating permanent records of those who are erased from history and whose voices are muted. In this spirit, Muslim Comics maintain a testimonial mission to chronicle the long-lasting effects of trauma: They speak *for* the oppressed/wronged Muslim; they speak *against* the power structures responsible for their subjugation; and they speak *to* audiences that may be able to alter present realities if properly informed and encouraged to remember. This triangulation between Muslim Comics, warscape, and witnessing will be the chief organizing principle of each chapter. The different kinds of witnessing discussed in the ensuing sections shed light on the complicated nature of seeing, speaking, and representing as public practices.

But witnessing itself is a complex and sometimes problematic act—not least in Muslim warscapes, where "witness" has religious as well as secular significance. As Kelly Oliver explains:

> It is important to note that witnessing has both the juridical connotations of seeing with one's own eyes and the religious connotations of testifying to that which cannot be seen. It is this double meaning that makes witnessing such a powerful alternative to recognition in reconceiving subjectivity and thereby ethical relations. The double meaning of witnessing—*eyewitness* testimony based on firsthand knowledge, on the one hand, and *bearing witness* to something beyond recognition that can't be seen, on the other—is the heart of subjectivity. (483)

The idea of witnessing is especially significant in Islam, since being a pious Muslim starts with a proclamation of *shahadad* (avowing that there is no God but God, and that Mohammad is His prophet), which itself is an act of witnessing. In some *suras* of the Qur'an, "witness" appears as a label referring to all pious believers willing to testify to Mohammad's message; in others, it is reserved for those who are labeled the *shaheed*, a term that literally translates to "witness" but has also come to signify a martyr.[5] This usage, which emphasizes self-sacrifice while defending a religious cause, has been appropriated by jihadism—even though this is a highly contested interpretation, with many Islamic scholars arguing that sacrifice of the self has no bearing on Allah's view of the virtues of the believer or the value of their testimony.[6] Nevertheless, this link between "witness" and "martyr" (a link present in Christendom as well: It denotes someone willing to act as a witness to their faith, even at the risk of death) is now well established and is explored in a number of Muslim Comics in a critical manner.[7] Muslim Comics generally problematize the valorization of the *shaheed* as an exceptional and ideal witness who testifies to the glory of Allah by sacrificing his life; instead, they focus on witnessing as a common and indeed inescapable condition of living in a warscape, where violence is ever present to the point of becoming banal. This push back against the cult of the *shaheed* is also an effort to disrupt the prevalence and centrality of the jihadi figure, which has far too long dominated the Western imagination.

Muslim Comics often embrace the idea of warscape witnessing as a way of resisting the jihadist *shaheed*, but that does not mean that they operate as simple, neutral "witness statements" or that they accept witnessing as a transcendent experience. One graphic narrative can move between secular witnessing (as attestation to the lived experiences of victims) and religious

---

5. The Qur'an states: "The day will surely come when We shall call a witness from each community to testify [. . .]. We shall call *you* to testify against your people: for to you We have revealed the Book which manifests the truth about all things, a guide, a blessing, and good news for those who submit" (16:89). In other *suras*, Allah describes Himself as a witness to the moral integrity of his subjects: "Say: 'People of the Book, why do you deny the revelations of God? God bears witness to all your actions'" (3:98).

6. The connection between *shaheed* and martyr is extremely controversial in the Islamic world. According to *True Islam*, there is no basis to make such a link in the teachings of the Qur'an: "The concept of shaheed, as interpreted by the majority of Muslim scholars to mean a martyr is totally un-Quranic. According to the traditional Muslim scholars, anyone who is murdered, drowns or is killed in a fire becomes a shaheed (martyr) and goes straight to Heaven" (True Islam).

7. In the OED, a martyr is defined as "a person who chooses to suffer death rather than renounce faith in Christ or obedience to his teachings, a Christian way of life, or adherence to a law or tenet of the Church."

witnessing (validation of faith and belief in a transcendental truth) as a meditation on misplaced convictions. Another graphic narrative can approach witnessing as an ethical question, differentiating between authentic witness (one who provides a truthful representation of facts) and false witness (one who manipulates facts for self-interest) only to blur the lines between the two: The authentic witness may falsely rely on manufactured facts, while the "false" witness may deliberately bend the truth to stay alive. And some eyewitness accounts can be complicated by the presence of a proxy witness—someone who has access to trauma via postmemory rather than memory, weaving objective facts with subjective feelings. Aminatta Forna touches on this when she argues that witness literature can operate as "an interplay of sometimes real events or a context that is real, with fictional events and characters, combined with the aesthetic qualities of fiction."

We can see precisely this kind of "interplay" in a graphic novel like *Zahra's Paradise*, which provides an account of the Islamic regime in an attempt to convey "the story of today's Iran" to a larger audience. Indeed, Amir claims that "nothing in *Zahra's Paradise* was invented; it is a sort of collage made up of real-life events strung together to make sense of what can sometimes seem too absurd to be true" ("Zahra's Paradise"). But more precisely, Amir and Khalil tell a fictional story inspired by a medley of headlines; the narrative often deviates from the main plot to include real-life events covered in the Western media, including the execution of two queer men as well as the killing of Neda Agha-Sultan, the young protestor who became the face of resistance in Iran. Some critics have argued that it is counterproductive to mix fiction with witness testimony, fearing that it will weaken the "moral and political urgency" of such testimonies; others (including myself) are convinced that traditional distinctions between fiction and nonfiction, and between personal recollection and political testimony, are increasingly breaking down (Beverley 40).[8] Why are Muslim Comics effective in creating witness accounts of warscape existence? Partly because the different levels of witnessing that occur in these narratives are a product of their commitment to dual audiences: On the local level, these comics are setting out to provide reliable testimonies of events and people, but at a global level, they utilize fiction as a way to communicate their larger messages to an international audience unfamiliar with intimate local details. Because these narratives can move so readily between accuracy and abstraction, between objective reality and subjective representation, they ultimately produce multifaceted witness testaments well suited to voicing and humanizing identities that are under

---

8. As Jessica Murray puts it, "classifications and boundaries, such as those between fiction and testimony, self and other, personal and political [have] become more difficult to maintain" (2).

constant strain and pressured by the permanent instability of the warscape in which they exist.

THE FOLLOWING CHAPTERS grapple with a diverse range of Muslim characters in warscapes spread over a vast geography (Palestine, Saudi Arabia, Iran, Syria, Lebanon, Turkey, and India). This broad scope is meant not only to insulate Islam from a simplistic East/West binary (where Western epistemology dominates the production and circulation of knowledge about the Other) but also to enable a comparative analysis of the challenges faced by different groups of Muslims inside and outside the Muslim homeland. I employ a transnational lens to evaluate common threads in the creation, evolution, and circulation of images of the Muslim. The exploration of multinational comics strategies for the transmission, appropriation, and propagation of images demonstrates that Muslim Comics do not all revolve around a single concept of religion or even understand it as an overriding component of identity; rather, a variety of Muslim experiences—from states of exception and statelessness, to communal suffering and mourning, to border existence, and so on—are discussed, with each touching on different theoretical concepts and each entangled with a different idea of bearing witness. Such an approach reinforces the notion that there is no single organizing idea that "makes sense" of Muslim identity but rather that Muslimness is a cluster of identities and affiliations.

Chapter 1, "The Politics and Aesthetics of Muslim Comics," interrogates the merits and shortcomings of the term "Muslim Comics." What are the main features of Muslim Comics and what history do they share? Should this label be reserved only for those who have Muslim backgrounds, or should it gesture toward a more collective endeavor in regard to strategies of representation that include Muslims and non-Muslims alike? Is there, or should there be, some sort of litmus test to determine the "Muslimness" of a text? I argue that Muslim Comics are less about the biography of the artist/author and more about the centrality and ambition of its engagement with Islam and Islamic life. Muslim Comics foreground Muslim experiences and represent sophisticated and complex Muslim characters as protagonists without succumbing to the flattened images or sensationalist rhetoric traditionally associated with Islam. Essentially, Muslim Comics emerge as an interventionist oeuvre dedicated to the pluralization and normalization of this faith group.

The ensuing chapters focus on the idea of Muslim existence in different types of warscapes: Starting with a self-contained extralegal site (Guantánamo detention center), expanding to a city (Tehran as a locus of civil unrest), then outward again to a region (Kashmir as a contested zone), and finally to a country (Palestine as a partially recognized and partially occupied state), I consider different types of witness accounts about the everyday experiences of Muslims situated in distressed areas. This movement allows me not only to highlight the triangulation between place, identity politics, and warscape existence but also to reconsider the ways various locations manage, regulate, and distinguish between "good" and "bad" Muslims—whether they be detainees, citizens, immigrants, displaced refugees, or others.

Chapter 2, "Reluctant Witnesses in Prison Camp Narratives," focuses on three Guantánamo narratives, namely Jérôme Tubiana and Alexandre Franc's *Guantánamo Kid: The True Story of Mohammed El-Gharani*, Sarah Mirk's *Guantanamo Voices: True Accounts from the World's Most Infamous Prison*, and Jay Cantor, James Romberger, and Jose Villarrubia's *Aaron & Ahmed: A Love Story*. These narratives directly challenge the long-established comics trope of the "dangerous Muslim." In stark contrast to the active and aggressive jihadi, they show the abject Muslim detainee in Guantánamo, subjected to violence on a daily basis—from casual beatings to full-fledged torture. The warscape conditions in Guantánamo not only produce a subjugated and victimized Other but eventually transform the Muslim into an utterly wretched figure comparable to the "Muselmann"—a term employed in Holocaust narratives to refer to the cadaveric and zombified existence of the broken prisoner. Eventually, all three works depict the Muselmann figure as a "reluctant" witness, who, despite having the ability to speak, cannot reclaim his voice or restore his impaired agency. It becomes clear that neither witnessing nor speaking can help the Muselmann end his abjection; rather, Muselmann status becomes a lifelong sentence, something held even after release from prison.

Chapter 3, "Vulnerability, Resistance, and False Witnesses," shifts attention to the Muslim homeland and explores Tehran as an emerging warscape within an oppressive Islamist state—as discussed in Amir and Khalil's *Zahra's Paradise* and Mana Neyestani's *An Iranian Metamorphosis*. The chapter picks up on the idea of "prison" as a large-scale, coercive state apparatus by centering on the torture and killing of hundreds of protestors opposed to the corruption of an Islamist state. As Amir attests, Evin Prison becomes the emblem of a country that has abandoned law and transformed into "a penal colony"—with continual crackdowns, incarcerations, and killings of its own citizens. In this warscape, witnessing is linked to a vulnerability-resistance dialectic: Even though speaking against the regime turns one into a target, remaining silent can be equally dangerous. Detainees are forced to testify—even if that testimony is a fabrication utilized as state propaganda. Indeed, when Neyestani is asked to write his own account of the events that led to his arrest, the authorities keep rejecting his statements until he is able to present them with the "right" explanation. Likewise, government officers in *Zahra's Paradise* visit homes of the dead detainees to coerce their families into signing sham confessions. The figure of the false witness in both comics points to a serious ethical and political dilemma: Why act as a witness when the very act of witnessing has been compromised and corrupted? If there is no way of speaking truth to the public, no way of preserving the story of the individual, no possibility of upholding justice or pursuing truth, then the future of witnessing itself is in doubt. In the end, the two comics contemplate the possibility of creating documents that will allow subjects to bear witness outside of the warscape.

Chapter 4, "*Shaheed* and Border Witnesses," weds the notion of witnessing with border existence. Malik Sajad's *Munnu: A Boy from Kashmir* and Naseer Ahmed and Saurabh Singh's *Kashmir Pending* focus on the everyday lives of Muslims as the fighting between rival factions turns Kashmir into a warscape. In this border territory, violence extends to all parts of everyday life—including schools and mosques. The two narratives challenge contemporary border theories (Gloria Anzaldúa, Emily Hicks), which understand "borderlands" as inherently positive and productive spaces that lead to a renewed sense of self rooted in duality—even plurality. For Sajad and Ahmed, border existence instead triggers a loss of individuality and an irresistible paranoia when the border space is contested and threatened by rival nations. In fact, as these comics illustrate, the border can produce ideologues entrenched in their own worldviews and detached from their original identities and communities. In the end, both authors distance themselves from religious witnessing, used predominantly in their warscape society as a recruitment tool. Instead of celebrating the Muslim martyr-witness, they introduce the border witness as an ambivalent speaker, one who prioritizes regional belonging and empathy—known as *Kashmiriyat* (communal coexistence)—over religious or even national dogmatism.

Chapter 5, "Surrogate Witnesses and Memory," explores the role of postmemory in Leila Abdelrazaq's *Baddawi* and Ari Folman's *Waltz with Bashir: A Lebanon War Story*, with the creators of both narratives acting as surrogate witnesses for Palestinians trapped in a warscape. In *Baddawi*, Abdelrazaq records her father's experiences growing up in a refugee camp, in an effort to give voice to millions of displaced "people, born into a life of exile and persecution, indefinitely suspended in statelessness." *Waltz with Bashir*, on the other hand, is an attempt to end Folman's amnesia as he tries to come to terms with his involvement as an Israeli soldier in the attacks against Palestinian refugees—later known as the Sabra and Shatila massacres. Both comics emphasize the way memory and postmemory influence the gaze of the witness as they create eulogies for lost, unrecoverable homes subsumed by emerging warscapes.

The conclusion of the book, "The Future of Muslim Comics," asks what we learn from new Muslim Comics aesthetically. Are there common characteristics that enrich the testimony of the witness by emphasizing a different ethics of reading and engagement? Can these characteristics be understood as an aesthetic movement that will serve as a counterpart to the long-standing tradition of (usually stereotypical) representations of Muslim characters in comics? This chapter argues that a new approach to aesthetics may ultimately lead to a new ethics of Muslim representation and indeed of cultural politics for Muslims; in these works, warscape aesthetics leads toward an ethical sentience and responsibility that moves beyond the artwork into the realm of action.

This book, finally, is about the ways in which graphic narratives can aid in developing strategies for Muslim existence through storytelling. By offering insights into current and emerging warscapes around the globe, these works imagine the effects of violence on diverse Muslim communities inside and outside Muslim homelands. New Muslim Comics not only challenge clichés and stereotypes but also present themselves as social and political documents, a new kind of witness statement where—to borrow from Edward Said's description of Joe Sacco's graphic novel *Palestine*—"accuracy" meets "gentleness" to capture the humanity of a people ("Homage" iv). At the same time, the book lends its weight to diversification efforts in comics and comics studies by pushing for a more global (rather than Western-dominated) engagement with difference. Charles Taylor notes that to make sense of identity, it is imperative to have "an orientation to the good" (47). He writes: "Now we see that this sense of the good has to be woven into my understanding of my life as an unfolding story. But this is to state another basic condition of making sense of ourselves, that we grasp our lives in a *narrative*" (47). If narrative is how we make sense of ourselves as well as Others, then we need effective interpretive tools that can guide our understanding toward "good." Only by embracing a new ethics of seeing can we move forward with the larger project of racial and religious toleration and inclusion. And Muslim Comics do just that.

CHAPTER 1

The Politics and Aesthetics of Muslim Comics

Before examining the nature and ambitions of Muslim Comics today, it will be useful to trace the history of Muslim characters in sequential art and then locate this history in relation to the evolution of comics studies. Such an approach will not only help navigate some muddled disciplinary boundaries but will also shed light on recent efforts within the medium to counteract its long history of racial demonization, religious vilification, and whitewashing. A large part of this chapter will dwell on the US comics tradition; my intent is not to privilege American comics by ignoring other established and commercially successful markets (such as *bandes dessinées,* manga, etc.) or create an artificial binary by pitting the US corpus against "native" Muslim ones. Rather, my hope here is to use the long and influential history of American comics as a way to contextualize developing trends and aesthetic patterns. It is also helpful to examine the evolution of the Muslim figure in this oeuvre in relation to the substantial Muslim diaspora in the US, acting as a contact zone of sorts.[1] Dissecting the representations of Muslims in this manner will bring certain ideological undercurrents to the surface and help identify strategies for (as well as deficiencies in) visualizing the religious Other.

---

1. There is a long history of comics in the US, which started with the comics sections in newspapers at the beginning of the twentieth century (*The Little Bears, The Yellow Kid*).

An important goal of this chapter is to attend to questions of race and racism. Many have noted that historically, the comics medium has been suffused with racial stereotypes that highlight—and often amplify—alterity in visual terms. A general xenophobic intolerance of immigrants and foreigners had encouraged anti-Muslim sentiments even before the events of 9/11. As Sam Keen puts it: "You can hit an Arab free; they're free enemies, free villains—where you couldn't do it to a Jew or you can't do it to a black anymore" (qtd. in Shaheen, "How the Media Created"). Given this history, it is not surprising to see some comics continue to tap into these kinds of collective dispositions and exhibit Islamophobic attitudes. At the same time, the recent impetus for adding fresh faces to the comics repertoire (as well as fostering a more inclusive labor force within the industry) reflects a broad shift toward diversification. Comics has always been an "outsider" form of sorts, and the medium's propensity to "reflect and affect" culture situates comics both as a record of collective attitudes toward alterity *and* a pioneering enterprise that constantly pushes for social change (Rifas, "Racial Imagery"). Muslim Comics are a product of that oscillation.

From Racialization to Racism

The elusive line between race and religion—not only in comics, but more generally in American popular culture—presents real challenges for those seeking to pin down the politics of Muslim representation. Much academic consideration of Muslim experiences in the US, for example, is subsumed into the field of Arab studies, which implicitly engages with the idea of "anti-Muslim racism." The racialization of Islam, according to Susan Stanford Freidman, has long reflected a vaguely paradoxical situation whereby "being 'Muslim' becomes an identity, an ethnicity defined in part through an association with a religion" (205). In literary studies, various contemporary anthologies and collections that study Muslim identity have to some extent reinforced the conflation of Muslim American writing with Arab American writing.[2] For some scholars, this mutual alliance is quite natural; Carol Fadda-Conrey, for one, argues that using the term "Arab American writing" could help to diminish the derogatory connotations of "Arab" and energize ongoing conversations about the Arab community's place in American multiculturalism.[3] For others, the conflation of Arab subjectivity with Islam is

---

2. See Akash and Mattawa; Darraj; Salaita, *Arab American*; Fadda-Conrey.

3. Fadda-Conrey contends that the Arab designation in this context would "denot[e] a minority collective whose members are connected not only through a shared cultural and linguistic Arab heritage but more importantly through a common investment in shaping and performing a revisionary form of US citizenship" (10–11).

deeply problematic: Steven Salaita points out that this pairing overlooks the plurality of religions within the Arab culture (Arab Christians, Druze, Bahai, etc.) while also minimizing the importance of non-Arab Muslims in conversations about religious marginalization in the West. An Arab-centered investigation, he further argues, leads to the homogenization of a multiethnic, multinational, polyvocal global *ummah*:

> I am hesitant based on long-standing religious diversity to compel Arab America into an Islamic posture, something that frequently (and mistakenly) occurs in popular media throughout the United States. Even among Muslim Arab Americans there are longstanding [sic] religious diversities that prevent scholars of Islam in Arab America from offering formulaic discussion. (Salaita, *Arab American* 6)

This taxonomic crisis is obviously relevant to Muslim Comics. How are we to situate Muslim Comics within a multidisciplinary field of analysis that regularly conflates race and religion and erroneously negates the racial and cultural plurality of the global Muslim *ummah*? Certainly, one major intervention that any scholar of Muslim Comics must undertake is to end the habit of using "Arab," "Muslim," and "Middle Eastern" as interchangeable labels.

The conflation of race and religion is apparent from the earliest moments of the American comics tradition and continues throughout the twentieth century. For example, in *Action Comics* #598 (1988), Superman is confronted by two villains, Khareemali, the Minister of Defense for the nation of "Qurac," and "Fist of Allah," a member of a terrorist group known as the Angels of Allah. Both characters are presented as Arab and Muslim. To begin with, Khareemali's appearance visually marks him as a cliché of an Arab despot: He is dressed in his green military suit (the shade of green traditionally associated with Islam); he sports a *ghutra* (a traditional Arabian headdress for men); he exhibits a thin mustache above his lips with a thick goatee underneath. His visual "Arabness" is complemented by his conservatism and misogyny: During his interview with Lois Lane, he cannot hide his chauvinist views. When she asks whether he has a problem dealing with women, he responds: "Indeed not . . . In their proper place. The females of Qurac know that place. Unlike their American cousins" (6). When Lois responds condescendingly ("Welcome to the 20th C." 6–7), Khareemali orders his guards to restrain her while he reaches for his whip. A Muslim/Arab man threatening a liberated white woman is a familiar trope; the minister's sexism and abusive demeanor embody Western images of toxic masculinity in Islam. Elsewhere in the same story, "Fist of Allah" appears in an armored suit, preparing to activate nuclear weapons on board a US navy ship. As his name suggests, he views himself as a conduit to impose Allah's will on earth, which in this case he has interpreted as building an anti-Western Arab coalition. Holding the captain of the ship hostage, he states: "The Angels of Allah have seized this American warship. Its crewmen are our prisoners . . . Prisoners in the war to unite the Arab brotherhood against the heathen world" (15). Muslimness and Arabness become indistinguishable, and the stereotypes pertaining to each position merge.[4] The enmeshing of identity categories hints at "the conditions of possibility of racing Islam and Islamifying race while politicizing Muslims and Arabs alike" (Gana 1577). Racialized, politicized Muslim representations in comics reflect a particular type of adversary that fixes the identity of the Muslim as vulgar, treacherous, violent, out of touch—and also racially Other.[5]

The racialization of Islam is part of a long history of comics utilizing racist stereotypes as visual indicators of Otherness. Chris Ware observes that "if you treat comics as a visual language and trace their origins, they point back, essentially, to racism" (*Dangerous Drawings* 39).[6] The popularity of exaggerated racial stereotypes and caricatures within the comics tradition, Leonard Rifas elaborates, is driven by the "us vs. them" binary.[7] The cartoonist, he explains, taps into populist anxieties about Otherness—be they marginalized minorities within the nation or foreigners threatening

---

4. Maryanne Rhett maintains that comics "pull from a common cultural knowledge" when portraying "Muslims and Middle Easterners as one and the same" (205); sequential art, she argues, replicates images and stereotypes drawn from "conventional wisdom" that echoes Orientalist construction of the Other (206). Rhett further observes that "modern sequential art—the graphic novel, comic book, and manga—plays with stereotypes and conventional wisdom about the Middle East and Muslims in such a way as to cut back on Said himself" (206).

5. This conflation continues to taint Muslim portrayals in post-9/11 narratives. In his study of superhero narratives published in the aftermath of 9/11, Fredrik Strömberg finds that while some of the negative Muslim stereotypes diminish, Arab/Middle Eastern/Muslim identities continue to be used interchangeably. Among the narratives he observes, he notes: "None of the Arab heroes is shown as belonging to a faith other than Islam or as being an atheist, although two characters were Muslims but not Arabs; this indicates a reluctance to separate the idea of Arabs and Muslims" (596).

6. Ware recalls his early illustrations: "I realized a great part of the 'visual rush' of comics is at least partially, if not almost entirely, founded in racial caricature" (*Dangerous Drawings* 41).

7. Rifas argues that "racism was built into the foundations of entire once-popular genres, especially jungle comics (in which white 'jungle lords' sometimes punched the faces of African challengers to maintain order in their realms) and war comics (which regularly showed white Americans fighting barbaric Japanese, Korean, or Vietnamese enemies)" ("Race and Comix" 28).

national interests: The Six-Day War ushered in Ra's al Ghul as an Arab villain in *Batman*, and 9/11 reinforced the image of the Muslim terrorist. The visual coding of Otherness, to put it another way, is "deeply embedded in our culture and our collective subconscious" and is driven by apprehensions about national susceptibilities that reinforce a clear division between friend and foe, insider and outsider (Robert Crumb qtd. in Rifas, "Race and Comix" 35).

Racist representations of Muslims—with visual cues that include skin color, facial features, and manner of dress—not only accentuate alterity in physical terms but also allude to moral shortcomings. Jack G. Shaheen's comprehensive study finds that comics dating back to the 1950s enthusiastically employed denigrating images of Muslims and Arabs in ways that implied a set of collective flaws embedded in Islamic culture and belief. In Shaheen's analysis, Muslims and Arabs regularly appear as sociopaths, prone to violence and deprived of "social consciousness":

> Arabs wade into personal combat against our gallant figures, spitting upon them and deriding them. They carry out acts of torture with Mephistophelian glee. Their features are frequently bestial, demonized and dehumanized. Their faces drip with hatred and fanaticism. [. . .] They are anti-American, anti-West, anti-Israel, anti-Jewish, anti-Christian. ("Arab Images" 123)

For Edward Said, the negative portrayal of the Arab world is a symptom of hostile media coverage in the West. In *Covering Islam*, he explains the anti-Muslim and anti-Arab bias as a politically motivated sentiment popularized by the media reports of the deteriorating relationship between the US and the Middle East during the 1970s.[8] Said characterizes lopsided coverage of "the world of Islam, the Arabs, and the Orient" as a politically motivated disinformation campaign to reinforce the idea that Islam is incompatible with Western values and modern democracies: "In many instances 'Islam' has licensed not only patent inaccuracy but also expressions of unrestrained

---

8. Said's methodical analysis of journalists pointed to partial and unbalanced reportage that targeted Islam as a whole:

> Negative images of Islam continue to be very much more prevalent than others, and [. . .] such images correspond not to what Islam "is" [. . .] but to what prominent sectors of a particular society take it to be. Those sectors have the power and the will to propagate that particular image of Islam, and this image therefore becomes more prevalent, more present, than all the others. (*Covering Islam* 144)

ethnocentrism, cultural and even racial hatred, deep yet paradoxically free-floating hostility" (xi). As a consequence, Islam became a fixed signifier, with racial components, that represented a clear and present danger for the West.[9]

These sentiments quickly infiltrated comics productions, and readers have for decades encountered a range of negative Islamic stereotypes and characters, from "towel-headed bozos" (*Action Comics* #598) to "bandits in bedsheets" (*Batman: A Death in the Family* #426–429), from America-bashing villains such as Yassir (*The Punisher: Nuclear Terrorists over Times Square* [1987]) to woman-hating Muslim militants (*Captain America* #1).[10] By the end of the twentieth century, Arabs and Muslims were lodged firmly in comics writing as "poorly developed caricature[s]" with no redeeming qualities (Dar 99). A particularly gripping example of such characterization can be seen in Joker's tirade in *Batman: A Death in the Family* (1988) as he appears before the United Nations Assembly to represent Iran (see figure 1.1):

> I am proud to speak for the great Islamic Republic of Iran. That country's current leaders and I have a lot in common. Insanity and a great love of FISH. But unfortunately we also share a MUTUAL PROBLEM. We get NO RESPECT. Everyone thinks of Iran as the home of the TERRORIST ZEALOT! They say even worse things about ME, would you believe? We've both suffered unkind ABUSE AND BELITTLEMENT! WELL, WE AREN'T GOING TO TAKE IT ANYMORE!! You'll no longer be allowed to kick us around. In fact, you aren't going to be able to kick ANYONE around ever again!

Shaheen points out the factual inconsistency in portraying Joker's affiliation with Iran through a headdress and robe associated with Arabs and in showing Batman speaking in Farsi when he visits Beirut. He writes: "Arabs are equated with terrorists who are equated with Iranians who are equated with Batman's insane arch-nemesis, the Joker. [. . .] The Joker's insanity is their insanity; his destructiveness is their destructiveness" (qtd. in Dar 102). Connecting the Arab and the Muslim with a supervillain attempting

---

9. As Laurence Michalak explains,

> The Arab stereotype did not originate in America. A negative stereotype of the Middle East has existed in Europe at least since the spread of Islam. Europeans feared Middle Eastern peoples as the formidable adversaries they indeed sometimes were. After all, the Arabs conquered Southern Europe up to Central France, and in Eastern Europe the Ottoman successors of the Arabs fought to the very gates of Vienna. Later, in the 19th century, the Middle East came to represent potential colonial possessions and subject peoples. (33)

10. See Dar; Strömberg.

FIGURE 1.1. Joker speaks at the United Nations on behalf of Iran.

to undermine modern society epitomizes the way racialization and racism work in tandem.

It is against this background of racial and religious politics that I set out to scrutinize the figure of the Muslim in US comics. I identify three broad categorical tendencies in the deployment of Muslim characters before the rise of Muslim Comics: the Orientalized companion, the barbaric jihadi, and the hybrid token—all of which convey different racial politics with various visual cues. These categories do not necessarily align with historical periods—although there are upticks in the appearance of characters belonging to certain categories at particular moments. That is to say, in tracing this history, I do not pretend to construct a complete account of the Muslim figure that follows a neat chronological order. Rather, my goal is to show how certain character and design trends continually recur in American comics and how those trends contribute to the flattened image of the Muslim—an image Muslim Comics strongly contest.

The Orientalized Other

The racialized pigeonholing of the Muslim has been intensified by Orientalist depictions of the East as the antithesis of the West. Numerous Muslim characters in comics—both friend and foe—have been conveyed in Orientalist terms. Abdul Alhazred, known as the "Mad Arab" (*Tarzan Whitman Variants* #15 [1978]), is a good example of the Orientalized adversary. Inspired by the works of H. P. Lovecraft, Alhazred is a supernatural being with the ability to disappear behind a green cloud and teleport himself, to mesmerize people, and to possess their bodies. His colorful costume (*salwar*, dagger, and a long *ghutra* that frames his hollow face to highlight his entrancing eyes) evokes the East without pinpointing a specific origin. When Alhazred gets wounded by Tarzan's knife during a fight, he neither shrieks nor bleeds. Tarzan asks, in surprise, "What kind of a man are you?" To this Alhazred responds: "No man." Straddling the line somewhere between exotic enemy and ghostly demon, he embodies the Orientalized villain, completely inscrutable and utterly unrelatable.

Alhazred's Orientalist characterization does not necessarily lean on the idea of Islam, but the protagonist of *Kismet: Man of Fate* illustrates the popular convergence of Muslim subjectivity and Orientalist aesthetics in comics (see figure 1.2). The first Muslim hero headliner, published by Elliot Publishing Company in 1944, Kismet is the embodiment of Islamic values. Originally from Algeria, Kismet wears a fez inscribed with a V (for "victory"),

THE POLITICS AND AESTHETICS OF MUSLIM COMICS • 31

FIGURE 1.2. The 2016 cover of *Kismet: Man of Fate*.

salwar pants, and a cape over his shirtless back. His name translates to "destiny" or "fate," and he possesses the ability to see into the future to anticipate "Allah's will." His signature statements ("By the beard of the prophet" or "By the star and crescent of Islam") as well as his refusal to drink alcohol or kill his enemies attest to his "authentic," if hyper-Orientalized, Muslim ethics. At the time of his creation, Kismet was an anomaly: Fighting alongside Western forces against the Nazis during the World War II, he was presented as an ally, determined to help "the conquered people of Europe carry on their ceaseless struggle against tyranny" (*Bomber* #1). However, this was a short-lived experiment: The character did not catch on, and the series was discontinued after only four issues.[11] According to Strömberg, the brief shelf life of this eccentric superhero was indicative of readerly indifference toward nonvillainous, non-Western heroes, which "were not culturally significant on a wider plane in superhero comics before 9/11" (579)—a point that I will revisit later in this chapter.

The innovative ambition behind *Kismet* raises the interesting question of whether Orientalism can be employed by comics artists in a progressive way. Craig Thompson's eagerly anticipated *Habibi* (2011)—hailed as an extraordinary exercise in visual syncretism that combined Arabic calligraphy, numerology, ornamentation, geometry, and arabesque—provides an intriguing case study. Thompson tells the story of Dodola, an Arab girl, and Zam, an African boy, nine years her junior; both are kidnapped by thieves to be sold as slaves. At one point, Dodola saves Zam from being killed and runs off with him; they hide in an abandoned ship in the desert. As their supplies deplete, Dodola prostitutes herself to travelers in exchange for food. Soon, her reputation as "the phantom courtesan of the desert" reaches the ears of the Sultan of Wanatolia, a fictional space that closely resembles Arabia. Dodola is captured yet again and is sent to the Sultan's harem as a concubine, where she attains the name Sfayi ("pleasure giver"). In the meantime, Zam leaves the desert to seek Dodola in the city, where he chances upon a group of *hijras*—eunuchs, living on the street as entertainers. Zam decides to embrace their way of life, and, after undergoing castration himself, eventually finds employment at the palace as a guard. He is reunited with Dodola, now rejected by the Sultan and awaiting execution. Against all odds, they manage to elope and leave the city for a simpler life in the country. Despite numerous obstacles—including Zam's depression generated by his emasculation—they persevere as a couple. The graphic novel ends with them adopting an enslaved girl to complete their unconventional family.

Thompson's meticulous lettering, detailed landscapes, and illustrations of Qur'anic *ayats* coupled with biblical verses create a stunning visual cypher. Reviews hailed *Habibi* as "a triumph of creativity" (*The Independent*) and a "graphically dazzling" masterpiece (*Telerama*). For Thompson, it was important to show the beauty and humanity in Islam:

---

11. Kismet was later resurrected by A. David Lewis in 2015.

FIGURE 1.3. Dodola becomes a concubine in the Sultan's harem.

Islam was being demonized by the media and I tried to humanize it, to discover its beauty, and to understand it. [. . .] My research led me to discover Arabic calligraphy, geometrical designs, decoration, and architecture—all these artistic domains that have developed in such an incredible way on account of a supposed prohibition on figurative art. (qtd. in Groensteen 150)

Nevertheless, Thompson leans heavily on Orientalist stereotypes—from the oversexualized female body of the harem slave to the nomadic predators of the Arabian desert, from the perversely hedonistic royal palace to the eerie community of *hijras*, Orientalist clichés about debauchery and depravity run amok (see figure 1.3). The question is: How does Thompson's overt investment in Orientalism complicate the alleged politics of his work? Do the Orientalist images take over the narrative and sabotage the progressive efforts of the artist, or do they support Thompson's attempt to reclaim the East by contesting Islam's traditional demonization?

A group of critics contend that Thompson uses Orientalist images knowingly and strategically as he creates a textual/visual amalgamation of the Qur'an and the Bible to invalidate the East/West binary and highlight the similarities between the two belief systems. Madeline Backus and Ken Koltun-Fromm hold the opinion that "within this space and gaze, Arabic calligraphy takes on the form and function of the sacred orient. Thompson deploys calligraphy as an image/text to naturalize the orientalist discourse as sacred space" (6). This Orientalist grounding of the narrative, in other words, serves to enhance the idea of the universal sacred. Thierry Groensteen similarly suggests that "the Orientalizing phantasmagoria of *Habibi* is balanced out by a realism rarely seen before in the portrayal of all these afflictions" and thus cannot be interpreted solely through an Orientalist paradigm (155).[12] He further argues that Thompson's wedding of realism with fantasy creates an alternative mode of representation that facilitates an unlearning of various misconceptions about Islam. Other critics, however, remain unconvinced when it comes to the question of Thompson's attempts to disrupt stereotypes. The harem and slave market scenes, for example, are full of Orientalist banalities that replicate rather than destabilize conventions. By emulating the style of French Orientalists like Jean-Auguste-Dominique Ingres and Jean-Léon Gérôme, Thompson stylizes his female characters as objects of a male voyeuristic gaze: women in the nude, stretched out on the sofa, taking baths, putting oil on their bodies, conversing in intimate groups—images that blend the exotic with the erotic.[13] Such hypersexualization, argues Nadim Damluji, places Thompson's neo-Orientalist creation firmly in the tradition of Othered, universalized Western depictions of the East. Damluji also takes note of the fact that Thompson had not traveled in the Middle East ("except Morocco," in his words), did not know Arabic, and ultimately was engaging in "cultural appropriation" and cultural cherry-picking "for the purposes of quelling his own guilt." He consequently condemns the "well-intentioned" artist and his myopic vision of the Orient as a generic place "devoid of history." Damluji suggests that the end product is a parody rather than a critique of Orientalism: "The problem in making something knowingly racist is that the final product can still be read as racist." Despite these and other critical reservations, *Habibi* found a receptive audience and was commercially successful. Clearly, the Orientalized Muslim still survives as a character type.

---

12. Indeed, Thompson views his work as a fairy tale that can reclaim some of the Orientalist conventions in empowering ways:

> Edward Said talks about Orientalism in very negative terms because it reflects the prejudices of the west towards the exotic east. But I was also having fun thinking of Orientalism as a genre like Cowboys and Indians is a genre—they're not an accurate representation of the American west, they're like a fairy tale genre. (qtd. in Damluji)

13. Damluji questions the reason behind oversexualized characters, specifically Dodola, who is raped repeatedly and has failed to attain agency due to her sexual enslavement—not to mention the shallow representations of other Arab characters as misogynists and sexual predators.

The Muslim Jihadi and Islamophobic Comics

The second character category is the jihadi. While the popularity of the Muslim as a villain, and indeed the presence of jihadi characters in comics, predates 9/11, after the terrorist attacks, the figure of the jihadi became a dominant trope. As Nadine Sinno puts it, 9/11 "provided fodder to preexisting nationalist narratives that demonized Arabs and Muslims, labeling their cultures and religious beliefs as backwards, militant, oppressive, and simply incompatible with Western values—this time more vociferously" (117). The Muslim, once merely an exotic adversary, was now an existential threat, appearing not as "a complex human being but only as a purveyor of possible future violence" (Bayoumi, *This Muslim American Life* 9).[14] Consequently, a certain level of Islamophobia becomes excusable—even sanctioned.

Two Islamophobic comics that appeared in the (long) wake of 9/11 are noteworthy in their attempt to weaponize the image of the bloodthirsty jihadi. The first is Frank Miller's *Holy Terror* (2011), a graphic novel that features the superhero Fixer and his love interest Natalie joining forces to thwart an Al-Qaeda attack on an iconic landmark that resembles the Statue of Liberty. As one might suspect, the hollow-eyed Muslim supervillain— dressed in a white cloak and turban and carrying a dagger and beads— faithfully inhabits the dehumanizing tropes associated with the Muslim since the Dark Ages. The cover art featuring Fixer striking the supervillain, Frank Mehring argues, is evocative of Captain America's memorable punching of Adolf Hitler on the 1941 cover, "pitting determined American white men against violent Muslim terrorists" (2). The opening quote of the book (splashed across two full pages), is attributed to the prophet Mohammad: "If you meet the infidel, kill the infidel." In its miscontextualizing of Qur'anic teachings, this epigraph deliberately reinforces Islam as an ideology indistinguishable from "destructive weapons, jihadists, barbaric extremists and fundamentalism" (Ali and Manna 41).[15] Mehring posits that by "appropriating a wide array of popular culture visual archives for a propagandistic call

---

14. As racist attacks against Muslims (or "Muslim-looking" minorities) increased by 1,700 percent around the US following 9/11, the state passed new legislation targeting Muslim Americans (e.g., the Terrorist Information and Prevention System [TIPS]). For Salaita, this erosion of civil rights was an attempt to enforce "imperative patriotism" and test the loyalty of minorities and contributed to a politics of exclusion ("Ethnic Identity" 154).

15. Miller skips the rest of the verse—which goes on to say that "if anyone of the [enemy] seeks your protection, then grant him protection so that he may learn the word of Allah and then escort him to where he can be secure" (Qur'an, Surah At-Tawbah 9:1–6).

for Muslim 'Othering,'" the book implies that fighting against Islam is an American moral obligation and a patriotic duty (2).

Indeed, the release of Miller's book on the ten-year anniversary of 9/11 lays bare his intent to capitalize on this national trauma. The ostensible evil of Islam also allows Miller to justify Fixer's own moral transgressions—he enjoys torturing Muslims, even as he brands Islam a violent cult. Miller's attempt to create a simplistic binary of good and evil—visually achieved with his use of black-and-white "silhouette aesthetics"—works in tandem with the book's overall debasing of Muslims and his refusal to distinguish jihadis and pious believers. As one reviewer puts it, "They're fighting Islam, not Al-Qaeda, and the book suffers greatly for it. [. . .] The result of all that was this: a hateful, ill-considered, simplistic, ugly, nasty little book" (Brothers). Miller, in an interview with NPR, doubled down on his Islamophobic stance, positioning the 9/11 terrorists as of a piece with general Islamic "culture" (which he summarizes as "sixth century barbarism") and claiming his comic as his attempt to "serve his country" by thwarting the Muslim invasion of the West (qtd. in Dar 104–05). While Miller's demonizing of all Muslims as violent criminals reduces his work to a xenophobic publicity stunt, it is worth remembering that the book was widely promoted by a major media company and was the top-selling comic in America upon its release.

Various iterations of the moral and ideological positioning seen in *Holy Terror* appear in other post-9/11 comics. Similar politics to Miller's, for example, are at play in Fawstin's *The Infidel: Featuring Pigman* (2015). Fawstin, who grew up in a Muslim household with Albanian parents, positions himself as an insider who can unmask Islam's sinister values. In *Infidel*, he introduces twin brothers Killian Duke, a former-Muslim-turned-atheist and the creator of a comic book character named Pigman (a superhero dressed in pig leather to repulse jihadis), and Salaam Duka, the foil to Killian, a Muslim who becomes radicalized after 9/11 after witnessing the rise of Islamophobia. Salaam occasionally confronts his Muslim-bashing brother:

SALAAM: Your goal's just to make Islam look bad.
KILLIAN: Simply telling the truth about it makes it look bad.
SALAAM: So you left Islam for what? Something better? As if that's possible?
KILLIAN: Anything's better. I follow a philosophy that, unlike Islam, teaches you how important living a happy life here on earth is.
SALAAM: [. . .] The West values life. The Muslim world values Islam.
KILLIAN: Enough. You're wrong, about Islam, about me. About a lot of things. In the end Islam will win because there's nothing Muslims won't do. Nothing.

Killian, like Miller's Fixer, presents himself as an American patriot who sees it as his duty to offend Muslims. Himself a comics artist, Killian enjoys being a provocateur and proudly defends his inflammatory art: "I love seeing this enemy get what it deserves at the hands of a ruthless hero. And since they'd kill me for no reason anyway, why not give them a good one?" When he runs into a group of Muslims near Ground Zero with educational pamphlets about Islam, he verbally attacks them, calling Mohammad a "liar" and a "pedophile." Salaam, on the other hand, is a typical, obstinate Muslim extremist; he cannot articulate the spiritual principles of Islam without succumbing to violence, and his predictions of Islam's triumph against the infidels become an expression of his blind submission to a twisted version of religious faith. Both characters, supposedly acting as mouthpieces for opposite ends of the spectrum, end up as shallow caricatures.

The comic within the comic adds another narrative dimension to *Infidel*. The graphic novel that Killian produces within the comic is essentially a revenge story that features the superhero Pigman on a quest to kill Osama bin Laden. Needless to say, the portrayals of Muslims in the meta-comic are negative if not outright hostile: Most are dimwitted simpletons who chant slogans as they blindly pursue death in a zombified fashion. After Pigman executes bin Laden, for example, he parachutes from a mountaintop to escape from enraged jihadis, who leap to their death as they pursue him. Pigman ponders their lethal devotion, referring to a commonly mistranslated passage of the Qur'an: "Madmen. Misogynists dying and killing for 72 'women' . . . Only in Islam." As an ex-Muslim, Fawstin justifies his stereotyping as a necessary part of educating readers about the dangers of Islam: "Islam is an evil ideology, a political religion that has retarded the humanity of everyone under its thrall. Just look at the countries who live by its 'ethics,' and you'll understand that it should be in the dustbin of history" (Biddle). Fawstin's resentment is evocative of other Muslim-bashing rhetoric from this period—most notably Christopher Hitchens's 2007 article in *Vanity Fair*, which warned of Britain's imminent takeover by Muslims, with a tagline that read: "How did a nation move from cricket and fish-and-chips to burkas and shoe-bombers in a single generation?"[16]

The hyperbolic evil invoked in the graphic novels of Miller and Fawstin finds a more humorous—though still problematic—counterpart in Rich Johnston's *Iron Muslim* (2012), a superhero comic that recycles the terrorist plot as it creates a parodic version of *Iron Man* in a Muslim context. The

---

16. In a series of interviews, Fawstin tried to establish his ethos as an insider who could relay the bigoted views of Muslims: "Although many people today would describe my parents and my larger Muslim family as 'moderate Muslims,' there was nothing moderate about the hatred for Jews or the abuse of women in my family" (Biddle).

comic features Al Stark, an Iraqi villager who, after losing his parents in an American-led raid, decides to join Al-Qaeda to take revenge: "The irony is that in Iraq under Saddam I was free to be an atheist. Now, I hide my rage under the respectable cloak of religious fanaticism." In an ironic twist on American racial/religious conflation, he is motivated to reinvent himself as a Muslim fanatic. Putting on an Iron Man–style uniform, he attempts to destroy the Statue of Liberty; soon after the assault, however, he feels guilty for assailing a culture he essentially admires: "I hate America, obviously. They killed my parents. [. . .] But I also love their Starbucks and their Apple Stores and their Big Bang Theory. Now that I am public enemy number one, will I be able to walk into a Best Buy to get the latest season box set without being whisked away to Cuba?" His regret eventually inspires a reversal of course, and Stark hires Hollywood publicists to shoot a propaganda piece to spin his actions in a positive light. The success of this PR campaign leads to him landing a spot in a group of heroes called the "Avengefuls." Johnston's parody presents itself as politically incorrect humor, but it still leans heavily on the toxic trope that any random Muslim is one event away from converting to radicalism and the idea that Muslim life can only be understood in the context of jihadism.

Not all adoptions of the jihadi character are immediately linked to 9/11, nor do all of them appear in overtly right-wing or fervently Islamophobic comics. In *A Suicide Bomber Sits in the Library*, withdrawn by its publisher (Abrams) just before its scheduled release in May 2019, Jack Gantos and Dave McKean tell the story of a young boy entering a library with explosives under his clothes. As the protagonist observes people around him reading books, he becomes intrigued, and this curiosity leads him to abandon his mission. The basic argument of the book—that reading, presented as a quintessentially Western pastime, might tame the savage terrorist—generated an immediate backlash. For Zainab Akhtar, the boy's epiphany about the power of books reeks of condescension: "Reading will help the ignorant brown Muslim boy question/renounce his beliefs, you see, in addition to being some vague kumbaya about how a specific interpretation of culture will save the barbarian." The overall impression, for many readers, was that a celebration of the transformative aspects of education fell prey to racist clichés about the backward, barbaric, suicide-bombing Muslim.

Across this character category, the hyperexaggerated features of the jihadi inspire simplistic narratives built around one-dimensional characters, usually brainwashed extremists unable to exercise their own agency. Viewed either as terrorist or potential terrorist, the Muslim becomes a fixed signifier that perpetuates racist tropes via fearmongering. Even if the Muslim protagonist is meant to disrupt a formulaic terrorist plot, the characterization quickly yields to familiar stereotypes of violence, backwardness, and extremism. The only possible way to pacify or save the Muslim perpetrator is through his integration into Western values and institutions—a colonialist logic. This highly problematic moral positioning essentially renders the Muslim devoid of intellect and history: a character type, but not a human character.

The Hybrid Token

The final category we will consider is, on the surface, a more positive one for Muslim characters. It eschews jihadi tropes and avoids openly Islamophobic portrayals in favor of likeable and relatable Muslims. However, while the graphic narratives in this category reflect an intent to recuperate the image of the Muslim, they still employ "exotic" or reductivist tropes and thereby sustain the "good Muslim / bad Muslim" binary. Mahmood Mamdani explicates the Islamophobic implications of such thinking: "We are now told to distinguish between good Muslims and bad Muslims. Mind you, not between good and bad persons, nor between criminals and civic citizens, who both happen to be Muslims, but between good Muslims and bad Muslims" ("Good Muslim" 767). The underlying logic suggests that Muslims can only occupy simple moral positions and are limited in their capacity to engage with moral complexities: There are only "good Muslims" (those who "would undoubtedly support 'us' in a war against 'them'") and "bad Muslims" (those who are "clearly responsible for terrorism") (*Good Muslim* 15). Such simplification essentially undermines the progressive ambitions of the comics in question: "Balanced" portrayals are achieved through numbers (introducing a "good" Muslim for each "bad" Muslim) rather than "balanced" dispositions of complex Muslim characters. Therefore, this category marks not a clean break from the others but a hybrid position, where sympathetic and usually token Muslim characters are presented through the recycling of old stereotypes—this time in a slightly less offensive but still problematic manner.

Sympathetic Muslims have gradually become something of a staple of big superhero franchises. A genre that has always been at the heart of the comics medium in the US, the superhero narrative is inherently aligned with national culture and shared values. As Ramzi Fawaz explains, superheroes are "perceived as exceptional Americans whose heroism could provide an aspirational model of ideal citizenship for the nation's impressionable young readers" (4–5).[17] In the latter part of the twentieth century, increasing racial and religious diversity in superhero comics became a new priority, part of an attempt to represent what Stan Lee described as "the world outside [the] window" (Dokterman 78).[18] A new string of racially diverse superheroes emerged, including John Stewart as the first African American incarnation of Green Lantern (DC Comics, 1971) and Carol Danvers as first female superhero in the Ms. Marvel series (1977). Over the past couple of decades, religious diversity has also come to play a part in the industry's drive for inclusion. Nonvillainous Muslim characters have started to appear in established franchises—first in supporting roles and later as central characters. However, this new inclusivity could be seen as only partially effective, given the subgenre's prioritization of action over characterization, as well as its traditional reliance on the good/evil binary.

Dust (Sooraya Qadir), who made her debut in 2002 (*New X-Men* #133), is one of the first examples of a "good Muslim" character to appear after 9/11. A native of Afghanistan, Dust discovers her mutant powers after being abducted; when her captors force her to remove her traditional clothing, she defends her honor using her telekinetic capability. Wolverine finds her unconscious after she overpowers her kidnappers, and he decides to bring her to the X-Corp Mumbai Headquarters. Waking up in an unfamiliar place, Dust transmorphs into sand; only after Jean Grey's telepathic appeasement

---

17. The early part of the twentieth century saw the rising popularity of the superhero narrative, which not only functioned as entertainment by projecting a world of fantasy but also carried an important symbolic mission to propagate national values and interests by invoking specific historical and political frames. Fawaz's overview of the superhero category reveals the intricate dovetailing of justice and nationalism:

> With its inception in the late 1930s, the superhero quickly became a popular national icon that wedded a fantasy of seemingly unlimited physical power to an ethical impulse to deploy one's abilities in the service of maintaining public law and order. The great superheroes of the 1930s and 1940s—among them Superman, Batman, Captain America, and Wonder Woman—were legendary crime fighters who protected civilians from the machinations of organized crime, saved innocent victims from natural disasters, and, in the case of Captain America, battled foreign threats to American democracy like the Nazi menace. (4–5)

Fawaz's description of the superhero as an "aspirational model" with utopian nuances that underscore physical capability and moral singularity sets up the parameters of an "ideal citizenship" for others to emulate. This moral positioning of the superhero is a clear sign of the genre's engagement with the ongoing efforts of nation-building signaling to the converging discourses of nationhood and selfhood.

18. There is indeed a handful of examples of diverse characters that appear as main characters: *All-Negro Comics* #1 appeared in 1947 as an attack on mainstream comics. Later, in 1966, Marvel Comics published *Black Panther*, featuring the first Black superhero endorsed by an industry giant.

does she feel comfortable enough to rematerialize. As the sand swirls around her, she reappears on a pile of dust, covered from head to toe in her black abaya (coat) and niqab (veil that covers the face except for the eyes), repeating the word "Turaab" (meaning "Dust"). Dust's centrality to the comic's plot is signaled by the cover of the issue, which prominently features her, reduced to a pair of eyes, gazing directly at the reader through the darkness. From the outset, her clothing marks her out as a woman who has (by the logic of the comic) miraculously escaped the fate of the average repressed Muslim woman. As Strömberg notes: "Dust's costume can be seen as both an invitation to be subjected to the male gaze and processes of Othering, and simultaneously as a signifier denoting an Arab/Muslim woman but with connotations of Western supremacy and male dominance" (587). Much later, Dust reunites with her mother at an American refugee camp; her mother is surprised to see her daughter still wearing Muslim apparel. Dust responds: "I never wore it because of the Taliban, mother. I like the modesty and the protection it affords me from the eyes of men" (*New X-Men: Hellions* #2). While Dust's explanation attests to her new autonomy, it also somewhat oddly reaffirms the patriarchal idea that a "good" woman is necessarily a "modest" woman—this is evidently the kind of logic that even a "good" and independent Muslim character inherently possesses.

In addition to gender normativity, colonialist tropes dominate the rescue plot, most notably the trope of the white male savior (see figure 1.4). The dust jacket shows Dust's pupils reflecting the image of Wolverine with his claws drawn, ready to attack. His position echoes the cliché of the white man trying to save the brown woman from brown men—even though Dust is perfectly capable of saving herself from her assailants.[19] Dust's portrayal does little to combat the Orientalist image of the Muslim woman as simultaneously an exotic caricature and a victim of patriarchy and continues to

---

19. Dar observes:

> In several instances, we can make the argument for the Western male gaze: She is an "oppressed" Muslim girl who was rescued from Afghanistan by Wolverine, a Western male mutant. Wolverine is told that the Taliban were trying to remove Dust's clothes, obviously to molest her, and since there weren't any "good Muslim men" around to take a stand against the Taliban's perverted behavior, who better to rescue her than Wolverine, or rather, "Western democracy"? (107)

Dar's observations echo Lila Abu-Lughod's description of Western arrogance in the treatment of Muslim women: "Projects of saving other women depend on and reinforce a sense of superiority by Westerners, a form of arrogance that deserves to be challenged" (789).

FIGURE 1.4. *New X-Men* #133 featuring Sooraya Qadir (Dust).

present her through a Western prism.[20] In the end, far from being a harbinger of change, Dust's depiction continues to iterate "post-9/11 anxieties about Islam, and in particular, Afghanistan" (Arjana 11).[21] Furthermore, Dust's "goodness" is offset by the pervasive presence of "bad" Muslims, including three Muslim men who try to hijack a plane. While it imagines

---

20. As Winona Landis argues, "these 'positive' Muslim characters actually play into stereotypical racial formations of Muslims [. . .] that objectify or 'Other' these characters through Oriental imagery and terms" (189).

21. See Sayeh the Seer.

itself as progressive, then, the work as a whole has little interest in undoing simplistic binaries—except for manipulating them slightly to make room for the token "good Muslim."

The contradictions of this hybrid category are also readily apparent in the characterization of Simon Baz, the Lebanese American introduced as the new Green Lantern in 2012. The inauguration of Simon Baz was immediately hailed as a significant step toward addressing the cultural pressures felt by Muslim minorities in the US. Indeed, Simon's experiences as a second-generation Muslim American and native of Dearborn, Michigan (a heavily Muslim American city), speak directly to the challenges of integration encountered by this community. Burdened by financial difficulties, Simon is initially a street car racer; as his circumstances deteriorate, he becomes a car thief. When he is caught by authorities in a stolen car loaded (unbeknownst to him) with explosives, he is immediately labeled a terrorist and sent to Guantánamo. During his interrogation there, a Green Lantern Power Ring finds him and breaks him out of prison. After his escape, Simon reinvents himself and joins the Justice League to fight against the Third Army, a rogue group wanting to take over the universe. Clearly, Simon is presented as a "good Muslim," who despite committing crimes is essentially a decent citizen. He is in no way a radical Islamist—and yet jihadi politics continue to dictate the arc of the story. The volume begins with young Simon watching the collapse of the Twin Towers on TV. The plane crash is reflected in Simon's pupils; outside his iris, there is circular shading that resembles Arabic calligraphy, linking Simon with a Muslim cultural topography and the threat of Islamic radicalization. Framing the comic around the terrorist attacks suggests that 9/11 is not only an epoch-making temporal marker that initiated the War on Terror but also the only event that matters in terms of the US perception of Muslim Americans. In a series of panels that follows, time speeds up as we see moments of racism and discrimination directed at Simon and his family over the years: bigoted slogans painted on the wall of the Islamic Center; his sister being attacked by white boys, trying to remove her hijab; Simon receiving a "routine" pat-down from airport security—all pointing to the way Muslim Americans are scrutinized as potential threats but also reducing Simon's history to his interactions with the Islamophobic legacy of 9/11. Indeed, this is the case with his entire family: His sister, Sira, loses her job at the Dearborn Office of the State Department after Simon's arrest, with her boss telling her that "people are worried about their security." Institutionalized Islamophobia is introduced as a way of setting up the "good Muslim" / "bad Muslim" test. Simon's incarceration at Guantánamo alludes to the possible fate of the young, angry Muslim susceptible to radicalization. His loyalties are put to the test by the interrogating agent questioning Simon's background: "Baz is Arabic. And Simon? That's a pretty common name in Lebanon. But it also sounds American." To this Simon responds: "I *am* American."

Simon Baz has been hailed as "one of the most prominent Muslim superheroes," but his characterization still bears the contradictory marks of the hybrid token category.[22] The diminishing prominence of Islam throughout the narrative creates the impression that Islam appears only as the source of Simon's initial troubles and is somehow negated by his later empowerment. In fact, there is barely any mention of Islam once he becomes the Green Lantern. He neither observes Islamic rituals nor embraces Islamic spirituality. Simon's Muslimness—as in other comics with Muslim characters—comes across largely as window dressing: Once he passes the "good Muslim" test, Islam has served its thematic purpose. Indeed, the larger Muslim community itself shows similar biases. Once the news of Simon's arrest spreads, his father worries about the repercussions for his family: "[My wife] won't leave the house. Your mother's friends won't talk to her. The Mosque won't let us in. We're as guilty as your brother." As one reviewer puts it, the harsh treatment received from the invisible Muslim American community is "offensive" as they have no "compassion, guts and campaigning smarts of their own."[23] In the end, the portrayal of Simon Baz as a Muslim falls flat. He may not be a jihadi, but his entire story arc begins with his criminality; he qualifies as a "good Muslim" not because he has strong ethics but because he is not technically a terrorist. *Green Lantern* misses the opportunity to present a Muslim character outside the familiar tropes; consequently, the tokenized inclusion of the Muslim Other as a superhero ends up undermining any broader message about diversity and belonging.

Islam's tightly restricted role similarly impairs the interventionist politics of the much-anticipated Kamala Khan as the new Ms. Marvel. Heralded

---

22. See ComicBookWire.
23. One reviewer argues:

> Nobody that's shown or referred to has any political convictions at all, whether framed in the context of Islam or not. [. . .] On the one hand, suggests Johns, they're victims, deserving of our pity because they're worn-down after doing their very best despite all the bullying. On the other, those from beyond the Baz's nuclear family seem predominantly dull-headed and hard-hearted, self-interested if not actively anti-social. [. . .] Nobody, it seems, is really to blame for anything, although it is the Islamic community which comes out of Johns['s] tales the worst. They alone are shown to have failed to have produced anything other than the meek, or the meekly criminal. ("What's the Point")

as the first Muslim female headliner, the sixteen-year-old Pakistani American Kamala quickly became an emblem of the successful integration of Muslim Americans into comics.[24] Unlike Dust, whose Afghani roots marked her as a foreigner, Kamala's position as a hyphenated American situated her as an insider—despite racist jabs and low-level bigotry ("Ugh Kamala—no offense, but you smell like curry," says her friend, Zoe). Most scholars agree that Kamala's strength lies in her relatability; from the onset, she establishes herself as a typical adolescent, carefully toeing the line between the obedient daughter and the defiant teenager, testing her parents' authority. According to Joseph Hughes, the series deserves praise for concentrating on different "aspects of Kamala's culture while simultaneously telling you that she's just like so many other teenagers" (qtd. in Kent 524). Her relatability, however, can come at the risk of erasing her cultural background and religious identity. In stark contrast to her brother, Aamir—who wears a traditional *salwar kameez* suit along with a *kufi* (skull cap) and a beard, and who voices a fundamentalist understanding of religion—Kamala does not engage with Islam to any great extent.[25] In this regard, the two siblings appear as polar opposites: Aamir's exaggerated commitment to religion reinscribes typical stereotypes about the pious Muslim, whereas Kamala's secular viewpoint marks her as a successful immigrant. However, the ease and rapidity of her integration makes her religious background read more like a hook as opposed to a serious exploration of Islamic identity. Her rebellious personality (she lusts after BLT sandwiches, sneaks out to attend parties without permission, and quickly takes off her scarf and turns it into a fashionable accessory around her neck the moment she steps out of the mosque) as well as her vocal criticism of the imam provide further evidence of her independence from Islam. The implication here is that when a mainstream series

---

24. As Katie M. Logan argues, Kamala's Muslimness adds to the richness of her character:

> In Kamala Khan, Wilson and Amanat have created a superhero whose patriotism and contributions to Jersey City emerge because of her Muslim heritage, not despite it. She challenges the assumptions many Americans have about Muslims and is a radical departure from how the media tend to depict Muslim-Americans. She shows how Muslim-Americans and immigrants are not forces that threaten communities—as some would argue—but are people who can strengthen and preserve them.

25. Kamala's mother calls him a "primitive mullah." Kamala's father mocks his son's laziness camouflaged under the pretense of devotion: As he mumbles a lengthy prayer before each meal, her father complains that "prayer is notable but when you spend all day praying it starts to look like you're avoiding something. Like finding a job, for example" (Wilson and Alphona).

tries to make a Muslim character palatable, the first step is to minimize or even undermine Islam itself. Consequently, Islam is not merely mollified but essentially nullified in order to make her relatable. If she is a "good Muslim," it is because she does not hesitate to abandon her Muslimness in the face of a crisis.

But perhaps more importantly, the plot twist that reveals Kamala as an alien undermines her "relatability" altogether. Once Kamala discovers that she has "inhuman" genes, it unsettles her: "I thought I was finally starting to figure things out. It seems like anytime you want to learn something, you have to unlearn something else. [. . .] I'm a Pak-American, part-alien, morphogenic nerd" (*Ms. Marvel: Generation Why*). The political implication of this twist is significant: It downplays Kamala's Muslim American identity and triggers a posthumanist ethics, shifting the dynamics of belonging. Fawaz argues that superheroes with alien genes have to negotiate their belonging and navigate ethical codes that transcend their immediate communities:

> The lack of definition surrounding the superhero's ethical purview—whether her commitments ended at the borders of the nation or the broader sphere of humanity or included all life in the cosmos—and to whom the superhero was ultimately accountable in the use of her powers made the figure a generative site for imagining democracy in its most radical form, as a universally expansive ethical responsibility for the well-being of the world rather than an institutional structure upholding national citizenship. (7)

This shift from community integration to trans-species assimilation on a cosmic scale decenters the importance of national belonging and reduces the angst over her religious and ethnic identity to an inconsequentiality. Who cares if the alien eats bacon or not?

The hybrid Muslim character is not unique to the mass-market superhero genre; it also appears in more experimental areas of comics, including comics journalism. Joe Sacco's groundbreaking work *Palestine* (1993) features an earlier example of this character category that combines personal testimony with travelogue to visualize the drawn-out conflict in the region. An American Book Award winner, *Palestine* offers a keen account of the suffering of a stateless people living under occupation. Sacco's reportage received praise even from Edward Said—in spite of Said's well-known cynicism about Western journalism covering the Middle East—who commended the journalist for his ability to capture the complexity of Palestinian people. In "Homage to Sacco," Said writes:

In Joe Sacco's world there are no smooth-talking announcers and presenters, no unctuous narrative of Israeli triumphs, democracy, achievements, no assumed and reconfirmed representations—all of them disconnected from any historical or social source, from any lived reality—of Palestinians as rock-throwing, rejectionist, and fundamentalist villains whose main purpose is to make life difficult for the peace-loving, persecuted Israelis. (iii)

Sacco collects oral stories and creates "visual and verbal counterarchives to official histories" (Chute, *Disaster Drawn* 205). A key component of Sacco's success is what Said describes as his "unhurried pace": the way he is able to move between familiar, newsworthy events and smaller-scale, personal stories to show the long-lasting effects of the conflict ("Homage" iv). Action-loaded spectacles (protests, armed clashes) are followed by detailed portraits of individuals suffering from forced displacement and indefinite detentions. Sacco's vision essentially creates a balance between the image of the flag-burning, stone-throwing Muslim and the traumatized Muslim subjected to mob violence, undue legislation, and chauvinist politics.

This distinctive pacing helps Sacco humanize his subjects, perhaps more effectively than many of the authors we have encountered so far; as he intertwines the personal with the political, he exposes the multiple layers of victimization inflicted on the Muslim subject. In one instance, he draws the hardened faces of young boys as they admit to throwing stones at Israeli soldiers: "We know when we throw stones we don't have much chance of injuring the soldiers . . . But there is something inside us . . . We have to show what is inside us . . ." (195). In these portraits, Sacco encapsulates the essence of the Intifada as a relentless and futile cycle of violence normalized as part of everyday life in the occupied territories. Sacco's visual style, which Hillary Chute describes as "dense, virtuosic, and often photorealistic," complements his desire to emphasize the humanity of an oppressed people (*Disaster Drawn* 201). For example, Sacco draws the story of an Arab refugee in Jabalia and his melancholic longing for a home he left behind during the Israeli attacks in 1948. The old man describes his narrow escape: "I walked with my wife, who was pregnant, for four days . . . The Egyptian army refused to take us in trucks . . . The Jews bombed us" (Sacco 15). Decades later, he returns to his home—now in Israeli territory—for a quick visit. Upon arrival, he discovers an empty space: "They destroyed everything. There is no sign that we ever lived here" (15). Sacco captures the intense emotional weight of the moment by showing three generations of family members gazing on the empty space that was once home. As Aryn Bartley explains, "the imaginative aspects of drawing allow Sacco to recreate and 'account for' otherwise erased details of everyday life" (70). Through this reenactment, he is able to record the psychological scars of the conflict. The "absence" is invoked not only by the physical demolition of a Palestinian home but also by a sense of systematic erasure of a people. The past no longer exists for this old man; likewise, the land no longer carries traces of his existence. It is very much a portrait of a real human, experiencing real suffering and loss.

But there are shortcomings to Sacco's approach as well. Sacco's work falls vaguely in the tradition of "New Journalism"—a type of reportage that dismisses objectivity as an unachievable principle.[26] He does not hide his prejudices and is willing to confess his ignorance (and sometimes arrogance), even double down on his naiveté as part of his journalistic gaze.[27] At times, Sacco's self-proclaimed "honesty" keeps the focus away from his subjects and positions him as an arbiter. Rocco Versaci contends that Sacco's "presence as an 'intruding' agent in the lives of these people [. . .] serve[s] to remind readers that he is filtering the events through his own unique perspective" (119). He is implicated in the story as a Western observer of abject Eastern subjects. Ultimately, the same familiar tropes and generalizations begin to creep into the narrative ("terrorism is the bread Palestinians get buttered on" [Sacco 7]). Again, Muslim subjects are viewed through the framework of violence and radicalization. In this regard, *Palestine* vividly illustrates the tendencies of this hybrid category: It plainly attempts to provide more honest and accurate representations of Muslim lives from an outsider's perspective but lapses back into the limitations and biases of the journalist's attempt to "translate" those lives (always imbricated with terrorism) for his Western readers.

WE SEE, then, how this category, reacting against Islamophobic narratives but falling short in embracing or even engaging with Islamic tenets in any genuine or extensive way, is invested in creating sympathetic Muslim characters yet still succumbs to old habits of representation: These characters

---

26. Versaci describes New Journalism as a new journalistic ethics: "In the process of 'fictionalizing' these facts, the New Journalists called attention to the mediation that takes place in any journalistic enterprise; that is, far from being unfiltered, works of New Journalism forced readers to consider the idea that truth is never completely objective and that the facts alone do not necessarily reveal a given event in the most meaningful way" (110).

27. In an interview, Sacco stated: "The important thing for me isn't so much objectivity, it's—I want the journalists to admit their contexts, their prejudices somehow. [. . .] Objectivity to me is a different word than honesty" (qtd. in Steinhauer).

continue to present a vexed conflation of race and religion, recycle Orientalist stereotypes, and subscribe to the "good Muslim" / "bad Muslim" binary, sustaining the impression that "unless proved to be 'good,' every Muslim [may be] presumed to be 'bad'" (Mamdani, *Good Muslim* 15). Such a split not only continues to privilege Western frames of reference but also legitimizes the us/them rhetoric that became more visible in the wake of the War on Terror. Consequently, as Strömberg argues, the inclusion of "good Muslims" in comics misses the mark:

> Despite the laudable attempts to resist racist configurations of Arabs and Muslims as terrorists, several of the stories still disappoint inasmuch as they are too eager to make their didactic point. The authors and/or the artists try too hard to show positive role models, thereby unintentionally evoking equally stereotypical clichés of Arabs and Muslims as well as of Islamophobes. This strategy then risks causing a reinscription rather than a substantial revision of the image of the Oriental. (596–97)

Therefore, while authors working in the hybrid category favor diversity and aim to increase the visibility of this faith group by making room for relatable characters, they do not actively reform the existing image of the Muslim. Instead, these projects present a watered-down version of Islam (if they present any version at all) and fall prey to existing conventions, reinforcing the idea that practicing or believing in the tenets of Islam is not compatible with the West.

Muslim Comics

This book is about what happens next—that is, the emergence of Muslim Comics as an interventionist and revisionist form of representation that engages with faith as an important—though not the only—component of identity, instrumental in shaping one's political and ideological attachments as well as one's everyday life. As discussed previously, "Muslim" is a slippery signifier: Unlike Christianity, it does not have a centralized, institutionalized, and hierarchical structure that defines what orthodoxy looks like for the estimated 1.8 billion Muslims around the globe. Furthermore, as Islam is spread over a vast geography, there are always regional and cultural rituals that interact in complex ways with the broader belief system. The understanding and practice of Islam in Palestine, Iran, Turkey, Egypt, or Syria can vary dramatically. Each region's political structures (secular or theocratic), linguistic traditions (Arabic or vernacular), legal orientations (constitutional or sharia), and cultural norms (patriarchal or matriarchal) feed into a plurality that resists sweeping statements about the composition of the global *ummah*. With this in mind, my definition of "Muslim" rests on a self-identification based on common values and shared perspectives that inform one's everyday responses and actions—regardless of how modest such attachments may be. In other words, I employ "Muslim" as a designation to recognize those who acknowledge Islam's constant and consistent—but not necessarily dominant—role in their subject constitution.

Muslim Comics, in this same spirit, are works that foreground Muslim experiences and discuss Islam's role in shaping the everyday life of their characters. That is not to say that Muslim Comics are interested in proselytizing by showing only the positive sides of Islam, nor does it suggest that Muslim Comics must refrain from criticizing wrongdoings within Islamic societies by ignoring real problems. Rather, Islam in Muslim Comics forms the social and cultural foundation to fill an epistemological abyss. By highlighting the complexity as well as the banality of fully realized Muslim lives, they participate in an imperative to combat simplistic misinformation. As Said writes:

> Very little of the detail, the human density, the passion of Arab-Moslem life has entered the awareness of even those people whose profession it is to report the Arab world. What we have instead is a series of crude, essentialized caricatures of the Islamic world presented in such a way as to make that world vulnerable to military aggression. ("Islam")[28]

"Muslim Comics" is not meant to act as an authenticity test but rather as a fluid label that can provide a new and powerful frame through which to analyze Muslim experiences. By replacing old habits of representation with fresh visual/rhetorical codes, Muslim Comics let Muslim subjects speak for themselves without requiring a mediator.

---

28. In *Covering Islam*, for example, Said makes a strong case about the journalistic predisposition to portray Muslims as irrational fanatics. Written as a response to the media coverage of the Iranian hostage crisis, the book conveys Said's frustrations with a lack of professional ethics as he criticizes the journalists for participating in propaganda campaigns that serve the political interests of the state. The vilification of the Muslim, Said argues, was a systematic effort to discredit not only Iran but all Muslim-majority states in the Middle East in order to establish the West's moral superiority. For Said, journalists who lacked expertise on the region forfeited their integrity by perpetuating archaic images that relate to the "dark" side of Islam (*Covering Islam* xi).

My definition of Muslim Comics prioritizes content over authorship. When it comes to Muslim writing more broadly, a group of writers has made the case for the biography of the author as an important aspect of such classification. Novelist and poet Mohja Kahf, for one, stresses the importance of Muslim authorship as a means of providing an insider's perspective: "A 'lapsed Muslim' author [. . .] is still a Muslim author for my purposes. I am not interested in levels of commitment or practice, but in literary Muslimness" (167).[29] What matters to Kahf is that the authors in this oeuvre can speak about Islam with knowledge and authority by articulating the perspective of those who have either been raised within the Islamic tradition or those who are familiar with Islamic tenets and can speak about them with proficiency and respect. I argue, however, that Muslim Comics are less about the religious affiliation of the author and more about the content and attitude of the text. As I demonstrate in chapter 2, books written by non-Muslims featuring Muslim lives accurately, honestly, and astutely, without using a Western filter, deserve a place in this category. Jérôme Tubiana and Alexandre Franc are not Muslims; still, their comic, *Guantánamo Kid: The True Story of Mohammed El-Gharani*, is a sensitive and powerful analysis of the injustice faced by Muslims whose rights are violated. Neither Tubiana nor Franc are insiders; their familiarity with Islam is more academic and anecdotal than practical and personal. Nevertheless, their access to an insider's perspective, their fidelity to an accurate depiction of Muslim persecution at Guantánamo, and their focus on Islam as a crucial and qualifying theme of their characters' subjectivity are sufficient to include their work within this oeuvre.

Muslim Americans and Muslim Comics

Early examples of Muslim Comics in the US are mostly graphic memoirs invested in the exploration of an identity crisis brought about by a sense of

---

29. Kahf identifies several distinct stages of Muslim American literature: The first stage, what she labels as "prophets of dissent from the Black Arts Movement," includes examples such as Marvin X's *Fly to Allah* (1969) as "the first book of poems published in English by a Muslim American author." Other phases consist of "multiethnic multitudes," "new American transcendentalists," and "New Pilgrims," which continue to engage with themes such as double consciousness, diasporic existence, national/transnational belonging, and Islamic modes of living. Kahf's emphasis on different stages of Muslim American literature offers an important warning against shoe-horning writers of Muslim descent into a preexisting framework; rather, Kahf recognizes the ideological, political, and aesthetic diversity of authors belonging to this cluster as an acknowledgment of the plurality of Muslim experiences in the US.

racial and religious difference. They exist across a spectrum: On one end of the spectrum are serious, somber, and self-conscious narratives that focus on the idea of "paralysis" brought about by double consciousness; on the other, more lighthearted treatments of the minor difficulties and embarrassments that stem from Islamic life experiences in the West. To begin with an example from the more serious end of the spectrum: In Toufic El Rassi's graphic autobiography, *Arab in America* (2008), the estranged protagonist is unable to form attachments as he tries to navigate a hostile "home" that constantly perceives him as the Muslim Other—if not the Muslim terrorist. The cover of the book conveys this idea of a paralytic in-betweenness: El Rassi only illustrates half of his face to convey his fragmentation; the background, with its vertical stripes and abundant stars, is evocative of a partial American flag. Underneath, he writes his name using both the Roman and the Arabic alphabet. This is not a gesture toward postcolonial hybridity or cultural mongrelization but a sign of an incapacity to develop a comfortable amalgamation of cultures that are popularly thought to be incompatible.

Arab in America begins "hours after the [9/11] attacks"—a familiar overture (we recall Simon Baz's opening). In this particular case, it is not simply a symbolic nod but a solemn catalyst for El Rassi to meditate on his identity as an Arab American. His double marginalization (due to race *and* religion) and the gradual shift in the mainstream culture around him, from what he describes as Arabophobia to Islamophobia, leads to a split identity.[30] He recalls specific moments from his childhood that underscore his sense of difference: In eighth grade, for example, after watching the school production of *Wizard of Oz*, he recognizes his "brown skin" as opposed to the "angelic white faces arrayed in the chorus" (6). He is unsettled by his growing awareness of the way "Arabs are variously depicted as inveterate liars, greedy schemers, oversexed maniacs with multiple wives who desire blonde women, crazed religious fanatics, or stupid savages who don't appreciate or understand the technological advancements in the West" (39). Following 9/11, his apprehensions turn into debilitating paranoia as he finds himself either the target of or witness to random racist attacks on the street ("Hey, look at Osama over there" [83]). His dark features, thick black hair, and prominent beard become a source of anxiety as he fears being misidentified as one of the terrorists. To illustrate his apprehension visually, he re-creates the front page of a newspaper that features mugshots of the terrorists; in the middle of the page, he

---

30. In this regard, El Rassi's discussions of Arabophobia and Islamophobia go hand in hand as the American media continues to treat them as inseparable entities: "In the newspapers and magazines or on television news 'Arabs' and 'Islam' is usually synonymous with violence and terrorism" (47).

FIGURE 1.5. El Rassi inserts his own picture among terrorist mugshots.

places his own image to show how his physiognomy blends in (see figure 1.5): "Could the average American distinguish me from a Muslim terrorist? I saw the photos of the hijackers and the fact is . . . they looked like me, and the images appeared everywhere" (19). The prospect of misrecognition—let alone his potential criminalization as a suspected enemy combatant—paralyzes him. As a permanent resident but not a citizen, he feels he is not fully protected against random accusations and fears being deported to Lebanon, his birthplace, or worse yet, to "Guantanamo Bay or being held incommunicado in some military prison somewhere in the world" (96).

The differences from earlier forms of Muslim categorization are apparent in El Rassi's work. The protagonist is highly conscious of his Islamic subjectivity; he is not naive as to the importance of his Islamic background but does not simply see himself as a "Muslim." He is deeply connected to his Arab heritage (even though he occasionally feels a "desire to cancel or obscure [his] ethnicity" [5]) but is less enthusiastic about being identified with Islam due to his secular background: "I was no Muslim. Religion was just not something I really cared about and again, the restriction on vices was always the major obstacle" (81). By refusing to automatically label himself as a Muslim (he is highly sensitive to the way Muslims are profiled as if Islam were a race), he makes a conscious effort to decouple religion from other markers of identity.[31] At the same time, El Rassi's detachment from the spiritual aspects of religion does not immunize him from the challenges experienced by more devout members of the Islamic community. The first panel of the book illustrates him reading an email from his sister, with the subject line reading "shave" (1). The ensuing panels show how both devout and nondevout Muslim Americans quickly become the targets of public uproar and hostility: El Rassi draws a group of protestors near a mosque, carrying racist signs and shouting jingoistic and anti-Muslim slogans (one protestor yells: "I am proud to be an American and I hate Arabs and I always have" [1]). Interestingly, he does not draw the mosque itself; instead, he focuses on the mob and especially the American flag, now transformed into an emblem of broad Islamophobic chauvinism. As for the effects of this sort of hostility toward Islam upon Muslim Americans, we see that it elicits a range of responses. El Rassi's friends adopt various "ways of operating" by succumbing to preemptive "tricks" that allow them to sidestep social and cultural pressures exerted by the majority (de Certeau 37). Through their examples, El Rassi is able to contemplate different models of identifications embraced by diasporic Arabs attempting to "deal with being alienated" (El Rassi 75), ranging from his friend Hamid's denial ("I'm not one of those crazy terrorists" [75]) to his friend Ahmed's dismissiveness ("How can I be part of a society that rejects who I am" [75]). The characters do not discover any sudden inspiration or magical resolve from the bigotry around them; none of them become nighttime vigilantes or superhero community defenders. Instead, they try to reconfigure their religious affiliation as part of their everyday existence.

---

31. Inaash Islam describes Islam as "key to contemporary Muslim American self-formation" (3). He further argues that "in the past two decades, we have undoubtedly witnessed a significant rise in sociological works that understand and describe the Muslim experience as being racial" (429).

What actually happens to El Rassi's community is that it is pulled into history as the personal becomes entwined with the political. They become aware of themselves as acting within a larger national, international, and historical context even when dealing with private issues such as religion. The global-historical insinuations of their everyday behaviors point to the dual function of the narratives of Muslim Comics: First, an emphasis on self-exploration designed to appeal to any minority subject grappling with a hyphenated identity. Second, a pedagogical function—an awareness of the comic as a document designed to inform the dominant culture about pervasive misconceptions about the minority. At times, El Rassi's "documenting" detours can be exhausting, with his inclusion of maps, sketches of historical figures, Orientalist paintings, album covers, and film posters all meant to explain large chunks of history—including the Lebanese civil war, the Palestinian refugee crisis, and a detailed account of Osama bin Laden's rise to power. But this is intentional.[32] As Frederick Luis Aldama observes: "By intermixing the life story with the historical (and even privileging the latter), El Rassi aims to use the autobiographical content—the experiences of being Arab in America—to teach readers about a not-so-black-and-white racism that permeates American society" (10). For El Rassi, this was a calculated risk:

> I tried not to think about audience because I didn't want to move in that sort of linear fashion. I tried to think of it more in terms of a journal or a diary. But then there were moments where I felt like I had to explain things. I couldn't assume everyone would understand it. So it does get a little pedantic. That's one thing I wish I had balanced, taking the teacherly approach and then the more autobiographical one. It goes back and forth. But I was thinking of [sic] terms of a subplot within a subplot. The main plot would be my experiences and the subplot would be more of a documentary, an explanation of things . . . It was a sort of balancing act. (qtd. in Markicevic)

The "balancing act" between the teacherly and revelatory aspects of the autobiography reflects the deep cultural fissures that mark his characters' lives—fissures that remain unresolved by the end of the book, as it ends with an image of a plane carrying El Rassi to his birthplace, Beirut. His last words, "Who knows, maybe I'll stay" (116), reflect his ambivalence about

---

32. Margaret Noori feels that the "recurrent diversion away from the main story, with numerous embedded narratives that provide specific cultural and political information," can be disruptive (63).

his future as a Muslim American. It is an ambivalence a million miles away from the clarity of a "good Muslim" / "bad Muslim" binary.

If El Rassi's solemn, autobiographical comic marks one end of the spectrum of Muslim Comics in the US, more recent comics that employ humor and optimism occupy the other. These lighthearted investigations of American Muslim identity are geared more toward a young-adult audience with an upbeat and casual (occasionally bordering on frivolous) tone sprinkled with messages of positivity and self-empowerment. Huda Fahmy's *Yes, I'm Hot in This: The Hilarious Truth about Life in a Hijab* (2018), *That Can Be Arranged: A Muslim Love Story* (2020), and *Huda F Are You?* (2021) and Wendy Díaz and Uthman Guadalupe's *The Secret of My Hijab* (2020) are just some of a flurry of graphic narratives created by hijabi women addressing their hyphenated identities.[33] These comics use wit and self-deprecating humor to connect with their audience: One of the advantages of being a hijabi, Díaz explains, is that she can use her veil to cover her nose when someone "takes off their shoes and they have stinky, smelly toes." Yet this humorous meditation on the Islamic veil still ends with an empowering and defiant statement: "The best of all is that it makes me uniquely me." The celebration of individuality is also at the heart of Fahmy's works. In *Yes, I'm Hot in This*, she discusses a series of experiences that contribute to her marginalization as a hyphenated subject: She relays her experiences of "flying while Muslim" (29); she recalls responding cheekily to a woman who tells her that her clothes are "not appropriate for America" (116); she mentions a stranger throwing bacon at her at a supermarket. Fahmy's responses are not angst-ridden or outraged but attempt to be funny and entertaining; even when she is stunned at the unexpected "bacon" attack, for example, she remains cheerful: "Oh no! Not bacon," she screams, pretending to vaporize as she sinks into her abaya (99). Squatting on the floor, she yells: "I'm melting! Meeelltttiiinnnggg" (99). Behind the slapstick, we can see a clear movement away from the traditional strategies of Muslim characterization: an earnest effort to normalize "foreign" Islamic habits; an interest in presenting pious Muslim American women as independent and relatable; a sense of humor; a level of postmodern irony and knowingness.

---

33. Fahmy's graphic memoir, *That Can Be Arranged: A Muslim Love Story* (2020), records her quest to find an acceptable husband for herself. The marriage plot is highly evocative of Jane Austen's novels (whom Fahmy calls "Jane bint Austen" and describes as a "low-key Muslim" [52]), dedicated to the pursuit of romance within the highly strict rules of gender relations. In the course of the book, Fahmy, who initially views her worth by the number of suitors she entertains, eventually learns to love herself.

Between El Rassi's pessimism and hijabi comics' sanguinity lies a vast terrain, with space for a huge range of works, from hard-edged superhero comics to nonfiction graphic narratives about queer Muslim immigrants. And, of course, each of these types of works can themselves be subdivided in all sorts of ways. We might take the case of nonfiction graphic narratives about Syrian refugees, a subject that has provided ample opportunity for a number of comics artists—from Sarah Glidden's *Rolling Blackouts: Dispatches from Turkey, Syria, and Iraq* (2016), to Olivier Kugler's *Escaping Wars and Waves: Encounters with Syrian Refugees* (2018), to Ali Fitzgerald's *Drawn to Berlin: Comic Workshops in Refugee Shelters and Other Stories from a New Europe* (2018)—to reflect upon Muslim lives in distress. In the US, Jake Halpern and Michael Sloan's Pulitzer Prize–winning work of graphic journalism, *Welcome to the New World* (2020), received much praise for its portrayal of the challenges faced by a Syrian family settling in Connecticut.[34] The early chapters illustrate the Aldabaans' life in Syria at the beginning of the conflict. The father, Ibrahim, is tortured in prison; outside, his family hides in their apartment to avoid tanks and gunfire. Once it becomes clear that their home is no longer safe, they make their way to the US, hoping to find refuge there. This is not the end of their struggle, however. They feel isolated in their American house, living apart from their extended family; when they speak on the phone with relatives, they complain about their seclusion, the lack of community support, and, more strikingly, the anonymous racist phone calls they receive ("Hey you fucking Muslim. [. . .] I'm gonna chop your fucking head off, Ibrahim, and I'll kill your fucking family" [92]). Despite these challenges, the comic ends with a hopeful tone. Once the family moves to a safer neighborhood, they feel they are beginning to make progress and find ways to fit in. On the final page, the two children, Ammal and Naji, contemplate their future as they walk through the beautiful neighborhood. There is a sense of reserved optimism as they gradually ease into their new lives in the US.

Halpern and Sloan take what we might broadly recognize as graphic journalism and redefine its parameters. Their approach is quite different from Sacco's: less self-referential, more focused on the problems of silence and isolation (rather than violence). They shy away from inserting their own views or offering political commentary. Rather, they "produce both knowledge and feeling" via visual storytelling without interfering as a mediator

---

34. The serialized comic commissioned by the *New York Times* was turned into a self-contained book after its great success.

(Worden 7).³⁵ The strength of graphic journalism, according to Todd Schack, is that it decodes the everyday and converts it to "emotive immediacy and [...] visceral impact" (109). Halpern and Sloan are invisible (or at least translucent) storytellers, who let their subjects do the speaking even when their speakers are not convinced of their own capacity to tell a story.

WE HAVE been concentrating on the American tradition here, but it is worth pointing out, however briefly, that Muslim Comics have become a major force in Europe as well—although the heightened visibility of Muslim characters there has arguably been met with more ambivalence from the industry and from mainstream audiences. In France, Norédine Allam, a cartoonist and colorist who worked on recolorizing the *Asterix* series, founded the *Muslim Show* to present a humorous take on the everyday lives of French Muslims. But even though the comic found success elsewhere in Europe, it met a different fate in France. In an interview with Warda Mohamed, Allam states: "The comic is hardly available anywhere and takes four to five weeks to receive after ordering from Fnac. Press and comic book festivals shun us. With Astérix and Léa Parker, I was invited to fifty festivals a year, now we are boycotted . . . Many think that this topic doesn't interest a wide audience. Unlike in the past, we are hardly ever invited anywhere!" ("Muslim Show"). In Germany, Muslim Comics have encountered similar resistance. After the Tunisian-born Muslim artist Soufeina Hamed began using comics as a medium to create dialogue and empathy, she experienced backlash, and her legitimacy as an artist was questioned. Yet comics artist such as Allam and Hamed are united under the Muslim Comics tradition in ways other than overt pushback: Both discuss the subtler pressures they have felt as they attempt to depict the everyday experiences of European Muslims (see figures 1.6 and 1.7). Both often imagine Muslim characters as surrounded by commentators and critics (sometimes helpful, sometimes hostile) to show the claustrophobic reality of speaking out as a Muslim Comics artist.

The main defining feature of Muslim Comics, then, is not any one style or ideological approach, or even the Muslim identity of the author, but the dedication to imparting Muslim experiences with accuracy, sensitivity, and

---

35. Halpern talks about his writing process as an intense form of scrutiny and fact-checking: "Because this book is not a memoir, but rather a work of journalism, the story also needed context and fact checking, beyond the families' own accounts and experiences. [. . .] As in any work of journalism, I did everything possible to probe for the truth and resisted the temptation to take anyone's account at face value" (Halpern and Sloan 174–75).

FIGURES 1.6 AND 1.7. A panel from Hamed's comics and a panel from *Muslim Show*.

compassion. These comics are determined to make a case for this faith group to enter into the national sphere as legitimate stakeholders. In this regard, they depict the everyday lives of Muslims to pacify "moral panic over cultural differences" (Petersen and Schramm 9). For decades, the overuse of the hyperactive, destructive Muslim adversary silenced all other subject positions affiliated with Islam. Muslim Comics directly address this silence. Giving Muslims the permission to narrate their own stories—as Said would argue—is not only a vital postcolonial imperative but an ethical obligation, one that allows readers to rethink Muslim identity de novo. Consequently, Muslim Comics come to reflect this plurality, displaying Muslim subjects in their localities while making global connections to underscore their various entanglements, challenges, and little victories.

Muslim Comics in Warscapes

Finally, a brief word on the other key theme of this book: warscape. If the term "Muslim Comics" designates an emerging oeuvre that aims to give voice to Muslim experiences, what is the special significance of Muslim Comics situated in warscapes? Warscapes—civilian areas that are always on the verge of transforming into battlefields, with the natural rhythm of everyday activities and interactions altered accordingly—position Muslims differently: Simply by dint of occupying that space, they become people facing constant ethical dilemmas, political doubt, and social tension—situations that defy hasty categorization as "good" or "bad." Thus, the warscape, a space rife with moral complexities and ambiguities, automatically complicates the blunt and unempathetic images of the Muslim and helps to articulate the everyday, human challenges of a range of Muslim subjectivities. It also sheds new light on the Muslim "homeland" and draws attention to Muslims simply trying to experience everyday life at home, even when that "home" could dissolve into violence and rubble at any second. Locating the Muslim as part of a larger discourse about "home" is a crucial step in contesting the cultural and physical ghettoization of the Muslim minority—whether they be Muslim immigrants in the West, secular Muslims in theocratic Muslim states, or Muslim minorities under Hindu occupation. In this way, Muslim Comics in warscapes offer a way to scrutinize the effects of "zones of contestation, incorporations and exclusions" on sophisticated, complicated Muslim subjects (Appadurai and Breckenridge 4).

Muslim Comics set in warscapes are interested not only in testifying to atrocities in their immediate communities but also in engaging with the global rhetoric of human rights. Joseph Slaughter discusses the parallels between bildungsroman and human rights narratives, which he envisions as "enabling fictions": "Each projects an image of the human personality that ratifies the other's idealistic visions of the proper relations between the individual and society and the normative career of free and full human personality development" (4). There are similar overlaps between warscape comics and rights-oriented narratives; Muslims presented as political leaders, subversive artists, independent thinkers, advocates, and activists constantly negotiate between vulnerability and resistance as they respond to their traumatic circumstances. The self-development of the Muslim protagonist in the warscape, I argue, necessitates a negotiation between local and global structures as well as the private and the public to show how state apparatuses, political institutions, and social and cultural networks both help and impede the free and full development of the individual. Accordingly, this book will also enter into a conversation about the shaping of the Muslim character in the context of human rights theory.

A great deal of scholarship on Muslim characters focuses on unfortunate histories, negative situations, terrible actions. Despite my focus on conflict areas, *Muslim Comics and Warscape Witnessing* is not driven by "misery literature." Rather, it aims to honor the human spirit. If trauma is at the heart of warscape existence, so is hope. As Nordstrom argues, affected people of "warzone cultures" seek solutions "beyond individual survival actions" to build a coalition from the ground up: "These many acts coalesce into political movements in their most fundamental sense and constitute, in essence, politics in the making" (11). This notion of "becoming" in warscape—the necessity of adapting to an increasingly hostile environment and then aiding, however modestly, peace-building efforts through art—shows human resilience and promise in the face of unimaginable affliction. *Muslim Comics and Warscape Witnessing* is a celebration of that resilience.

CHAPTER 2

Reluctant Witnesses in Prison Camp Narratives

> These prisoners, who are not prisoners, will be tried, if they will be tried, according to rules that are not those of a constitutionally defined US law nor of any recognizable international code.
> —Judith Butler, *Precarious Life*

In the previous chapter, I identified three character categories that use various visual codes to create easily recognizable Muslims. Of these three categories, the second one, which primarily consists of supervillains or jihadi terrorists, was especially successful in fixing the identity of the Muslim as the antithesis of the West. Jack Shaheen reiterates the negative treatment of the Muslim in his analysis of comics dating back to the 1950s, stating that

> one is about as likely to find a good Arab as the camel is to pass through the eye of the needle. Zestfully, Arabs wade into personal combat against our gallant figures, spitting upon them and deriding them. [. . .] Their features are frequently bestial, demonized, dehumanized. [. . .] They are anti-American, anti-West, anti-Israel, anti-Jewish, anti-Christian. Despising freedom and democracy, they give their allegiance to tyranny and servitude. ("Arab Images" 123)

The long-standing popularity of the radical Muslim trope is a reminder of the industry's willingness to capitalize upon (and therefore exacerbate) racial and religious resentments already brewing in the popular sphere.

Especially in the aftermath of 9/11, the traditional image of the Muslim as a bloodthirsty fanatic took center stage in comics. I have already mentioned Frank Miller's *Holy Terror*, arguably the culmination of this tradition.[1] When accused of spreading Islamophobia and hatred, Miller boldly and unapologetically doubled down ("My new comic book [. . .] is naked propaganda"), adding that propaganda could be "virtuous" when used against enemies like radical Muslims: "I'm too old to serve my country in any other way. Otherwise, I'd gladly be pulling the trigger myself" (Nickerson). Miller was quickly castigated by many in the comics world, even though *Holy Terror*'s defamatory tone and retreat to negative stereotypes was not unique. Rather, it was typical of the industry's silent complicity with cultural denigrations of the Muslim Other, its subtle endorsement of the conflation of race with religion (and Islam with violence), and its apparent reaffirmation of the popular suspicion that "Arab = Muslim = Terrorist" (Dar 100). Miller's work was Islamophobic and promulgated the idea of the Muslim as an active and dangerous agent, a powerful figure moving against the Western state—but it was an Islamophobia supported and nurtured by the comics enterprise as a whole.

This chapter responds directly to the obvious and visible trope of the Muslim jihadi as the belligerent, dangerous extremist determined to slaughter innocents for no reason other than his own fanaticism. The comics discussed here move away from this icon of the active, aggressive jihadi and focus instead on a less prominent image of the Muslim that emerged during the US War on Terror: the abject Muslim prisoner. In stark contrast to the familiar narrative of the "dangerous Muslim," these comics illustrate that Muslims are no longer the elusive, mysterious perpetrators of violence, but a prominent and highly visible target population to be confined, interrogated, and even tortured to keep America safe. In documenting the suffering and victimization of the abject "average" Muslim—an image rarely considered in comics up until this point—these graphic narratives act as testimonials, bearing witness to the lives of those condemned to a warscape existence. In doing so, they point to a reversal in visibility politics: If the jihadi figure is one to be brought out into the open and fought head-on, the abject inmate is meant to be hidden away, condemned to existence in a clandestine warscape rather than confronted on a battlefield.

---

1. As one reviewer put it: "Longtime Miller watchers have viewed [the publication of *Holy Terror*] with apprehension, hoping that his dark views about the source of that national trauma wouldn't turn the comic into a vulgar, one-dimensional revenge fantasy. They were wrong. It's even worse than that" (Ackerman).

The way I define "warscape" in this chapter is also slightly different. Typically, this book is invested in emerging warscapes in Muslim homelands to explore how conflict areas and topographies of violence influence the everyday life of the Muslim. This chapter, however, focuses on the figure of the alleged but unproven terrorist forcefully removed from the Muslim homeland and locked up in an offshore prison. I argue that the extralegal detention centers established over the past twenty years—Bagram (Afghanistan), Abu Ghraib (Iraq), Guantánamo (Cuba), and so on—represent a new and untraditional type of warscape, where all legal rights are suspended. For Moustafa Bayoumi, the state of legal limbo renders these centers "empty spaces":

> Outside of time and space, yet regulated like a prison, these are not the ends of the earth but more like floating penal colonies for the uncondemned (for even the condemned get a hearing where they are condemned). In these places, there is no means of challenging one's fate. Rights have evaporated like a kettle whistling itself dry. ("A Bloody Stupid War" 40)

The US government's covert operations against the "uncondemned" ultimately came to light in 2003, when the Associated Press released a number of damning interviews conducted with former detainees; the sites gained further notoriety in 2004, when photographs from Abu Ghraib that substantiated systemic abuse of prisoners were leaked to CBS's *60 Minutes*. That same year, the army charged its own General Antonio M. Taguba to lead an investigation into the treatment of prisoners, whose right to a fair trial was revoked indefinitely to keep them incarcerated. The general's report concluded that within the prison system, excessive use of force led to "sadistic, blatant, and wanton criminal abuses" (Hersh).[2] This carceral ecology, I argue, nurtures the warscape existence of the abject, condemned yet uncondemned Muslim prisoner, which emerges as a new type of comics character.

---

2. A copy of the report obtained by the *New Yorker* listed a series of misconducts:

> Breaking chemical lights and pouring the phosphoric liquid on detainees; pouring cold water on naked detainees; beating detainees with a broom handle and a chair; threatening male detainees with rape; allowing a military police guard to stitch the wound of a detainee who was injured after being slammed against the wall in his cell; sodomizing a detainee with a chemical light and perhaps a broom stick, and using military working dogs to frighten and intimidate detainees with threats of attack, and in one instance actually biting a detainee. (Hersh)

All three graphic narratives featured in this chapter are set in the Guantánamo Bay detention camp (or "Gitmo").³ Jérôme Tubiana and Alexandre Franc's *Guantánamo Kid: The True Story of Mohammed El-Gharani* (2019), Sarah Mirk's *Guantanamo Voices: An Anthology: True Accounts from the World's Most Infamous Prison* (2020), and Jay Cantor, James Romberger, and Jose Villarrubia's *Aaron & Ahmed* (2011) put the infamous prison under the microscope and push back against the carefully crafted "Guantánamo narrative" of keeping America safe.⁴ By shedding light on the irreparable trauma suffered by the detainees—a group that included innocent as well as guilty Muslims—these comics emerge as "Guantánamo counternarratives" that not only contest the myth of the dangerous, ever-active Muslim offender but also expose the strategic transformation of the prison into a warscape. *Guantanamo Voices*, for example, opens with an interview with Mark Fallon, former chief of Middle East counterintelligence operations for NCIS, that reveals the government's self-aggrandizing justifications of the prison (as a site in which high-profile Al-Qaeda operatives could indefinitely be isolated) as largely a fabrication. Upon visiting Gitmo for the first time to verify the identities of the detainees, he is astounded: "'What the fuck? Who are these guys?' [. . .] It became clear that we ended up with a bunch of guys warlords had turned in for a bounty with no evidence they had any value. We called them . . . dirt farmers" (Mirk 28, 30). To Fallon's surprise, Guantánamo had become a dumping ground for a number of random, ill-fated Muslims, in some cases already abject figures used as pawns by regional warlords, who traded them in to American agents for various favors. In another section, a simple statistical panel exposes the government's false narrative: Out of the 799 Guantánamo prisoners, 75 were thought to have litigable cases, and only

---

3. The Platt Agreement (1903) was signed between the US and Cuba at the end of the Spanish-American War to specify the conditions under which the US government can aid Cuba against foreign intrusion. Yet rather than a passive protector, the US leased land to build a naval base all the while hiding behind "the paternalistic narrative of rescue" (Kaplan 835). For Amy Kaplan, the rhetorical choices in the agreement ("occupation," "complete jurisdiction," "control") not only demonstrate the imperialist strategy behind the US interests but also corroborate the way "coercive state power has been routinely mobilized beyond the sovereignty of national territory and outside the rule of law" (832). This was a sore point for Fidel Castro, who tried to revoke the charter after the Cuban revolution, referring to the original arrangement as "a knife in the heart of Cuba's sovereignty" (qtd. in Gregory 412). Consequently, despite framing the agreement as a shield to protect Cuba against threats to preserve its independence, in reality, it served as a sign of American exceptionalism, "bear[ing] the marks of these ligatures between colonialism, violence, and the law" (411).

4. See United States, Congress, House.

16 were actually charged and prosecuted by 2019 (108). The irony of this fundamental incompetence reverberates profoundly in these Guantánamo counternarratives: What should be a fortress containing the most dangerous examples of the radicalized Muslim Other is revealed as a bureaucratic boondoggle largely filled with the powerless and misidentified.[5]

Guantánamo Kid tells the true story of Mohammed El-Gharani, one of the youngest detainees in Gitmo, born in Saudi Arabia to a family from Chad. He sells prayer beads and water to tourists on the streets of Medina from a young age. Disadvantaged by his status as a nonregistered citizen, constantly threatened by the local police for his illicit trade, Mohammed decides to move to Karachi temporarily to learn English and study information technology. To obtain a valid passport and visa, he is advised to change his age (from fourteen to eighteen) and name (to Yousef Abakir Saleh) for a small fee at the consulate—which later proves to be a fatal mistake. In Karachi, Mohammed quickly settles into a comfortable routine. Soon after 9/11, however, he becomes an unexpected target: The fact that he is a practicing Muslim with a heavy Arabic accent attracts attention during a routine crackdown by police on the local mosque. Inter-Services Intelligence detains him on suspicion of being a member of Al-Qaeda, and after a brief, coercive interrogation, they label him a terrorist and "sell [him] to the Americans" for $5,000 (27).

Like *Guantánamo Kid, Guantanamo Voices* is also rooted in true stories; journalist Sarah Mirk conducts a series of interviews with ex-detainees, lawyers, and servicemen affiliated with Gitmo to present various perspectives on the infamous site. She explains that she initially wanted to use photographs to supplement the oral accounts of prison life that she had collected, but when her camera was confiscated for security reasons, she decided to collaborate with a group of artists to illustrate the interviews. Characterizing her collection as "a nonfiction accounting of real life," Mirk was determined to produce a candid representation of Guantánamo while respecting the artistic autonomy of the twelve illustrators working on each section of the book: "Before I sent the script to the artists, I scoured public domain archives and put together a folder of visual references that would help them draw each scene. Clearly, each comic is not a photo-realistic representation of the world, but we tried to draw details accurately whenever possible" (182). Thus, Mirk's collection becomes a kind of hybrid piece: nonfictional stories conveyed through creative visual reconstructions.

Unlike the other two works, *Aaron & Ahmed* is a graphic novel; it tells the story of the relationship between a suspected terrorist and his interroga-

---

5. See Khan; Perera; Kurnaz; Slahi.

tor at Guantánamo. Having lost his fiancée on one of the planes that struck the Twin Towers, Aaron leaves his job as a psychiatrist in a mental hospital in Kansas and joins the interrogation team at Guantánamo, largely motivated by revenge. When he meets Ahmed, an alleged associate of Osama bin Laden, he decides to experiment with a new technique: To form a bond of trust, Aaron slips estrogen into Ahmed's food, and then uses therapy to uncover his past. Gradually, the sessions between Aaron and Ahmed become more of a prelude to a romantic relationship. Aaron attributes Ahmed's affability to the estrogen—but, unbeknownst to him, Ahmed has been avoiding his food out of suspicion it has been tampered with. Eventually, Aaron and Ahmed flee the prison together and manage to smuggle themselves into a jihadi camp in Pakistan. In the end, Aaron's initial performance of piety turns into an authentic appreciation of Islam, which makes him vulnerable to radicalism—especially after being tapped by the "old man in the mountain" to hear his sermons. After they make their way back to New York, Aaron is "activated" as a suicide bomber and ordered to destroy the New York Stock Exchange. Unable to dissuade him, Ahmed follows Aaron and, without hesitation, sacrifices himself by using his own body to shield Aaron from snipers. The last panels show Aaron back in the psychiatric ward in Kansas, this time as a patient.

Even though the three works considered in this chapter represent different genres—biography, interviews, and fiction, respectively—as "Guantánamo counternarratives," they share an interest in a basic theme: the idea that a particular type of warscape environment developed over the past two decades is producing the precise opposite of the energized and active jihadist cliché. Rather than being the aggressor, the Muslim detainee in these counternarratives appears consistently as an abject figure, completely controlled and ruthlessly used by the West. By portraying Guantánamo as an insulated and impenetrable theater of violence, and by focusing on "violated bodies and eroded subjects, dehumanized individuals and collapsed everyday worlds," the authors create a grotesque ecosystem that offers no rights or protections to the powerless detainee (Nayar, "Human Rights" 319).[6] Indeed, the figure produced in this warscape, I suggest, is best understood not as emanating from the traditional "Muslim character" categories of American popular culture but rather in terms of the historical

---

6. As Pugliese writes:

> Guantánamo's penal apparatus pivots on the exercise of a virtually unfettered state power that can produce murder and corpses with impunity. The ontotautological transmutation and reduction of the Muslim inmates into *Muselmänner, Figuren,* and dolls facilitates the murderous operation of this penalogical system. (182)

figure of the "Muselmann"—the term used by Jewish prisoners to describe the "living-dead" inhabitants of the concentration camp. For Joseph Pugliese, the "reincarnation of the Muselmann" in Guantánamo attests to the analogous "operating logic" of the prison camps that reduces its inhabitants to bare life (160).[7] I trace this transformation to show how the Muselmann status of the detainee has lasting effects beyond incarceration, creating a sustained form of captivity that outlives the prison. I then turn my attention to the witnessing potential of these narratives, to argue that comics as a medium is not only *appropriate* to capturing the dehumanizing effects of this metamorphosis but rather *essential* in recovering and chronicling the muted voices of the wrongfully incarcerated. Essentially, these narratives bear witness to the anguish of the Muselmann—even when the Muselmann is not capable of testifying himself.

The Abject Muslim and Warscape Desubjectification

All three counternarratives present Guantánamo as a warscape—not only because it is a militarized detention center but also because of its unique standing as a nonbattle zone and extralegal site where violence is an everyday occurrence. The anticipation of violence—in the form of physical and psychological abuse—turns the prison into a state of exception, an "indeterminate space" outside the formal mechanisms of legal scrutiny and accountability.[8] When the protagonist of *Guantánamo Kid* asks for legal representation, the response is telling: "Not here in Guantánamo [. . .] no rights

---

7. "Guantanamo is not Auschwitz," writes Joseph Pugliese; but he also acknowledges similarities in "the structurality of the camp," arguing that specific features of the camp "appear to be constitutive of [Gitmo's] operating logic and that, across different spatiotemporal configurations, continue to be reproduced" (176). Indeed, Mirk notes that human rights activists repeatedly compared the conditions in Guantánamo to those of a "concentration camp" (v).

8. The Sixth Amendment reads:

> In all criminal prosecutions, the accused shall enjoy the right to a speedy and public trial, by an impartial jury of the State and district wherein the crime shall have been committed, which district shall have been previously ascertained by law, and to be informed of the nature and cause of the accusation; to be confronted with the witnesses against him; to have compulsory process for obtaining witnesses in his favor, and to have the Assistance of Counsel for his defence.

Guantánamo's unique geopolitical situation allowed the Bush administration to remove any links to traditional war from operational procedures so that they could evade the normal protections afforded to prisoners.

here" (Tubiana and Franc 42).⁹ In this regard, Gitmo represents what Judith Butler labels "the new war prison"—a different type of warscape that

> literally manages populations, and thus functions as an operation of governmentality. At the same time, however, it exploits the extra-legal dimension of governmentality to assert a lawless sovereign power over life and death. In other words, the new war prison constitutes a form of governmentality that considers itself its own justification and seeks to extend that self-justificatory form of sovereignty through animating and deploying the extra-legal dimension of governmentality. (*Precarious Life* 95)

Governmentality in a warscape, in other words, is almost precisely the opposite of what Michel Foucault imagines "governing" to be. That is, while Foucault explains governance as the transformation of human beings into subjects via the mechanisms of power, in a warscape, governmentality works against the subject, as central institutions of power seek to *de*subjectify select groups (777). Traditionally, Muslim characters in American popular culture are marked by a striking blend of extreme devotion and high levels of autonomous agency: They are utterly loyal to their faith but also frequently act as self-motivated "lone wolves" unbound by Western mores and rules. Warscape desubjectification, the unmaking of the self through a series of hostile deprogramming techniques, targets the individual's autonomy and eradicates any sense of agency. Consequently, through various warscape mechanisms of governmentality infused into the everyday lives of the prisoners, and through a regular exploitation and degradation of the prisoners' devotion to their faith, the camp/warscape accelerates the Muslim detainees' descent into abjection, until they are eventually relegated to Muselmann status—a zombified, bare-life existence.

Of course, the loss of autonomy is not unique to the warscape prison—all prisons, after all, create controlled environments with hierarchical structures and physical consequences to rule-breaking. But Guantánamo is not just a site of discipline and control; rather, it emblematizes a regime dedicated to the complete disintegration of the individual. The traditional prison (at least ostensibly) seeks to reform, to reshape the prisoner into a subject who retains enough autonomy to function within the larger mechanism of power; the warscape prison is openly uninterested in any future function for those within it. And whereas the traditional prison desires to reshape the

---

9. The anticipation of violence, as Omar El Akkad describes, can take the form of "a linguistic violence, a bureaucratic violence, a violence of apathy, [. . .] a violence of forgetting" and can be as devastating as physical abuse (Mirk vii).

prisoner's understanding of society (and the prisoner's position within it) through rehabilitation, the warscape prison seeks to eliminate understanding altogether. This purge starts with the manipulation of the prisoner's perception. By controlling the sensory input of the prisoner (via goggles, headphones, blindfolds, etc.), the guards use confusion as a means of dulling the arriving prisoner's mental faculties.[10] In *Guantánamo Kid*, upon entering Camp X-ray, Mohammed describes his complete bewilderment and lack of understanding of his situation; he does not know where he is or even which country he is in. Conventional prison design is replaced by generic military architecture emerging as a warscape: "I saw soldiers everywhere, and guns, like it was a war zone. There were high metal fences, too. My cell had no walls, no roof, no shelter from the sun or the rain. Just wire netting" (39). Visually, the comic foreshadows the helplessness of the prisoner, with broken lines emanating from the sun drawing attention to the heat engulfing Mohammed as he sits in his cage, unprotected from the elements. The enmeshing of the lines with the prison bars suggests the blurring of natural and architectural oppression. Mohammed's spatial and temporal disorientation is enhanced by drugs administered to further obscure his bearings and undermine his self-reliance: When he wakes up with an IV in his arm, the heavily medicated Mohammed is unable to act or react. Pramod K. Nayar sees the calculated stupefaction of the detainee as part of the deprogramming tactics that elicit the "dissolution of the sense of an agential self" followed by "the loss of capability to determine the body's course of action" ("Human Rights" 325). This dissolution is captured by Mohammed's posture: Sitting in his cage on his knees, with his head bowed down, he embodies an abject sense of defeat.

After the initial disorientation tactics, various strategies of dehumanization are employed, the most symbolic of which is the assigning of numbers to prisoners to replace their names. When Mohammed becomes simply "number 269," he feels the loss of his entire personal history, "stripped of

---

10. In *Aaron & Ahmed*, Guantánamo's conversion from a naval base to a detention center is featured under the banner of a newspaper clipping that reads "Bush signs executive order making terror suspects 'non-combatants.'" In a two-page spread of the prison that follows, the vertical structure of this closed ecology is conveyed: We see detainees gathered in a pen, dressed in orange jumpsuits with black head coverings, sitting on their knees as their hands remain shackled behind them; soldiers on the floodlight towers remain on guard with their heavy weaponry; higher-ups (literally placed higher on the page) sit around a table engaged with planning; outside the detention area, soldiers interact casually in groups of two or three. The "faceless" detainees, "likened to caged and restrained animals," mimic the leaked photos of abuse, which further communicates their dehumanization (*Precarious Life* 73). The aerial image capturing the compartmentalized life of the inhabitants of this warscape reinforces the idea of impenetrability: The lawful world remains behind once the prisoner enters the warscape.

the specificity of culture, place, and history," turned into a "thing" to be managed by the state (Malkki 11). This point is reiterated by Moazzam Begg (Prisoner 558) in *Guantanamo Voices* as he recalls the experience of being attached to a random number as akin to a form of erasure: "I am not a family member. I am not a husband. We're no longer people. We're numbers" (Mirk 77). Reduced to mere numbers, the prisoners are treated as an inferior, quasi-subhuman race.[11]

A more literal sense of dehumanization is exercised under the auspices of "Psy-Ops" in *Aaron & Ahmed*. Aaron's mentor, Negroponte, explains to him how he has designed psychological experiments to turn Muslims into dogs (see figure 2.1). Kept in a kennel, the Muslim is exposed to "a combination of sleep deprivation, followed by hypnosis, and severe operant conditioning." After intense deprogramming, the Muslim detainee starts acting like a dog, doing "tricks": In one scene, two shackled detainees are shown sitting on their knees on the floor, made to "play dead." For Negroponte, the aim is to create pathologically delusional, bestialized detainees, evoking the leaked photographs that showed Muslims on dog leashes. Reflecting on the photographic images, Butler writes: "There is something more in this degradation that calls to be read. There is a reduction of these human beings to animal status, where the animal is figured as out of control, in need of total restraint" (*Precarious Life* 78). Especially significant here is the symbolic implication of the dog—a "fallen" animal, considered to be haram in Islam.[12] This is not just an instance in which humans are relegated to animal status; it signifies how Islamic ideas are utilized by the interrogators as deprogramming tools. The dog's "impurity" threatens the devout Muslim, who aspires to remain "pure" through actions, rituals, and Qur'anic teach-

---

11. Inmates complain about the racial insults uttered by the prison guards, illustrating the way Islam becomes a racial category. Mohammed explicates: "There was racism in Saudi Arabia, but in Guantanamo I learned that there are truly racist people" (Tubiana and Franc 32). He makes this statement as a guard walks by his cage and calls him "Fucking n——," a slur that Mohammed does not even understand until it is explained to him by another detainee (32). Bayoumi argues that the measures taken by the government against Muslims in and outside the US have, "in effect, turned a religion, namely Islam, into a race" (Bayoumi, "Racing" 269, 270). Alka Pradhan, a human rights lawyer featured in *Guantanamo Voices*, echoes this point as she notes that racism is not an isolated incident here and there but is enmeshed with the whole prison structure: "We created an entire new legal system for brown men. If these were white men from France and Germany, there's no way Guantanamo would exist" (Mirk 140). Racialization of religion fuels the prevailing racist/Islamophobic environment, which, in turn, intensifies the abjection of the Muslim detainee.

12. Amit Baishya writes: "A stereotype exists that Islam evinces an intense dislike for animals, especially 'fallen' animals like dogs. [. . .] Dogs, and especially their spit, are considered haram in Islam" (53).

FIGURE 2.1. Negroponte explains to Aaron how to turn inmates into dogs.

ings that emphasize personal hygiene. Again, the Muslim subject's devotion and "submission" to Islamic tenets is used to develop a new form of surrender—to Western power—that will ultimately undermine the subject's basic sense of self.

The weaponization of Islam is perhaps the most subtle tool employed in the abjectification of the Muslim prisoner. Here and elsewhere, we see that within the warscape, with its constant surveillance, religious adherence becomes a litmus test of an inhabitant's threat status. In *Guantánamo Kid*, the guards purposefully make it difficult for the inmates to fulfill their faith rituals, from praying to following basic dietary restrictions. Since the guards refuse to tell them the time, the prisoners can only estimate when they should perform their prayers. Those inmates who exert the extra effort to fulfill their religious duties are then identified as problems: Inmates who successfully do *namaz* are targeted, ridiculed, and beaten (48). Even the Qur'an, initially handed out to prisoners as part of a propaganda campaign for the media, is employed as a tool to provoke the inmates. During one of the regular searches of Mohammed's cell, a guard picks up the Qur'an, rummages through its pages, and then kicks it to the floor. Mohammed feels more pained than angered by the insult:

> I cleaned the Quran and put it back in its place. I wouldn't kick the Bible, ever. It's a holy book too. But when I saw people kicking the Quran, it made me sad. It's one of the more serious things Americans did to us. Something I never thought I'd see in my lifetime before I became a prisoner. It happened several times. Sometimes they tore up the Quran, sometimes they threw it in the toilet. (62)

Although Mohammed is shocked by the soldiers' disrespect, he understands their action in the context of what he now realizes is a warscape: A religious insult is a quasi-military gesture of authority, meant to provoke the Muslim prisoners and to elicit a punishable reaction from them. He responds the only way he can: by imagining himself outside of the warscape, in a world where warscape rules do not apply. As he wipes the Qur'an, for example, he has a vision of the calligraphy lifting from its pages and turning into a bird flapping its wings, escaping from the cage—a visual cue that suggests the liberating effects of the verses. In other instances, the army distributes cans of processed meat that include pork. Mohammed notes that they get little food in the prison to begin with, just enough "to keep one alive" (50). But for the devout, this nonmeal is entirely "inedible" (44). Protests fall on deaf ears; as prisoners hold out their opened cans of food, one guard yells: "You're not in a Muslim country! This is all you're getting" (44). In this instance, mental and physical torment overlaps, showing the holistic approach to warscape desubjectification. Depriving prisoners of halal food is an effort to exert total control, to break subjects physically and mentally by making them choose between religious duty and sustenance. Clearly, warscape management of everyday life—from food to sleep, from prayer to hygiene—is used for the demoralization of the Muslim detainee, not only to break him down as an individual by robbing him of his vitality and agency but also to break him away from Islam through a sense of spiritual defamiliarization.

From Abject Muslim to Muselmann

If desubjectification turns the Muslim into an abject prisoner, the use of torture transforms him into the Muselmann, "a new living dead man" (Agamben, *Homo Sacer* 131).[13] "Muselmann," a German term for "Muslim," originally gained currency as an epithet applied to the Jewish captives of Nazi camps. Afterward, it was used in numerous writings by Holocaust survivors (most notably by Primo Levi) to describe the wretched state of the camp inhabitants.[14] There are two explanations for the ironic renaming of Jews as Muslims in survivor tales. The first is that, in anticipation of death, the prisoner manifests a sense of fatalism traditionally associated by some with Islam. In this regard, Muslims, who practice their faith by showing absolute submission to the will of Allah, come to represent the defeatist attitude of the captives as they surrender to preordained suffering. The second explanation relates to the physical posture of the prisoner: Frequently forced, out of fear or exhaustion, to crouch on the ground, they were imagined as permanently stuck in the Islamic position of prayer. Giorgio Agamben writes:

> The most likely explanation of the term can be found in the literal meaning of the Arabic word *muslim* [sic]: the one who submits unconditionally

---

13. A new taxonomy was invented for suspected terrorists: Labeling them "enemy combatants" rather than "prisoners of war" allowed the administration to circumvent the Geneva Convention. In a speech defending this decision, Dennis Hastert, the Speaker of the House at the time, declared: "These aren't military people. They don't belong to a country, they don't wear a uniform, they're not part of an army. It's a unique situation and we'll have to deal with it in a unique way" (qtd. in Butler, "Guantanamo Limbo"). Subsequently, this simple speech act paved the way for the CIA to implement "provisional and exceptional measures" to obtain "actionable information" by using "special interrogation techniques."

14. The term appears in numerous testimonies about the concentration camps, including David Rousset's *L'univers concentrationnaire* (1947), Eugen Kogon's *Der SS State* (1946), and Elie Wiesel's *La Nuit* (1958).

to the will of God. It is this meaning that lies at the origin of the legends concerning Islam's supposed fatalism, legends of which are found in European culture starting with the Middle Ages. [. . .] But while the Muslim's resignation consists in the conviction that the will of Allah is at work every moment and in even the smallest events, the Muselmann of Auschwitz is instead defined by a loss of will and consciousness. (*Remnants* 45)

Not all prisoners in the Nazi camps were regarded as "Muselmann" figures; rather, the label was reserved for those who had assumed a "cadaveric" existence, occupying the lowest end of the prison hierarchy.[15] As Sharon Oster explains, there was a severe "breakdown of human solidarity between prisoners deemed *Muselmänner* and those who ultimately looked away" (305)—a division within the prison population between the abject, detached from the world of the living, and those who averted their gaze from the abject in order to retain their hope and humanity.[16] In this sense, the term suggests that even within a population already marked by abject Otherness and dehumanization, a select group can be distinguished as experiencing further alienation, suffering a complete dissolution of the self and awaiting imminent death with utter apathy.

All three narratives examined in this chapter portray Guantánamo as a place that creates "Muselmann"-type figures through torture, which reduces the abject prisoner into a zombified existence, half living, half dead, and therefore not entirely human, with no rights—as they remain completely outside of the law and unrecognized by it.[17] In these comics, the American military is shown taking advantage of legal loopholes in order to torture

---

15. Malini Johar Schueller explains "how the term Muselmann, in common use in Auschwitz, spread to other camps as well. In Majdanek the living dead were termed 'donkeys,' in Dachau they were 'cretins,' in Stutthof 'cripples,' in Buchenwald 'tired sheikhs' and in women's camps Muselweiber/female muslims" (244).

16. Engdahl writes: "'Muslims' was the nickname for the prisoners who had given up: an anonymous and continuously topped-up mass, people in whom the divine spark had gone out, who had grown too empty to actually suffer" (11).

17. The conditions in Guantánamo, explains Agamben, have certain legal parallels to those in concentration camps:

> The detainees of Guantanamo do not have the status of Prisoners of War, they have absolutely no legal status. They are subject now only to raw power; they have no legal existence. [Similarly,] in the Nazi camps, the Jews had to be first fully "denationalised" and stripped of all the citizenship rights remaining after Nuremberg, after which they were also erased as legal subjects. (qtd. in Raulff 610)

Agamben's emphasis on the collapse of the "legal subject" in relation to "raw power" provides a foundation for understanding the mechanisms of abjection that lead to the Muselmann figure.

Muslim inmates; the mistreatment of detainees becomes an institutionally endorsed activity designed to enhance the degradation of the Muslim.[18] Consequently, the anticipation of torture, "rendered as environmental and totalising," hangs over the prisoner; its "inevitability conditions the detainee's experience" (Coundouriotis 1069).[19] The Muselmann, then, signifies the Muslim body condemned to endless violence without death. As Schultheis Moore contends:

> Guantánamo as a paradigmatic state of exception in effect denies the possibility of reading the detainees as anything other than what Agamben theorizes as bare life—the life that may be taken with impunity and without sacrifice in the state of exception, the political life that is nonetheless beyond the reach of the law and therefore demonstrates the power of sovereignty and sovereign violence. (30)

The tortured body of the prisoner marks the final physical transformation of the abject Muslim into the Muselmann, reducing him to bare life.

In *Guantanamo Voices*, Abu Zubaydah, incarcerated without any evidence of guilt, endures unimaginable torment: He is initially kept in solitary confinement for months with no human contact, then beaten, and after that

---

18. Torture, of course, was not endorsed openly by government officials; rather, to elude the anti-torture clauses in the US Department of Justice, the Bush administration approved "special interrogation techniques"—alternative methods that do not inflict *severe* suffering or pain, consisting of a series of stress positions, including "beatings, exposure to extreme cold or heat, threats of death, sleep deprivation, various forms of psychological torture or mistreatment, painful stress positions, and in one instance, giving a prisoner urine to drink" (Human Rights Watch, "Getting Away"). Torture, defined as an act of inflicting severe pain or suffering, was not officially sanctioned by the US Department of Justice, which "proscribes acts inflicting, and that are specifically intended to inflict, severe pain or suffering, whether mental or physical" (Convention against Torture and Other Cruel, Inhuman and Degrading Treatment or Punishment, Section 23440A). But the Bybee Memoranda (also known as the "torture memos," drafted by John Yoo in 2002) tried to create a loophole around the idea of "severe" by contending that unless pain was "equivalent in intensity to the pain accompanying serious physical injury, such as organ failure, impairment of bodily function, or even death," it could not qualify as torture (Bybee report, supra note 25, at 172). In other words, the justification of torture rested on the idea that what was implemented as pain was simply a simulation of harm and death that was neither "severe" nor significant enough to leave marks on the body (thus the techniques were described as "stealth technologies").

19. In *Guantánamo Kid*, even before Mohammed is physically battered, he is psychologically tormented as he hears other prisoners scream with pain: "Somewhere or other they were torturing prisoners. When you hear then screaming, you are really scared—you think you'll be next" (40). These words are uttered as Mohammed lies down on his makeshift bed in a fetal position, covering his ears.

waterboarded "on 83 occasions" (Mirk 39). A series of four panels show this progression: We first see him sitting naked on the floor of his cell; the next panel tells us that he has been "slammed against the wall," showing a pool of blood on the ground (39). The final panels move to waterboarding, blood mixing with water as he is subjected to "controlled drowning" (39). This particular simulation literally brings the Muselmann closer to the image that Levi invokes as "the drowned"—the "anonymous mass" of "non-men" who make up the mass of the imprisoned, "the divine spark dead within them" (Levi, *Survival* 90). The unseen body of Zubaydah—too uncomfortable to look at—similarly represents a cadaveric existence, sentenced to a cycle of brutality. Indeed, the last panel on the page features a motionless arm lying on top of the blood-water mixture: "He became completely unresponsive, with bubbles rising through his open mouth" (Mirk 39). By using the limb as a metonym for the broken body, the artists omit the kind of bodily tableau that might turn the vulnerable prisoner into a spectacle and encourage intrusive voyeurism from the reader that would further the exploitation of the imprisoned subject. And this self-imposed censorship also benefits the reader: It spares him or her from the horror of the scene by acknowledging that "the sight of the living Muselmann is a new death scene, not to be endured by human eyes" (Consonni 254). In this way, the reader is also released from making a decision about whether to look or to avert his or her eyes.

Traditionally, the Muslim figure in Western comics is unquestionably the antagonist. In these warscape counternarratives, the Muselmann can be the protagonist—but only sometimes; at other times, he is the nameless, faceless character that remains in the background to illustrate the omnipresence of torture. In *Aaron & Ahmed*, as Aaron and Negroponte make their rounds from one torture chamber to the next, conversing about the effectiveness of various methods, neither of them pays close attention to the tortured. Here the visual perspective shows the disconnect between the rationalization of torture and its actual performance. Through focalization, the panels convey one (visual) reality while the conversation reflects an alternate (textual) reality. For example, the dialogue between Aaron and Negroponte takes place as the panels depict the waterboarding of a prisoner. Two officers pour gallons of water on a restrained detainee (the reader can hardly make out the face behind the barrage of water). The flood of the water obscures the image; bubbles gush out, each of them carrying mostly monosyllable words: "I" "am" "dying." When we finally get a glimpse of the victim—unconscious, secured on a wooden board, with bound hands and feet—we have a clear view of a Muselmann: Eyes closed, mouth half open, the quasi-lifeless body rests on a plank of wood surrounded by interrogators, closely watching this "new living dead man" to determine whether they can continue with their interrogation. As Aaron passively surveys the spectacle, Negroponte confesses that he does not think of the detainees as humans but as bodies in the service of his experiments. He knows well that these interrogation methods rarely garner useful information: "No one will talk. Supposing the poor bastards knew anything in the first place." Still, he pushes them physically and mentally to see how far things can go. As Negroponte resumes his moralizing speech about keeping America safe, the background images shift back to the "carnival of torture." The dissonance between the image and the text is striking: The false alignment of cause (terror) and effect (torture) shows the hypocrisy behind the failed "special interrogation techniques."[20] Yet the futility of the act does not necessarily annul it. If the tortured victim is the Muselmann, forced to oscillate between life and death, Negroponte represents raw power, illustrating "what people do when their power is absolute."

Agamben argues that bodies labeled as *homo sacer* can be tortured and killed with impunity; in Guantánamo, the intent of torture is not to kill but to create sustained suffering to eliminate the prisoner's sense of control. In fact, the *refusal* to kill becomes another torturous act in the management of the inmates. In *Guantánamo Kid*, Mohammed remembers the inhumane treatment of the prisoners when they went on hunger strikes: "With no food or drink, I was feeling sick, dizzy, weak, thirsty. But they wouldn't let you die. They force-fed us through a tube up our nose" (79). This narrative is accompanied by a series of panels showing him in and out of the prison hospital as they administer an IV to keep him alive. The last panel emphasizes the brutality of force-feeding: Strapped to a chair, with his head secured, Mohammed is held down by two soldiers as they insert a feeding tube in his nose. Mohammed's mouth is open—as if to scream—though the scream itself is not represented in the panel. A similar episode of force-feeding in *Aaron & Ahmed* shows the lack of empathy or even basic recognition of fellow humanity that dominates the prison warscape. A soldier jokes as he helps restrain Ahmed and works to shove a funnel down his throat: "Looks like one of those Strasbourg geese doesn't he?" Ahmed is silent, but his posture shows that he is in severe pain—yet the soldiers remain nonchalant, completely unresponsive to the human suffering before them. Their blithe attitude suggests that they are "so without any human recognition of or

---

20. Danielle Celermajer writes that "a large body of evidence now exists indicating that information obtained under torture is unreliable at best, and that, as a technique, torture is far from the best means of obtaining intelligence" (90).

identification with the pain" that, far from being disturbed by their participation in abuse, they are vaguely amused by it (Scarry 36). Their undignified joke is perhaps an admission of the detainee's undignified life. Analogous scenes in *Guantanamo Voices* similarly emphasize the Muselmann's ignominy: Emad's seven-year-long hunger strike is interrupted at various points to force-feed him, and we see him, too, pinned down with a hose in his nose (140). Why is there such a focus on force-feeding as a visual component of these narratives? Perhaps to convey the fundamental irony of existence as a warscape Muselmann. Denied all opportunities to control their own bodies, these prisoners finally enter into an existence in which they are entirely at the mercy of their captors—but also cannot be allowed to die of their own accord. The self-willed death of a prisoner is on some level a statement of self-control and therefore a failure of the institution to manage biopower: The Muselmann can be killed with impunity but cannot be allowed to regain subjectivity and power through sacrificing himself. Self-inflicted harm (starvation) expresses the prisoner's desire to be heard as a victim, to gain respect as a fellow human being, and to regain control of his body by being in charge of the terms of his existence: That dignified, qualified subsistence is denied to him in the warscape prison.[21]

In these narratives, the docile, abject Muslim detainee replaces the more recognizable active and energetic jihadi seen in *Holy Terror,* where Muslim characters are almost always either in physical motion (jumping, yelling, etc.) or engaged in strategic actions (e.g., Amina seducing a soon-to-be-dead victim), or in Ryan Inzana's *Johnny Jihad,* in which jihadist recruits are constantly active (running, jumping over walls, learning how to operate machine guns, etc.) as they ready themselves for Al-Qaeda missions in training camps. The Muslim detainee in Guantánamo is not the animated, untiring, and resolute jihadi; by controlling the everyday lives of the prisoners, this new war prison turns them into passive receptors, "their bodies

---

21. Lauren Wilcox argues that

> torture turns prisoners into objects of the sovereign's ability to act directly on their bodies or, in Michel Foucault's terms, to "take life or let live." Only representatives of the United States are allowed to inflict pain and violence on the bodies of detainees—the detainees themselves are forbidden the same right. The exercise of biopower on the bodies of the hunger strikers is a perverse form of biopower's power to "make live," as it is exercised directly on the bodies of the negative subjects of biopower, the dangerous bodies of "terrorists." Force-feeding has the effect of making the "terrorists" legible and forces a type of normative status onto them, as infantilized "dependents." (114–15)

micromanaged so that they will be useful and compliant" (Wilcox 105).[22] And unlike the jihadi, who has a specific purpose in life (and even in death, which he faces with enthusiasm), the Muslim detainee's future is taken away: "You're never going to see your family again. You could be facing execution by firing squad, lethal injection, or gas chamber" (Mirk 78). In these narratives, the Muselmann is pacified, immobile, and helpless.

Muselmann and Witnessing

However abject a victim may be, traditionally there is one last recourse to agency, even for those prisoners not allowed to commit suicide: the ability to bear witness to their suffering. If torture dehumanizes the detainee, testifying about the horrors of warscape should restore his agency and therefore humanity—an idea that surfaces in the writings of Annette Wieviorka, who views witnessing as an essential process for the victim to regain his or her voice and to "reintegrate[ ] into the community of humankind" (18). Even this recourse, however, is denied in the Guantánamo counternarratives; rather, the Muselmann is neither eager to take on a new role as the "bearer of history" nor able to emerge as a new "social figure" to hold institutions accountable (Wieviorka 88). Consequently, in these counternarratives, the witnessing potential of the Muslim-as-Muselmann is diminished. To go back to *Holy Terror*: Miller depicts the Muslim warriors who unleash terror on Empire City as frenetically active, constantly vocal and fervent witnesses always yelling recognizable phrases from the Qur'an. When "Allahu Akbar" rings out as a battle cry, it serves not only as a declaration of faith but also as a confirmation of the Muslim militant's willingness to sacrifice himself and to control the narrative around him. In death, they join the cult of the *shaheed* (heroes who bear witness to God's existence and die to achieve his glory on earth) and become celebrated heroes within radicalized circles. Miller and others repeatedly promote the idea of the dangerous, fanatically energetic Muslim as a real and always active threat, as well as a vocal and

---

22. While "bad" (i.e., unrepentant, uncooperative) Muslims are physically punished or placed in isolation for months on end, "good" (i.e., compliant) Muslims are given various privileges and rewards. In *Guantánamo Kid*, one of the "good" Muslims keeps feeding false information to the interrogators to receive "coke and pizzas" (Tubiana and Franc 43). Mohammed, on the other hand, not only refuses to cooperate with authorities but engages in acts of resistance in his limited capacity. At one point, he shows defiance by throwing feces at the guards. Mohammed links desubjectification with dehumanization; without an autonomous subject, there can be no recognition as human. And if he loses his humanity, he sees no reason to remain civil, so he begins to act animalistically.

self-promoting one. Clearly, he equates religious witnessing with fanaticism, much as he associates Islam with terrorism.

As opposed to these active and fanatical figures, the Muselmann in Guantánamo counternarratives manifests diffidence and reticence: The eagerness of new arrivals to proclaim their faith gradually gives way to rote responses, animalistic shrieks, and eventually uncommunicative dumbness as the warscape grinds them down. If the radicalized Muslim is the vocal witness, who asserts his belief by yelling Qur'anic mantras, the Muselmann is the muted witness whose speech is limited and generally unheard. Whether it be the wordless scream of Mohammed on a feeding chair or the muffled noises of a nameless detainee during waterboarding, there are physical and psychological barriers to speaking even within the prison—not to mention the complete silencing of the prisoner's voice as far as the outside world is concerned.

The section that features Moazzam Begg in *Guantanamo Voices* vividly illustrates the prisoners' inability to assume the position of the witness. Shortly after Begg comments on the dehumanizing effects of assigning numbers to prisoners, the reader sees him sitting on the floor and eating bread with other inmates, their heads down as a fellow prisoner in an adjacent cell is shackled to the ceiling and brutally beaten by two soldiers (see figure 2.2). Begg averts his gaze and stares at the food before him; by refusing to look up, he expresses a new inability to witness the suffering of another. At this point, he confesses that he is "no longer a person," capable of showing compassion. His lack of sympathy marks the extent of his dehumanization—his unresponsiveness stems partly from his inability to stand up against the authority of the soldiers and partly from his numbness to the normalization of violence unfolding around him. He cannot allow himself to empathize with the victim—even when he knows that it is a matter of time before the roles are reversed and he becomes the target.

The muted, apathetic Muselmann is not a departure only from Miller's bellowing jihadi but also from Levi's characterization of the Muselmann as the *ideal* witness. Levi attributes the Muselmann's initial muteness to his inability to convey the shocking particulars of his abject existence; still, he insists that the Muselmann's perspective eventually becomes essential to shedding light on the horrors of the camp: "We, the survivors, are not the true witnesses [. . .] We survivors are not only an exiguous but also an anomalous minority: we are those who by their prevarications or abilities or good luck did not touch bottom" (*The Drowned* 83). The larger problem, however, is that the Muselmann figure, while having witnessed the normally unwitnessable, is unable to fully grasp the extent of their victimization. Therefore,

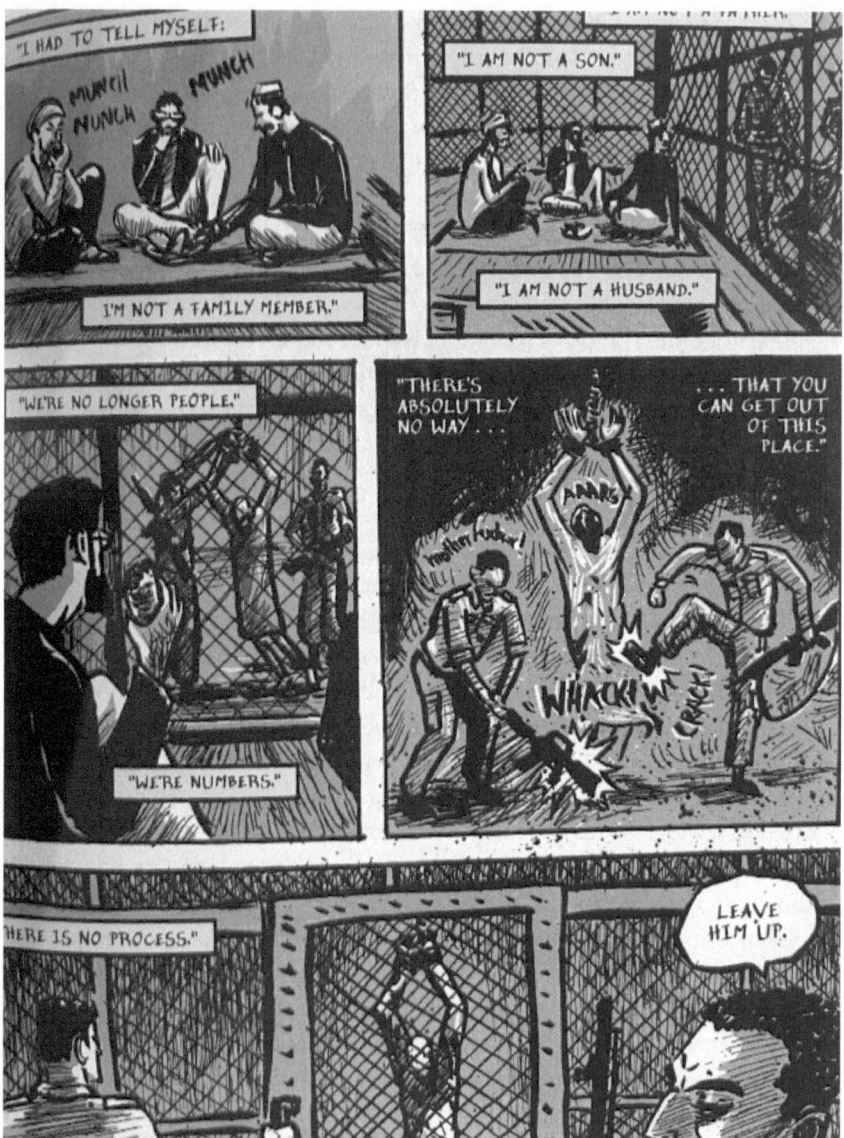

FIGURE 2.2. Begg and his friends eat as an inmate is being tortured.

the "true witness" is one who cannot testify: "Those who did so, those who saw the Gorgon, have not returned to tell about it or have returned mute, but they are [...] the complete witnesses, the ones whose deposition would have a general significance. They are the rule, we are the exception" (*The Drowned* 84). Agamben elaborates further as he discusses the notion of the "complete witness":

The witness usually testifies in the name of justice and truth and as such his or her speech draws consistency and fullness. Yet here the value of testimony lies essentially in what it lacks; at its center it contains something that cannot be borne witness to and that discharges the survivors of authority. The "true" witnesses, the "complete witnesses," are those who did not bear witness and could not bear witness. They are those who "touched bottom": the Muslims, the drowned. (*Remnants* 34)

This paradox of "not being able to bear witness" even when one appears to be "the complete witness" is a direct consequence of the limits of language: Seeing and speaking do not necessarily align neatly. As others have argued, language is ill-equipped to capture the intensity of suffering. Indeed, it took Levi decades to intercede for those who lost the ability to speak for themselves and invent a "new, harsh language" to articulate genuine and unadulterated experiences of the Muselmann. For Levi, acting as a surrogate witness for the Muselmann offers a way to reclaim the Muselmann's humanity, to help him "become a man again [. . .] neither a martyr, nor debased, nor a saint" (*Periodic Table* 151). Yet the Guantánamo Muselmann faces additional obstacles: Even before they were removed from their society and detained, they did not necessarily have the ability to communicate to the Western audience that needs to hear about the realities of Guantánamo. Once they are released, they have neither the emotional and physical ability to speak nor the capacity to compose a "new, harsh language" to bear witness to the conditions that dehumanize them.

So, then, we are left with a problem highly relevant to the Guantánamo comics: How does one testify if he cannot speak, especially when he does not have access to Levi's "new, harsh language"? This question brings us back to the merit of comics as a multimodal medium. As Dominic Davies writes, comics are well suited to document trauma precisely because they can "invoke it, play with it, revise it, challenge it, and in their most innovative moments, move beyond it" (8). Comics, then, have the potential to "unmute" the Muselmann: Not only can the visuals take over when language fails, but the form also assigns meaning to raw, inarticulate sounds, transforming monosyllabic utterances into comprehensible statements. If the Muselmann cannot find proper language to convey the intensity of his suffering, the image of the body in distress serves as its own evidence and testament. As Consonni attests:

It is the body of the survivor that constitutes integral testimony; the living Muselmann fills the testimonial lacuna. The presence of the Muselmann, the testifiable, replaces the memoir by the body. Almost every survivor was a Muselmann to some degree—or at least close to becoming one, whether in the physiological sense of depletion or in the philosophical sense of surviving one's own "being-towards-death." (250)

The idea of testimony inscribed on his body runs throughout the comics we are examining, as when Mohammed, after his release from Guantánamo, studies the injuries he had suffered over the years: "Torture had left its mark. Backaches, problems with my vision, stomach, knees . . ." (Tubiana and Franc 129). The list of injuries becomes its own narrative, one that the Western comics reader needs little translation to appreciate: They *see* the legacy of the internment rather than hear about it. The scars, of course, can be psychological as well; in *Aaron & Ahmed*, an inmate is made to wear women's underwear on his head, restrained by three soldiers mocking him as he is stripped naked for their amusement. The prisoner is completely silent, unable to protest for fear of receiving more beatings; the pictorial illustration, on the other hand, expresses the cruelty and the malice endorsed by those in authority positions in Guantánamo. Perhaps no words can convey the humiliation of the Muselmann—but the image comes close.

That is not to say that the comics artists are simply content to supplement or replace verbal descriptions of pain with visual ones. Rather, there is an incentive for comics artists to imagine new and visceral ways in which pain might be illustrated without reproducing the same spectacular, silencing intensity. An important comics device, in this sense, is fragmentation. In *Guantánamo Kid*, Mohammed recalls each torturous act by using his body as a map to trigger his memory:

> They tortured me with electricity, mostly on my toes. The nails of my big toes came off. [. . .] Sometimes they'd string you up like a chicken and hit you in the back. Sometimes they chained you up with your face on the ground. You couldn't move for 16 or 17 hours. You had to piss where you lay. If you said yes, they stopped the torture. If you said no, they kept it going. It could go on all day. [. . .] Sometimes I'd say: "I'll say yes to whatever you want." (42)

This narrative is accompanied by a series of images that depict in fragmented fashion the violent acts perpetrated on Mohammed's body: a hand putting out a cigarette on his arm; a foot pressing on his head as he lies on the ground with his hands shackled behind his back; a fist slamming across his face. Yet there are two absences that make these moments strangely incomplete. The first is the clinical and impassive nature of the images; that is, as Mohammed relates the facts of the torture, he remains emotionally detached. The images, too, clearly show pain, in a technical sense, but there is no emotional emphasis to the moment, and the details are captured without sentiment or melodrama. The aloof, calm nature of the images is perhaps a coping mechanism—as if to suggest that there is an attempt here to avoid reliving trauma by consenting to a kind of self-willed emotional amnesia. The insularity of the images, therefore, conveys the untranslatability of suffering as well as the inability of seeing: In all these panels, Mohammed's eyes remain tightly shut—as if refusing to see the harm coming his way.

But there is something else lacking in these images: Reduced to mere body parts, the torturer remains anonymous. None of the panels fully show the soldier doing the torturing; his presence is disembodied, shrunk to a body part executing harm (an arm slapping Mohammed, or a leg kicking him, etc.). This is partly because Mohammed, sometimes forced to wear a blindfold and at other times choosing to shut his eyes in fear, cannot return the torturer's gaze and thus rarely has a clear image of his tormenter—a situation that literally evokes Agamben's suggestion that the Muselmann is always faced with the "impossibility of seeing" (*Remnants* 54). But there is also room to think that the torturer has lost his claim to humanity, that he cannot appear as a full human being because he is excluded from *humanitas*—human nature, civilization, and kindness.

In other instances, a more wholehearted move into abstraction offers a way to reverse the dehumanization of the subject. When Mohammed defies orders to stop communicating with other detainees, he knows he will be disciplined by "the team"—the "immediate reaction force" deployed to restrain difficult prisoners. The team's arrival is illustrated in realistic detail: Each individual is drawn with heavy gear entering the block. However, the drawing shifts to abstraction once the team begins to inflict pain upon Mohammed directly. From this point forward, the five soldiers are drawn as identical paper-cut figures, bent over a stick figure, signifying the detainee (see figure 2.3). Each solider has an assigned role as they pin a body part to the floor: "There's a rule in their rulebook, their S.O.P.: it says that if you comply and lie face down, hands and feet crossed behind your back, they won't spray you with pepper spray. They just have to come into the cell, shackle you, and take you out. But actually, even when we lay down, they sprayed us anyway. So we never lay down" (71). Beyond dehumanizing the torturers, this abstract drawing shows the difficulties of bearing witness to torture for the abject victim: Mohammed is simultaneously present in the scene (as a stick figure) and absent from it (he is deindividualized). Nevertheless, abstraction allows Mohammed to speak about pain without

FIGURE 2.3. Mohammed explains the methods of torture.

reliving the actual trauma and also allows him to comment on the role of the soldiers (viewed as inhuman machines) in a relatively neutral and unbiased way. Abstraction helps the Muselmann describe suffering objectively, as an incident, without being personally invested in the spectacle of the moment.

With or without his voice, then, the Muselmann can indeed testify. Still, as Guantánamo counternarratives suggest, the Muselmann is neither the ideal (as in Levi) nor the complete (as in Agamben) witness, but something slightly different: the reluctant witness. He bears witness by refusing to bear witness: by closing his eyes, averting his gaze, keeping his head down, remaining detached, and finding ways to evade (while simultaneously hinting at) the emotional toll of testifying. In this regard, the Muselmann's backward gaze does not reveal a "liberatory agenda" but more what Margaretta Jolly labels a "limit case," a narrative "forged out of extreme suffering, often told reluctantly [. . .] in the hope that in doing so the experiences they depict will never be repeated" (5). The witness accounts of the Muselmann of Guantánamo, such as they are, would seem to bring at least some new transparency to a warscape regime—yet the act of testifying does not help the Muselmann end his abjection. As the ending of each narrative reveals, the Muselmann's testimony does not automatically empower him, nor does it reconnect him with humanity.

Once a Muselmann, Always a Muselmann

There is no simple, positive resolution for the Muselmann in Guantánamo counternarratives; the Muselmann's status does not change once he testifies, nor does he find some sort of closure that can end his abjection. Rather, Muselmann status is a permanent condition that cannot be shed even after the detainee leaves the warscape. In *Guantanamo Voices,* Shelby Sullivan-Bennis, a lawyer representing a number of detainees, describes the only venue available to the prisoners while imprisoned: a hearing at the Periodic Review Board (PRB), which is not a legal body but a system put in place to assess the rehabilitation of the detainees. She outlines the process as the panel depicts a detainee waiting to be reviewed. As he stares at his own reflection on the one-way mirror, it becomes apparent that this is a process that actually furthers the inmate's self-alienation and sense of self-abstraction. There is no control and no relief from abjection: "The PRB says 'we're not telling you to confess to things that you did not do.' But the practical outcome is the same. If he reads it over and says 'that's all untrue,' the detainee is accused of a 'lack of contrition.' They're accused of making false statements because they're denying the allegations" (Mirk 149).

The prisoner understands that there can be no justice or redemption for the Muselmann. Mansoor Adayfi of *Guantanamo Voices* addresses this irrevocable damage as he reflects on the fifteen years he spent in prison: "We would never get back the years of our lives that were taken away from us" (Mirk 127). The image that accompanies this reflection—an image of himself behind bars surrounded with anonymized fellow prisoners—suggests that he will continue to view himself as helpless and imprisoned for the rest of his life. The final panel of this chapter, which illustrates him at his home, sipping coffee alone, presents a bleak picture. He might be out of the cage, but the feeling of being caged does not leave him: "I struggle to survive. I live in uncertainty" (127). The extralegal status of the prison warscape, and the fact that there is no clear legal process to exculpate the innocent, causes further damage: Their unproven guilt becomes a life sentence that cannot even be legally remedied. Similarly, in *Aaron & Ahmed*, Ahmed's Muselmann status ends only because he sacrifices himself to protect Aaron. In a full reversal, the final images of the book show Aaron back in the psychiatric ward, in total isolation, naked and alone in a padded cell, trying to scratch his eyes out. His own encounter with Muselmann status—a status he neither entirely possesses (as a legal citizen with rights) nor evades (as a radicalized prisoner held under special conditions)—has reduced him to bare life, a serious threat not to America but to himself.

Guantánamo Kid ends up echoing this argument: There is no normalcy for the Muselmann, no ability to reintegrate into ordinary life after leaving Guantánamo behind. Mohammed is one of the lucky ones whose case is dismissed by a judge. He hopes to go back to Medina to reunite with his family, but his lawyer informs him that Saudi Arabia is refusing to take him back (Tubiana and Franc 117). Going to Chad—a place he has never been—is Mohammed's only option, after the Chadian ambassador to the US promises him safe passage. But even there, he is jailed upon arrival. He manages to escape to Khartoum, Sudan, to meet up with fellow ex-detainees, but there he is jailed yet again. The cycle of imprisonments and the reality of moving permanently through legal gray zones shows the impossibility of starting anew for the marked Muslim. The final lines of the graphic narrative read: "I had left home to study, but had been prevented from doing so. I had been treated like a criminal, and they had taken eight years of my life. I was thinking the same thing then as I had back in Guantánamo: I need to make my life better where I am. It is what it is" (149). Mohammed tries to regain some sort of agency by working toward improving his conditions; however, after passing through the warscape of Guantánamo, the change he seeks is elusive. Wherever he goes, he brings his Muselmann status, and the conditions of the warscape, with him. Katie Taylor, coordinator of Life After Guantánamo, explains: "Yesterday, my electricity went out. You don't really think about it, you just deal with it. Whereas a torture victim or someone who has been detained indefinitely might think 'What have I done to make this happen? Why are they doing this to me?!'" (Mirk 160). As she utters these words, we see the detainee referenced in this passage sinking deeper into paranoia as he goes out and sees a CCTV camera. The reluctant witness continues to bear the scars of the warscape that he can only partly bear witness to. In this regard, the Guantánamo Muselmann is doubly muted: Faced with "total loss of purpose," denied legal status, he is reimmersed in silence (Engdahl 12).

What, then, is the purpose of the Guantánamo counternarrative? Is it merely a corrective to the earlier tradition of Muslim-as-jihadi comics? Is it an attempt at giving the Muselmann an opportunity to set the record straight? Is it an experiment in creating "a new, harsh language" that can adequately address trauma? I suggest that the deeper significance of this new oeuvre and the introduction of the abject Muslim character as Muselmann has to do with the desire to amend willful misreadings and mischaracterizations of Islam. For decades, readers of comics understood Islam as a violent ideology, recognizing a clear binary between the civilized Westerner and the ferocious Muslim. Ryan Inzana's *Johnny Jihad* reiterates just that in its depiction of the Kabul Stadium, temporarily converted to a public courtroom to settle disputes. The protagonist notes that the spectacle "was like something out of a Mad Max movie. Violators of Sharia would be punished in front of a huge audience. It was the Thunderdome." Even in civil cases, the figure of the vicious and zealous brute appears as proof of Islam's incompatibility with Western norms such as law, justice, and reason. Correspondingly, Muslim agency has generally been described as dangerous and harmful and, perhaps more to the point, unstoppable: Even a superhero cannot entirely prevent or even seriously dissuade the fanatical Muslim from scheming and acting against America. The threat stemming from Muslim agency is imagined as permanent, something that can only be temporarily abated by the greatest of heroes. The Guantánamo counternarratives reimagine Muslim agency as something fragile, something easily breakable, and once broken, unrestorable. And the one recourse the Muslim-as-Muselmann would seem to have—bearing witness to this destruction of agency—can only be carried out incompletely, and reluctantly.

Still, even this imperfect and abstract testament has a value. The visual/verbal record of the creation of the Muselmann forces the non-Muslim reader to reflect on their own position in the system that allows such targeted reduction of agency. It demands that they empathize with those who are no longer capable of feeling empathy for their fellow prisoners, or even for themselves. In this regard, even if testifying cannot restore the Muselmann's agency, it can keep the reader's own humanity intact.

CHAPTER 3

Vulnerability, Resistance, and False Witnesses

The Guantánamo narratives of the previous chapter explored the aftereffects of the forced removal of Muslim characters from their native lands; the detainee (eventually reduced to the abject Muselmann figure) becomes a reluctant witness, unable to develop or reclaim his voice even after leaving the foreign prison warscape to return to the homeland. The comics in this chapter engage with the challenges of warscape existence and witnessing *within* the theocratic Muslim homeland. They show the very different impact of internal, Islamist pressure on the native witness, as opposed to the foreign, Islamophobic attitudes exerted on the suspected "enemy combatant"; while the latter is continually and relentlessly coerced to testify, rendering them permanently abject, the witness in the theocratic Islamist state experiences cycles of pressure, resulting in constant movement between feelings of helplessness and confident defiance. Ultimately, the only way to escape this cycle, which we may call the vulnerability-resistance dialectic, is to conspire with the oppressive theocracy itself, becoming a false witness in the service of the state (not an option for Guantánamo detainees, who are always and permanently separated from the non-Islamic state that imprisons them).

The two comics discussed in this chapter, Amir and Khalil's *Zahra's Paradise* (2011) and Mana Neyestani's *An Iranian Metamorphosis* (2012), are set in a polarized Tehran, where the authoritarian state's total Islamization of civic life has led to the marginalization of secular, leftist, and liberal-leaning citizens.[1] Hamid Dabashi notes that the struggle between Iranian pro- and antigovernment groups reveals "the distance between Muslims as free citizens of their democratic republic and the Islamic tyranny that the Shia clerics, and their oligarchical cliques and praetorian guards are exercising" ("A Persian"). The implementation of oppressive theocracy has contributed to a general erosion of Iranian democracy—as evidenced by election fraud, diminution of civil and political rights, and the weakening of the separation of power between the branches of government—and has inspired widespread pessimism among Iranian youth stuck in a perpetual cycle of helplessness and anger. This cycle is, on the surface, a relatively simple one: The protestors who occasionally inundate the streets are motivated by a desire to remove the conditions that make them vulnerable; at the same time, their collective resistance increases their political visibility and therefore makes them more vulnerable.[2] This vulnerability-resistance dialectic guides my reading of the two comics as I link witnessing to political and artistic agency, arguing that those who seek to escape this dialectical trap by testifying on behalf of the state can only be characterized as false witnesses, willing to sacrifice truth for protection. By setting up this character position, the two comics question the fundamental ethics of witnessing and challenge the notion that all forms of testimony are productive and legitimate.

INITIALLY SERIALIZED as a webcomic, *Zahra's Paradise* is a graphic novel that focuses on Mehdi, a protestor gone missing after participating in demonstrations in support of Mir Hossein Mousavi during the 2009 elections. The twenty-month-long protests, known as the Green Movement (and referred to by some as the Persian Spring), were triggered by Mahmoud Ahmadinejad's

---

1. Dabashi writes: "From the very ideological predicate of the constitution of the Islamic Republic on the supreme political authority of the Jurist (velayat-e faqih) to such repressive organs as the Council of Guardians and the Expediency Council, the pernicious mutation of a once-revolutionary reading of a cataclysmic faith is now in full view" (*Islamic Liberation* 95).

2. Human Rights Watch reports that

> Iranians use the term "*nahad-eh movazi*" literally "parallel institutions" to refer to the various extralegal agents of state coercion that have grown in formality, organization, and capacity. Iranian newspapers regularly use the term "parallel institutions" and "plainclothes ones" to refer to the networks of *Basiji* [militia], *Ansar-e Hizbollah* [partisans of the party of God], various intelligence services outside of the Ministry of Intelligence, and the secret prisons and interrogation centers at their disposal. ("'Like the Dead'")

premature declaration of victory against his challengers.[3] In the midst of this political turmoil, Mehdi's mother, Zahra, and brother, Hassan, embark on a dangerous quest to uncover the circumstances of Mehdi's disappearance. Hassan chronicles each step of their investigation in his blog—which he resumes after a hiatus due to his own imprisonment. As they dig deeper, they learn to navigate the Kafkaesque bureaucracy of the theocratic state. They eventually piece together a timeline that starts with Mehdi's incarceration and ends with his death and surreptitious interment at "Zahra's Paradise"—coincidentally, the name of the largest cemetery in Iran. The final chapter moves toward a climactic illustration of formal funeral rites performed after the exhumation of Mehdi's body, while also highlighting Zahra's transformation from a grieving mother to a resolute dissident and Hassan's formation of a coalition with his "hacktivist" friends to air government secrets, including kill lists and extrajudicial exploits. The work concludes with a list of 16,901 names of citizens either missing or dead since 1979, designed as a monument to those silenced by the government. In this sense, *Zahra's Paradise* becomes a symbolic repository of disappeared witnesses, made visible through the testimony of survivors determined to amend public memory.

Mana Neyestani's memoir, *An Iranian Metamorphosis*, is similarly engaged with the bureaucratic repression of the Islamist state—directly evoking Kafka in its references to Gregor Samsa's transmogrification into a cockroach in *The Metamorphosis*. Published a year after *Zahra's Paradise,* the graphic memoir details Neyestani's incarceration in 2006 after his illustration of a cockroach uttering an Azeri word in a children's book sparked civil unrest in northern territories with large Azeri minorities. Neyestani concentrates on the personal impact of the incident, which he argues was based on a misreading of his work. Despite their effusive public apologies, Neyestani and his editor were turned into scapegoats by the state, who used the incident to justify the arrest of Azeri agitators and eventually the installation of a pro-government editorial board at the newspaper. Treated as a "matter of national security," the protests mark the beginning of Neyestani's journey through the justice system and institutional bureaucracy that ends with three months of incarceration in Evin for "bigotry and anti-Turk activities" (24). In prison, Neyestani struggles not only to adjust to the severe condi-

---

3. The twenty-month-long protests, explains Parsa, "shook the foundations of the Islamic Republic" as demonstrators chanting slogans such as "Where is my vote?" and "Death to the dictator!" filled Freedom Square (57). However, civil unrest reinforced the erosion of democracy as the state erected disciplinary and punitive measures that led to arrests and executions by the IRGC (Islamic Revolutionary Guard Corps). She notes: "By August, at least four-thousand people had been arrested. At least 115 were executed in prison. Mousavi was eventually put under house arrest" (57).

tions and isolation but also to break through the bizarre judicial red tape preventing him from bringing his case before an impartial judge. When he is released temporarily from prison, he flees the country to seek asylum in a Western country.

Both comics see the ever-intensifying clashes between protestors and security forces as indicative of the emergence of more permanent warscape conditions in Iran; both comics also imagine themselves as witness accounts invested in the exploration of warscape vulnerability as an underlying condition of Muslim citizenship in a theocratic state. Similar scenes depicting the tensions between civilians and the state were present in the most influential Iranian graphic novel, Marjane Satrapi's *Persepolis*. Marji remembers her parents demonstrating "every day" in the street against the shah: After the revolution, her mother marches to protest against the enforcement of the veil; Marji and her maid secretly join the crowds shouting and yelling "from morning till night" (38). The series of protests show an emerging warscape that relatively quickly begins to replace Iranian democracy. Marji, despite her young age, is particularly attentive to the vulnerability of the dissidents: She watches with alarm when a photograph of her mother taken at a protest is featured in a Western magazine, prompting her mother to color her hair blond to maintain her anonymity. Marji is also aware of the prison as a central institution of the new warscape, one that emphasizes the helplessness and vulnerability of the average citizen's body (see figure 3.1): She overhears her parents' conversation about how her uncle Anoosh was "tortured terribly" (60) in prison and how a family friend, Ahmadi, "suffered the worst torture" before he was "assassinated" (51). Clearly, Amir and Khalil and Neyestani inherit the type of warscape conditions described in *Persepolis*. They add to Satrapi's visualization of a nation still in distress some twenty years later as they depict the tensions between the Islamist autocracy and pro-democracy Muslims. And like Satrapi, they show how the exercise of political and artistic agency triggers a never-ending cycle between vulnerability and resistance.

Typically, vulnerability has been constructed as a binary opposite of resistance: The vulnerable subject, the thinking goes, cannot fully assert the self because of his or her weakened state and therefore cannot fully commit to resistance.[4] And since vulnerability conveys "a capacity for damage, a liabil-

---

4. Sabsay writes:

> Etymologically, vulnerability comes from late Latin *vulnerābilis*, from Latin *vulnerāre*: "to wound," from *vulnus*, "a wound." According to Oxford Dictionaries, to be vulnerable is to be "exposed to the possibility of being attacked or harmed, either physically or emotionally; [or] (of a person) in need of special care, support, or protection because of age, disability, or risk of abuse or neglect." (285)

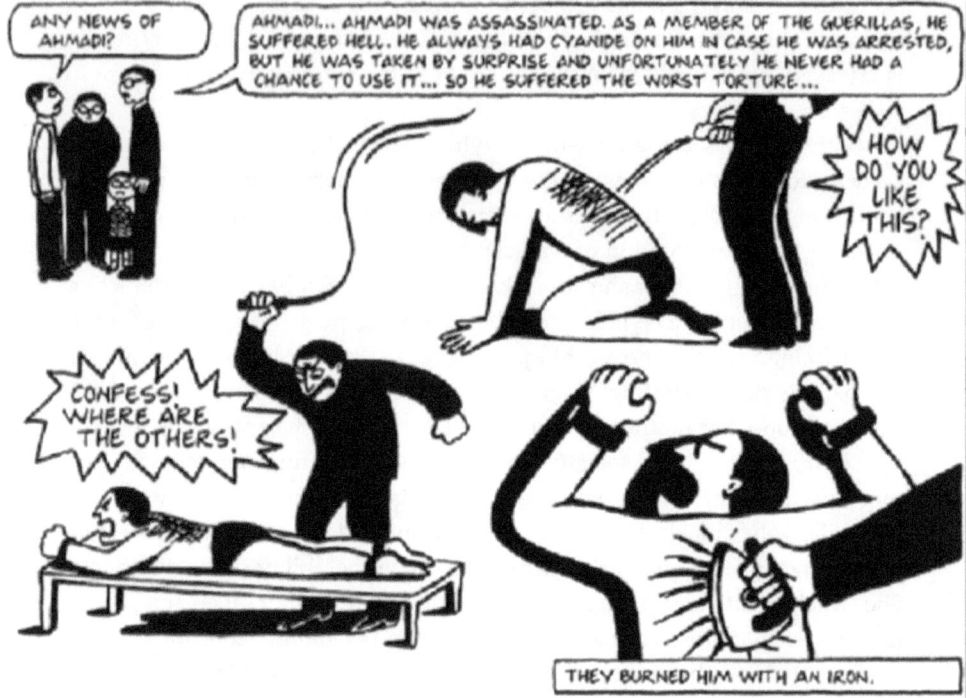

FIGURE 3.1. The prisoners are subjected to torture.

ity to harm, an exposure to risk, aggression, or attack," it is reasonable to expect the vulnerable "as a group [to be] marginalised, silenced, othered" (Ganteau). Lately, however, scholars have started to rethink this binary and imagine ways in which vulnerability might actually elicit resistance. Judith Butler, for one, contends that vulnerability and resistance might be constitutive of each other, with the political subject exercising agency not by "vanquishing" vulnerability but by leaning on it as motivation to effect change ("Rethinking" 24).[5] For Butler, therefore, "resistance relies fundamentally on the mobilization of vulnerability" ("Rethinking" 24). In a similar vein, Leticia Sabsay declares: "While the precarization places the question of affect and bodies at the center of debates, the politicization of the vulnerability of bodies as a form of resistance has acquired a new significance" (283). Drawing on these recent discussions, though perhaps in a less optimistic way, I explore how this new theorization of vulnerability and resistance can lead to fresh

---

5. Butler writes: "I want to argue against the idea that vulnerability is the opposite of resistance. Indeed, I want to argue affirmatively that vulnerability, understood as a deliberate exposure to power, is part of the very meaning of political resistance as an embodied enactment" ("Rethinking" 22).

perspectives on the agency (or lack thereof) of the witness. I ultimately argue that both comics conceive of witnessing as a speech act that is simultaneously invigorated and endangered by the vulnerability-resistance dialectic.

Vulnerability in a Muslim context deserves special consideration: If being a good Muslim necessitates "submission to the will of Allah" (as the literal meaning of Islam denotes), then there is an inherent assumption that self-surrender is the precondition of piety. Yet such an understanding erroneously links Muslim subjectivity with a lack of autonomy—a belief perpetuated by Iran's Islamist state as it heavily promotes the idea of "submission," weaving a particular type of theology into the fabric of Iranian nationalism in order to inspire indiscriminate obedience and sycophancy among its citizens. But a deeper engagement with Qur'anic teachings on the subject reveals a much different conception of submission, one that stresses the importance of an understated self, a self that recognizes Allah's power and vows to fulfill religious duties *without* relinquishing autonomy. Submission, according to the Qur'an, does not signify zombification but an erudite and humble approach to the Islamic theology. This nuance—which essentially marks the gap between Islam and Islamism—is underscored by Amir and Khalil as they describe the way protestors co-opt religion as part of their resistance to the theocratic state. Khalil repeatedly illustrates demonstrators chanting "Allahu Akbar" (*takbir*) from rooftops as an expression of simultaneous private faith and public defiance; later, when crowds gather in front of Evin Prison to hear news of loved ones, they pray together as soon as they hear the *ezan* in the distance. The blending of Islam with resistance becomes a statement against the Islamist state's abuse of faith, a vision of solidarity within the *ummah* as it pushes back against the hollowed-out version of religion deployed by the repressive government, which remains indifferent to "the realities of a nation in the tightening grips of a debilitating moral and material crisis" (Dabashi, "The End" 477). In the case of the theocratic warscape, therefore, religion is not only a tool used to control everyday life; private faith can also be something that inspires the citizen to oppose the politicization of religion.

Public Warscape and Agency

Our two comics have a particular interest in how warscape existence under an authoritarian regime that vows "to rein in the totally out-of-control revolt of the youthful population" presents a challenge to witnessing (Dabashi, "The End" 479). There is a level of theatricality to the Tehranian warscape: Parts of the urban environment have turned into backdrops for regular displays of violence and repression. Armored police vehicles, constant patrols of *basij* militia on motorbikes, thousands of Chinese-built surveillance cameras—all of these have become part of the basic performative infrastructure of certain parts of the city. Perhaps most infamous are the more institutionalized warscape elements, notably the prisons, surrounded by walls of barbed wire—institutions where violence is hidden from public view, but which themselves testify by their monumental presence to its constant, invisible employment. These warscape spaces represent and broadcast the necropolitical power of the state—what Mbembe describes as the "ultimate expression" of sovereign ability to decide whether "to kill or to let live" (66).[6] We might expect our comics to show citizens standing up against this power (and against these warscape spaces) by having them bear witness against them—and to a certain extent they do. But the authors are highly sensitive to the infiltrative and corruptive nature of necropolitical power, and therefore they temper expectations by showing that witnessing does not exist in any kind of straightforward manner once the normal rules of citizen life are replaced by the rules of the theocratic warscape.

We can begin with Hassan, who consistently imagines the state response to the Green Movement in terms of a stifling triangulation of religion, state, and necropolitics.[7] In a series of panels, he laments: "God has abandoned us all . . . His truth was written on the walls and smeared on the floors of the hospital. We are left with the scarecrows: God's deputies and their deputies, all the way down to their pawns: the *basij* paramilitary militia. They hold Iran hostage as if God's shadow on earth were but a shroud of death" (Amir and Khalil 25). The narration is accompanied by provocative yet seemingly disconnected images: an orderly cleaning the bloodstained walls and floors

---

6. Drawing on Foucault, Achille Mbembe explains that "the ultimate expression of sovereignty largely resides in the power and capacity to dictate who is able to live and who must die. To kill or to let live thus constitutes sovereignty's limits, its principal attributes" (66).

7. Misagh Parsa reflects on Ahmadinejad's strategy:

> Ahmadinejad advocated greater egalitarianism within Iran and continuing confrontation abroad. He packed his cabinet with IRGC veterans, and replaced thousands of reformists and technocrats in the state bureaucracy with clerics and IRGC members. He unleashed restrictive measures against the press, cultural activities, and women's freedoms, and targeted human-rights and labor activists as well as universities. Corruption and cronyism grew. Anger at them was the context for the Green Movement. (57)

of a hospital; a number of scarecrows featuring the faces of Iran's supreme leader Ayatollah Khomeini and Ali Akbar Rafsanjani; a panel showing black boots—a synecdoche of the *basij* and the repressive apparatuses deployed by the state. The final frame of the sequence depicts a number of graves, with pictures of the dead attached to the tombstones. The "covert cultivation of death" by the necropolitical state renders citizens as punishable and perishable bodies and presents the average Iranian citizen as highly vulnerable—and silenceable (S. Murray, "Thanatopolitics" 718).

Initially, *Zahra's Paradise* presents this necropolitical insistence on submissive citizenship as something that might be countered by activist witnessing.[8] If the necropolitical power of the state renders citizens vulnerable, that vulnerability is soon transformed into resistance, and eventually oppositional advocacy, especially in the form of mass demonstrations. Millions gather at the Azadi Square (Freedom Square) to express their political agency, and special attention is paid to the energy and vitality of these demos: Given the power and centrality of death in Iranian society, and the sense that those living around the vast cemeteries of the city are merely future inhabitants of them, it makes sense that those who choose to resist the necrotization of everyday life seek to show their strength through mass displays of vital and animated frustration—it is a way for them to proclaim that they are still alive. Khalil offers an illustration of a Tehran "shuddered by the cry of defiance" in a two-page spread, with Mousavi supporters surging through the city with political signs and slogans, refusing to be silenced. The main square, filled with vulnerable, resistant Muslim bodies, turns into what Arendt calls a "space of appearance"—an empowering space where "men are together in the manner of speech and action" [199]).[9] Khalil's portrayal depicts not only the enormity of the Green Movement but the potency of the political communication it inspires, as people share "their hope, their

---

8. Engin F. Isin argues that in the twenty-first century, there is a need to revise the existing conceptions of belonging to account for new articulations of political agency signified by the "activist citizen":

> Citizenship understood as political subjectivity shifts our attention from fixed categories by which we have come to understand or inherit citizenship to the struggles through which these categories themselves have become stakes. It also shifts our attention from already defined actors to the acts that constitute them. Rather than asking "who is the citizen?" the question becomes "what makes the citizen?" (383)

9. Arendt defines space of appearance as a place "where I appear to others as others appear to me, where men exist not merely like other living or inanimate things, but to make their appearance explicitly" (198–99).

98 • CHAPTER 3

FIGURE 3.2. Protestors fill the square.

optimism, their solidarity" by the sheer act of occupying the public square (Messman). Onlookers shout out messages of camaraderie from their balconies with their children waving flags and banners (Amir and Khalil 40–41). And Khalil's realistic, almost photographic re-creation of the protest also centers on images circulated via social media (see figure 3.2). By recycling images taken by common Iranians, Khalil not only records the collective nature of the public outcry but imagines it as viral, something that can draw in and recruit more Muslim activist citizens.

And yet collective resistance also begets more scrutiny and maltreatment and enhances the chances of bodily harm, injury, and death. The protestors take "a risk with their own bodies, exposing themselves to possible harm" contra the necropolitical power of the state (Butler, "Rethinking" 12). Thus, the images of vital collective action are offset by a series of panels that show Zahra and Hassan at the morgue going over photographs of unidentified bodies.[10] The headshots show evidence of abuse, revealing bruised faces, cuts across the cheeks, or missing teeth—attesting to the systematic destruction of the young, the almost industrial conversion of youthful defiance into death. In her read-

---

10. Salmi observes that "panels depicting Zahra and her son Hassan's conversations, set against the white background of the page, alternate with portraits of corpses against the black background of the morgue, creating the effect of a chessboard"(183).

ing of this section, Charlotta Salmi discusses how the alternating black and white background creates the effect of a chessboard: "The visual chess analogy shows citizens as pawns in the state's violent games and demonstrates the dark logic behind theocracy" (183). The allusion reinforces the idea of the precarious life of the "pawns" regarded as disposable bodies.

Those bodies are almost always buried in the titular cemetery, Zahra's Paradise (Behesht-e Zahra), which serves as the convergence point of theocracy and necropolitics in the city. There, the level of the deceased's approval by the regime determines the level of visibility one is accorded in death: Khomeini's mausoleum complex dominates an entire section of the cemetery, designed to act as an unmissable, gold-domed landmark, while "lot 309," which holds anonymous bodies buried by order of the Intelligence Ministry, is rendered officially invisible ("That place does not exist: it has no name and no record" [Amir and Khalil 163]). When Hassan and his uncle Bahodar pay a visit to inquire about Mehdi, the state-appointed director boasts about the cemetery's scrupulous record-keeping as proof of the bureaucratic strength of the Muslim nation: "We don't want to bury the wrong person in the wrong grave; this is an Islamic Republic you're talking about!" (161). For him, the interment of the dead, which requires a death certificate, a burial permit, and an identity card, along with fees for the burial plot, transporting the dead, and washing the body, is an affirmation of administrative efficiency and control. Bahodar, on the other hand, sees the place as "an airport terminal for departing souls" (159). While they wait, Bahodar and his old schoolmate, Parviz, now the director of the cemetery, exchange morbid jokes:

> PARVIZ: Welcome to Zahra's Paradise.
> BAHODAR: It's been a while!
> PARVIZ: An eternity! (chuckle)
> BAHODAR: At least I'm visiting you on my own volition . . . That may not be the case the next time.
> PARVIZ: Haha! We accept you dead or alive! (159)

Behind their smiles, however, there is an undercurrent of nervous vulnerability. Even death has become unpredictable and uncertain in the theocratic warscape: Dissidents, labeled as "enemies of God," are disappeared, their memories erased—Zahra's Paradise is closed to them.

Finally, Amir and Khalil's Tehran is marked by an excessive use of necropolitical aesthetics designed to promote the figure of the martyr. Bahodar notes the uncanny feel of the place, stuffed with garish monuments to martyrs: "They've turned the cemetery into a Hollywood B movie set . . . Even death we can't get right, in this country!" (158). Throughout the city, war memorials and monuments serve as propaganda that not only normalizes but also glorifies death in the service of the state; everyday life is consumed by perpetual mourning. Martyrdom, woven neatly into the fabric of nationalism, is endorsed as "something positive and communal [. . .] perhaps even sacred" (Cole qtd. in Shams 896). In *Zahra's Paradise*, the taxi driver complains about the "morbid street names" honoring the fallen soldiers of the Iran-Iraq War (Martyr Beheshti Ave., Martyr Bahonar Ave., Martyr Hemmat Expressway, etc.). The obsessive renaming exemplifies an economy and infrastructure of death co-opted by the state, determined to use the figure of the *shaheed* to cement the bonds between political ideology and religion.[11] The direct consequence of this urban relabeling is the removal of the boundary between the cemetery and the city. As the taxi driver attests: "Everything's named after death in this city! Almost makes you wonder whether Tehran isn't just a suburb of Zahra's Paradise" (Amir and Khalil 84).[12] In this sense, Tehran is figured as an ever-expanding necropolis, with the living joining the dead in "a strategy of sublimation that transformed a gruesome, bloody conflict into a sacred, desirable aspiration for those who adhered to the state ideology of warfare" (Shams 896).[13]

WHILE NEYESTANI SHARES the belief that Iranian cities are an emerging warscape, his vision of the city is in some ways a very different one. In *An*

---

11. Amir Moosavi writes about wartime literature, stating that "in novels and short stories published during the war, martyrdom was repeatedly portrayed as an inherently meaningful action for a war that was promoted on nationalist and religious grounds. To die as a martyr was an achievement, an honorable act, enviable by those unable to make a similar sacrifice" (2). Moosavi further notes that

> the Iranian government has used various methods to remind the country of its war martyrs. This has included renaming highways and streets after those who died in the war and creating massive murals across the country depicting high-profile military commanders as well as locals who were martyred at the front (see Karimi). Furthermore, Holy Defense Week (Haftih-yi difa'-i muqaddas), September 22–29, has become Iran's most important annual remembrance of the war with public events and television and radio shows devoted to commemorating the legacy of the war for the entire week. (4)

12. Shams explains that "Iran's war graves have been bestowed with deep political significance, turning Zahra's Paradise into a political landscape within the Islamic Republic" (895–96).

13. Stuart J. Murray argues the martyr comes to participate "in a textured and irreducible reality, part of an everyday language or way of life that feeds the imagination, with hope or with despair" ("Thanatopolitics: On the Use of Death" 207).

Iranian Metamorphosis, Neyestani depicts the warscape not as a zone of vulnerable bodies inspired to resist (or die) en masse but as a zone of enforced isolation and brutal dehumanization. Within the comic, Neyestani himself does not participate in the demonstrations (logically, since they were partly inspired by his offensive comic), but when he hears shots being fired into crowds, he cannot help but imagine the "bloodshed" orchestrated by the security forces (52). In a series of panels, he visualizes lonely dead bodies bleeding out as soldiers in the distance appear like shadow puppets, holding their smoking guns (52). The vision is not one of joining together but of an atomized group, both soldiers and victims reduced to hollow and isolated images, stripped of anything connecting them to society, or to humanity in general. Unlike Hassan, whose connection to the warscape as an active participant strengthens his role as an insider, Neyestani positions himself as an outsider disconnected from the city and the country around him. His detachment is partly due to his inadvertent role in initiating the unrest; it also stems in part from his sense of artistic agency, as opposed to political agency, as central to his identity. In this regard, Neyestani embraces a sensibility less oriented toward political than artistic resistance; for him, the ability to exercise free speech is an artistic imperative, which sets him apart from the majority of the demonstrators, who understand free speech in political terms.[14]

The prioritization of independent artistic agency influences Neyestani's choices as an illustrator as well: As opposed to the docu-graphical realism employed in *Zahra's Paradise*, *An Iranian Metamorphosis* offers a distinctively rendered, somewhat abstract, allegorically rich sketch of the Iranian warscape. Khalil's large-scale, detailed, and accessible illustrations of unrest are replaced by highly stylized depictions of protestors without individualized features lumped together.[15] We see the warscape represented through

---

14. Khadem writes:

> The book does not narrate the cartoonist's experience against the backdrop of any large-scale political upheaval, but only a short-lived local unrest. Apart from a brief but powerful reference to the years of the Iran-Iraq War and a few allusions to the ultra-conservative government of Mahmoud Ahmadinejad, the book does not delve into any critical moment of contemporary Iranian history. There is nothing about the Green Movement—except one quick mention in the "Epilogue"—and only an implied reference to the dark episode of mass execution of political prisoners, which plays an essential role in Satrapi's narrative. (481)

15. Achim Hescher argues that the graphic memoir is "riddled with metalepses," which he describes as "illogical transgression of ontological borders" ("Transgressing" 59). He explains that the recurrent images of the cockroach as well as the cartoon child further complicate the plot; in these instances, it becomes difficult to determine whether these metaleptic uses allude to dreams or are employed as narrative devices.

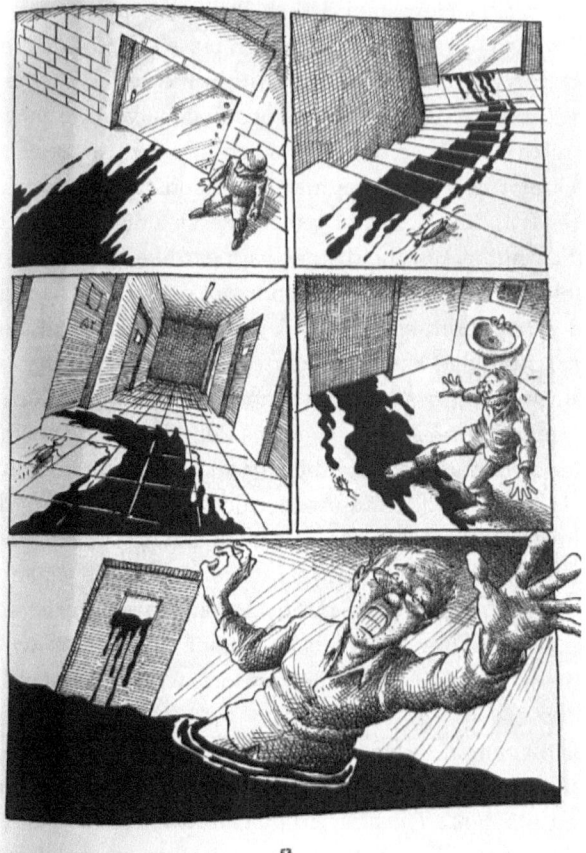

FIGURE 3.3. Neyestani feels as if he is drowning in blood.

the depiction of a mob, standing with fists raised to the sky, their mouths gaping to indicate yelling. Neyestani's decision to forgo realism suggests his desire to move away from a focus on the material conditions of warscape and the way they affect the general population; instead, he depicts the emotional impact of his vilification—on a personal level. Still, that loneliness does not translate into psychological immunity from the warscape. In an earlier panel, a cockroach (the leitmotif of the comic) moves around the corpses of slaughtered protesters. This imagined depiction of carnage infiltrates his subconscious, generating nightmares: He dreams about the blood of the protestors reaching his prison door, oozing under it, gradually turning into a flood that overwhelms and engulfs him (53). Neyestani wishes to remain disconnected from the protests, but he cannot avoid the warscape unfolding around him (see figure 3.3).

This greater focus on personal consequences and guilt, rather than collective resistance, influences Neyestani's depiction of himself as an ineffective witness stranded in the necropolitical warscape. During their time at the courts, Neyestani and his editor, Mehrdad, are condemned to a condition of abject helplessness. When they are escorted to the Prosecution Office, they wait for four "agonizing" hours before being granted an audience with Judge Mortazavi, who directly accuses Neyestani of accepting money from the Americans to instigate unrest. The judge, drawn in caricature, appears as a tall, menacing figure, sketched from a lower vantage point to enhance his fearful stature. With one foot raised—as if to crush a pest—the judge represents a punitive rather than a restorative justice system: "You will be destroyed . . . to teach people like you a lesson for wanting to serve America" (64). The latter part of the statement is accompanied by an image of his foot coming down to squash Neyestani, who is now reduced to a size of a small glass figurine. The verdict—to send him back to prison—is crushing; Neyestani conveys this literally as his figurine self is shattered to pieces and swept away by a broom as if he is dirt (64). He is not inspired to resist or to reach out to others to create a movement: He is broken. Back in prison, when an official informs him that "police opened fire on people" in Azeri cities, Neyestani, unable to handle the trauma and guilt of the announcement, drifts away, staring at a childish drawing of a house someone has made on the cell wall, imagining himself as a stick figure safe at home with his stick-figure wife. In comparison to Khalil's photorealistic depiction of the protestor-witness, Neyestani's reduction of himself to a crude, stick-figure cartoon is haunting.

Prison

Despite the differences in their visions, the artists agree upon the central symbolic element of the necropolitical, theocratic warscape: the prison. Butler writes that "the freedom to gather as a people is always haunted by the imprisonment of those who exercised that freedom and were taken to prison. And when one arrives in public or common spaces with radical and critical views, there is always an anxious or certain anticipation that imprisonment will follow" ("Rethinking" 20). In both comics, prison is presented as the ultimate warscape institution, a site designed to exploit the vulnerability-resistance dialectic by implementing mechanisms geared to break and reprogram the prisoner-citizen. Khalil illustrates the notion of the carceral system cannibalizing the prisoners in a two-page spread featuring Khomeini and

Khamenei as giant, all-consuming machines: "Look at that: they turned Islam into a penal colony where time is a measure of pain" (169). With an image reminiscent of Fritz Lang's "Moloch" furnace in *Metropolis*, Hassan imagines the new Islamist political-legal system as a semi-sentient being, set on devouring the faceless youth it is supposed to serve (see figure 3.4). The theocratic state is able to exercise its power by weaponizing Islam and deeming demonstrators "terrorists" or, eventually, as "dust and dirt,"—rhetorically demoting them, not just to flawed citizens but to subhumans (Amir and Khalil 41, 54).[16]

Both comics eventually turn their gaze to life inside the prison, providing a blunt critique of the way necropolitical mechanisms are used to reprimand, discipline, and reform citizens. Both artists attempt to make the hidden visible, to highlight "the oppressive material conditions of imprisonment," and to lay bare the victimization of everyday Iranians whose lives have been disrupted or destroyed by a punitive incarcerative system (Sevcik 18).[17] The two protagonists spend months in prison, and they each wrestle with physical and psychological trauma afterward. The experience essentially alters their subjectivity, and along with it, their perception of citizenship. Hassan describes Evin, the main political prison, as an "educational" site intended to reprogram the citizen by stripping away any sense of political agency and replacing it with empty religious mantras: "Evin's all about continuing education. If you cannot memorize God's word, they'll scrawl it into your flesh. God save us from our teachers" (Amir and Khalil 53).[18] Mana also describes his prison experience as a form of self-estrangement; not only does his isolation bring him to the brink of madness, but the fake

---

16. The use of the "terrorist" label is especially significant in justifying torture. The terrorist "acts outside of the norms of modern humanitarian law" and presents a significant threat to the established way of life (Kahn 5).

17. While the two comics cannot be categorized as "prison writing"—a genre that focuses on literature produced by prisoners during their incarceration—they neatly align with this type of writing as they chronicle the nitty-gritty details of prison life. Doran Larson argues that "prison writing is a genre bound not only by its subject and authors but in its expressive tropes, and those tropes at once determined by, actively resistant to, and thus indicative of both global and local conditions of composition" (143). There are significant differences between the two comics in terms of the positionality of the witness: *Zahra's Paradise* is a fictional account that focuses on Hassan's blog, which essentially bears witness to Mehdi's imprisonment and death; Neyestani's memoir positions him as a firsthand witness stuck in a legal limbo while also incorporating pre- and post-prison experiences to capture the farcical escalation of events.

18. Nicknamed "Evin University" due to the sheer number of intellectuals, academics, and artists confined in the premise, the prison represents both the state's raw power and people's resistance to it.

FIGURE 3.4. Khomeini and Khamenei appear as all-consuming machines.

identity given to him as a protective measure before his transfer to the political prisoners section leaves him unsettled. Under a mugshot that features his disheveled image and his identification number of "1245134620," Neyestani writes: "Mana Neyestani existed no more. I was Reza Keshavarzi; a swindler arrested for writing bad checks" (86). For his editor, Mehrdad, who receives the same protective treatment, the erasure of his name signifies the erasure of his identity: "My whole life I was proud of the one thing only: being a man of letters. Now I have to deny it" (90). Their disguise deeply unnerves them and causes them to withdraw further into their shells. By capitalizing on their vulnerability in prison, then, the state is able to manipulate and indeed dissolve their sense of self to force obedience and compliance.

In the previous chapter, we discussed Guantánamo as a fully self-contained warscape prison, separated from any surrounding society, and acting, in effect, as its own nation-state. Is the prison-in-the-warscape (Evin) ideologically and philosophically different from the prison-as-warscape (Guantánamo)? Two factors distinguish them: First, as opposed to the Guantánamo prisoners—reduced to the figure of the Muselmann, torturable but not killable—prisoners in Evin can perish without fear of legal liability and with minimal political consequences. Second, unlike the methods of desubjectification used in Guantánamo to reduce the prisoner to bare life, the Iranian prison system is keen to resubjectify the prisoner to "produce self-governing subjects" (Smith 244). Resubjectification, the transformation of the citizen into a compliant, indoctrinated subject, is an attempt to minimize the role of participatory citizenship, an attack on the Aristotelian idea of the human as a rational being with the capacity to partake in the political life of the polis.[19] In *Zahra's Paradise*, Hassan admits to losing his appetite for politics after his release from Evin; when discharged, malnourished with a shaved head, he vows to discontinue his blog and pull away from political life: "Let somebody else save this cursed country" (35).[20] Fully acknowledging his vulnerability, Hassan is determined not to sacrifice his life for a political cause—even if that means relinquishing his ability to resist. Neyestani similarly favors disengagement: He repeatedly has nightmares in which he attacks his former self for his naive confidence in the freedom of press. He eventually decides that the only way to keep his humanity is to disavow his Iranian citizenship and become a fugitive. He willingly gives up his ties to a state that intends to punish him for his artistic sensibility in exchange for a new allegiance to a nation that can keep his autonomy intact.

But if acknowledging his own vulnerability temporarily zombifies Hassan (and robs him of his humanity as a consequence), the awareness of his brother's deeper and more existential vulnerability eventually reignites his passion for subversive politics and restores his humanity. His reentry into the political arena as a witness, invested in exposing the government by giving voice to the powerless through his blog, attests to his rekindled desire to disrupt the state's "forcible erasure of human life" (Sevcik 14). Hassan refuses to let his brother fade into oblivion: "They want to wipe Mehdi off the face of time, confiscate the sound of his name, the promise of his return. There can be no witness. Now it's my turn to publish. I'll test the power of my blog against their press" (Amir and Khalil 59). By narrativizing Mehdi's final hours moment by moment, Hassan seeks personal closure as well as public accountability. In this way, he turns his personal suffering into activ-

---

19. Aristotle defines the human as "a living animal with the additional capacity for political existence" (qtd. in Agamben, *Homo Sacer* 11); robbing an individual of his or her political agency is a form of not only pacification but also dehumanization. In this line of thinking, the depoliticization of the human subject reduces him to "a living animal." Andrew Norris takes this a step further, arguing that "if politics was an 'additional capacity' with Aristotle, now politics is of our essence, and life has become its object" (39).

20. This idea is consistent with real testimonies included in a Human Rights Watch report; one prisoner states: "I went in as one person and came out another person" ("Like the Dead").

ism. Quickly, Mehdi becomes an emblem of the youth who vanish before "our very eyes with no record, no paper trail. No name, no receipt—just a blur. This blog is all that is left of them" (27). Khalil conveys Mehdi's symbolic erasure on a paratextual level by refusing to draw his face: Mehdi is either featured with his back turned to the reader, or his face is blurred or left blank. In this sense, like the unmarked tombs in "lot 309" in Zahra's Paradise, the visual effacing of Mehdi speaks to his unrepresentability as a conventional political emblem while also gesturing toward the dissident's dehumanization by the state.

What cannot be represented visually, however, can be extrapolated from the testimonies of others; if Hassan cannot give voice to Mehdi directly, he can bear witness to his last moments by capturing the voices of those who were around him. By visiting Ali, Mehdi's young cellmate recently released from prison, Hassan learns more about Mehdi's imprisonment at Kahrizak Detention Center. Ali describes the physical conditions of the prison, referring to it as a kind of disposal site: "One day we were dancing in Freedom Square, the next we were sinking into a human landfill" (125). The image of the courtyard—high walls, barbed wire, and a tower in the corner—conveys the claustrophobia of the prisoners' animalistic existence, unable to speak, move, or even "swat a fly," locked into a state of permanent disorientation and deprivation (125). The physical torment is constant: At one point, the guards entertain themselves by forming a "human corridor," through which the prisoners are forced to walk to get back to their cells, beaten as they go. The brutality of the walk is captured in a large panel that runs diagonally across the page, featuring guards drinking and smoking as they gaze at the violent spectacle with amusement. Ali recalls that Mehdi "didn't take this sitting down. It took five guys finally to subdue him" (126). Prisoners are struck, humiliated, stripped of their clothes, urinated on; with no agency, the dehumanized body is reduced to a receptacle of pain and degradation. Back in their cell, which Ali defines as "a large coffin" with ground "covered in vomit, shit, and urine" overpowered by "the stench from rotting corpses nearby," he spends the night "trembling" while Mehdi—determined not to be reduced to a necropolitical commodity, and still determined to convert vulnerability into resistance—cracks jokes to change the mood. By encouraging Ali to share these memories of Mehdi, Hassan ultimately also inspires Ali to end his traumatized silence. Borrowing a lighter from Hassan, Ali sets a *rial* with Khomeini's face on fire: "I will speak my truth, even if it is from the funeral pyre" (131). Unlike the reluctant witness of the Guantánamo narrative, Ali is able to reclaim his voice as Hassan's blog gives him an opportunity to repurpose his trauma.

Neyestani's firsthand representation of prison, in contrast, focuses less on physical torture and more on the psychological torment of isolation.[21] After being processed, he is escorted blindfolded to his cell; the cries he hears from other cells seem to foreshadow his own suffering. Most of Neyestani's apprehensions stem from the widespread rumors of the use of torture in Iranian prisons. He reminds himself of the number of people who were killed in detention; he mentions Zahra Kazemi, an Iranian Canadian journalist killed during an interrogation carried out by Judge Mortazavi, the same judge he is assigned to. In an illustration, he draws Kazemi and Mortazavi as black silhouettes: Kazemi tied to a chair, beaten by the judge holding a bat as blood pours out of her mouth. The next two pages offer up a gruesome spectacle: Neyestani himself suspended from the ceiling, with an oversize interrogator using his face as a punching bag until he is no longer recognizable. Yet there is a twist. Neyestani writes: "If the scene from the last two pages were real, the story would have been more interesting (and, of course, more successful). But I'd rather tell you exactly what happened. After all, it was my fate, however boring. I have to admit that the last two pages were what I was afraid of while waiting in the interrogation room" (43).

This image of a torture never actually experienced serves two purposes: First, Neyestani forces his readers to consider the psychological impact of torture, the agony of anticipating or meditating upon the *possibility* of various types of torture—a pain the reader can also experience to a limited degree, therefore allowing them to better comprehend the state of terror associated with prison life. Second, and equally important, by introducing torture imagery and then admitting that it was only a fear and not a reality for himself personally, Neyestani establishes his integrity as a storyteller who values veracity over sensationalism at the risk of disappointing the reader. Certainly, he constantly anticipates torture ("I knew that there were hidden detention centers where some political prisoners were taken to be tortured" [65])—but Neyestani does not let fear dictate truth and does not waver from providing an accurate account of his own experiences. More to the point, perhaps, even though Mana himself is not physically beaten, he *is* subjected to "white torture," a less severe form of maltreatment designed to break a

---

21. Prisoners reveal the traumatic effects of soft torture: "The individuals who were interviewed by Human Rights Watch emphasized that their time in absolute solitary was far worse than any physical or verbal abuse they experienced. They spoke of fear of losing their minds, of worrying that another day without any human contact would break their will" (Human Rights Watch, "Like the Dead").

prisoner's resolve and to reinforce the feeling of helplessness.[22] For example, Mana's confinement in the infamous section 209 of Evin brings him to the brink of mental collapse.[23] After a few weeks of isolation with his editor, they run out of things to say to one another: "We were two shipwrecked soldiers living on isolated islands" (76). They both start experiencing sensory deprivation: "There were no smells except the odor of our sweats. There was nothing to hear. Dead silence" (75). They listen to the call for prayer as a way to mark the passage of time, but even in between prayers, they imagine hearing the constant call of *ezan* in their heads. Neyestani obsessively observes the sunrays move across the cell floor until they vanish at dusk. At times, in the oppressive heat of the unventilated cell, he imagines attacking the rays to make them move faster. If the state was instrumental in his dehumanization, the prison conditions are conducive to the breakdown of reality. Neyestani's memoir, in this sense, is both solipsistic (self-absorbed) and communalistic (outward-looking) in documenting his personal ordeal to warn others.

False Witnessing

Ultimately, both Neyestani and Hassan cast themselves in the position of the witness as they record the vulnerability and suffering of Iranians both on a collective and a personal level by chronicling the details of prison hierarchy,

---

22. For Khadem, "[Neyestani's] narrative voice not only uses this violent and dismal point to stop and create an ironic distance between his experience and a stereotypical 'torture,' but implies another torturous condition: the narration of pain as intimately as it has happened, without any bruise or blood, or without jostling it into a narrative cliché" (483).

23. It is reported that

> some prisoners were held in general wards before being taken to the solitary sections of Evin. Others were picked up by plainclothes men and taken directly to the solitary sections. In Section 209, prisoners were walked down stairs into a basement, where there were at least four halls, approximately twelve cells per hall, and a separate row of solitary cells for female prisoners. The cells measured about one meter by two meters, with a ceiling height of about four meters. A light at the top of the cell (most prisoners estimated about 40 watts), is on twenty-four hours a day. The cells in Section 209 have a toilet and a sink inside the cell. The floor is made of what most prisoners described as chalk. Prisoners are generally given a blanket, a pair of slippers, and a disposable cup. The walls of the cell are all white. Some prisoners were granted twenty minutes per twenty-four-hour period in a caged outdoor area, but others never saw the open air except on their way to and from court. (Human Rights Watch, "Like the Dead")

abuse, and necropolitical power. Hassan collects oral testimony from victims and documents the harassment of protestors confined within the prison archipelago in his blog. Neyestani, perhaps encouraged by those who carved the walls with their names to mark their presence in his prison cell, captures the destructive, exploitative carceral ecosystem: "I've never seen so many miserable people in my life. I really want to draw everyone in here" (121). His desire to document these characters echoes Hassan's sentiments about writing disaffected people into history; the agonistic descriptions disrupt the state's propaganda and create a visual archive. As Larson explains,

> It is by writing [. . .], by responding both to the fixed schematic of power and to the singular characteristics of their particular conditions and treatment that prison writers, first, bear evidence to the failure of fixed strategies to overcome a diverse set of aleatory tactics, and, second, in their singular responses, expose a particular system of justice's failure to bear responsibility for its penal regime. (152)

Carceral witnessing, then, sustains the vulnerability-resistance dialectic, marking each protagonist simultaneously as "an object of violence and a subject of resistance" (Smith 244).

And yet, while both comics describe witnessing as a form of resistance against tyranny, they are also careful not to fetishize witnessing as an inherently laudable and virtuous act, an easy route to salvation, or a means to erase or even significantly offset the realities of the new warscape springing up around them. On the contrary, by introducing the figure of the false witness, they illustrate how certain forms of witnessing, once corrupted by the pressures of a warscape, can sustain and perpetuate oppressive power structures rather than unsettle them. Differentiating between the witness, who speaks *against* the system publicly at the risk of harm and ostracization, with the false witness, who speaks *for* the state as a submissive collaborator, allows the two comics to rethink and complicate the vulnerability-resistance dialectic. The presence of the false witness, one who agrees to testify by falsifying facts, is an indicator of the potential collapse of the vulnerability-resistance dialectic to the benefit of the state.

There are different types of false witnessing depicted in the comics. In *Zahra's Paradise*, government officers visit the homes of the deceased to strong-arm their families into signing fabricated confessions in exchange for government pensions. They also capitalize on the families' religious sentiments by promising to treat those who are killed under state care as *shaheed* (religious martyrs). Thus, this particular form of false witnessing occurs at the intersection of necropolitics and theology: The state's ability to kill also grants it the ability to bestow martyrdom. By portraying these deaths as collateral damage in the service of the theocratic state, the officers sustain the idea that Khameini's acts are divinely ordained and politically justified. As families are pressured to sign official documents relieving the government of guilt, they become complicit in a cycle of violence. When Hassan and Zahra are finally granted an audience with the Ministry of Intelligence, the officials employ these kinds of tactics to frame Mehdi's death in a positive light: "Our condolences on the martyrdom of your son" (Amir and Khalil 209). Zahra's bafflement and shock elicit a more profitable payoff from the officials: "Yes, the news of his death has shocked us, too. [. . .] Of course, you understand the political sensitivity of your terrible tragedy. Foreigners will no doubt conspire to blame his death on the Islamic republic. [. . .] If you sign right now, top of the line benefits. Better than we ever gave mothers of martyrs of the Iran-Iraq War" (209). By creating a narrative about Mehdi's *shaheed* status and asking the survivors to validate that fictional account, the authorities attempt to invalidate the entire notion of witnessing. Mehdi's mother immediately recognizes the trap and dismisses the offer: "I did not raise my son to be a sacrificial lamb on the altar of the Islamic Republic" (211). She refuses to bear false witness to the imagined martyrdom of her son, fully understanding that such a refusal will be taken as a form of resistance that makes her vulnerable to various repressive state mechanisms. Essentially, Zahra chooses the right to speak freely over all the other freedoms remaining in her life.

False witnessing as a means of escaping from state-induced harm is also discussed in *An Iranian Metamorphosis*, although the emphasis here is more on the prisoners themselves, rather than their survivors. By framing false witnessing as a patriotic "duty," Maleki, the state attorney, puts the burden on the victims: "We need you to keep the country in order" (126). At first, Neyestani is asked to write a confession to implicate himself as a foreign provocateur. When his official statement fails to duplicate the cover story prescribed by the prosecutor, he tries to produce a more "convincing" and "credible" version without admitting guilt. Maleki frames false witnessing as a necessary "penance" that must be paid before he can leave the prison and return to his former life (55). Neyestani is initially able to escape from Maleki's clutches without having to lie; other journalists are not so fortunate. He mentions Shahram, whose exposé on the use of torture gets him arrested. After being tortured himself for weeks, he agrees to confess to "spying and sex scandals" on national TV, performing his false testimony for a mass audience (156).

FIGURE 3.5. Neyestani re-creates Leonardo da Vinci's *The Last Supper*.

Eventually, however, Neyestani is forced into the world of false witness by becoming a state informant. When asked to report on other cartoonists as foreign agents, Mana reluctantly starts to fill pages with random "gossip" about his peers and develops worthless profiles of them where he rambles about his criticism of their cartoons (47). His strategy, then, is to submit to the state but remain subversive with the kind of "information" he provides to keep himself morally uncompromised. Still, the tension between self-interest and betrayal weighs heavily on him. He re-creates Leonardo da Vinci's *The Last Supper*, which highlights Jesus's foreknowledge of the inevitability of treachery, to express his sense of unease (see figure 3.5). He draws cartoonists sitting around the table, interacting with each other, and places himself at the end of the table, writing his worthless confessions. By obeying his captors while providing mere gossip, fusing "complicity and critique" together, Neyestani hopes to escape from the trap of the vulnerability-resistance dialectic—but ultimately, he knows that such an evasion is a hollow one and still comes at the expense of others (Salmi 171).

In Guantánamo, prisoners were also under heavy pressure to provide "actionable information" under "enhanced interrogation tactics"—a point that Ali raises in *Zahra's Paradise* as he calls Kahrizak Detention Center "Abu Ghraib redux," adding: "Rumsfeld would be impressed" (Amir and Khalil 126). But unlike the Guantánamo prisoners, who are kept alive to participate in an endless performance of interrogation and confession, political prisoners in Iran are constantly threatened with death, and only by becoming an active false witness can they protect themselves. The Guantánamo prisoner eventually becomes the Muselmann, unable to reintegrate into his original world; in the case of the political prisoner in Iran, false witnessing offers an opportunity to be reabsorbed by the state, as something less than what they were before. And even though false witnessing requires the relinquishing of political agency, it also offers a (bleak) way out of the vulnerability-resistance dialectic: By disavowing resistance, the false witness—now a protected collaborator—eventually escapes the conditions of vulnerability for good by surrendering entirely to them. In this way, the two comics maintain a cautionary stance about witnessing, contending that not all speech acts related to testimony are legitimate and redemptive.

DESPITE THEIR DIFFERENT GENRES, the two Muslim Comics considered here are both committed to shedding light on the everyday lives of Iranians in their homeland and the impact of the warscape conditions created by the Islamist regime. But their ability to speak openly about these atrocities also complicates their position as "insider" narratives: Both works are only able to bear witness to the Iranian warscape because their creators are no longer in it. Amir left his home country at the age of twelve as part of "a massive exodus" a year after the revolution. He recalls how the state labeled the critics of the revolution as "mofsid fil-ard" (corruption on earth) and "moharebs" (enemies of God) and started a campaign of mass executions and incarcerations during what Amir describes as a "reign of terror" ("Zahra's Paradise"). Neyestani's position as a fugitive asylum seeker also places distance between him and Iran. This is not to say that the comics are products of total freedom or the work of authors now immune from threats: Amir discusses how he has continued to feel the state's wrath since the success of *Zahra's Paradise*: "Since we started serializing *Zahra's Paradise* on the web in February 2010, we have received a number of strangely threatening messages—which we presume may be coming from the government in Iran—as well as statements meant to discredit our work, since it reaches deep inside of Iran and is read there" ("Zahra's Paradise"). Neyestani enjoys the freedom of creating graphic novels from afar, stating that a creative endeavor of this nature is "something I couldn't do in Iran"—and yet he is highly aware that, unlike Amir, his present refugee status in France is temporary (Karim 40). They are still linked to those in Iran through their new version of a vulnerability-resistance dialectic, although their vulnerability is greatly lessened and the power of their resistance arguably is equally limited (given that their work is not accessible to most within the warscape). If bearing witness within the warscape is impossible, or counterproductive, the possibility of creating documents that allow for bearing witness outside of the warscape perhaps offers a way, however imperfect, to move forward.

Both comics creators, therefore, occupy a liminal position as "ghorbat" writers, located "outside one's home and longing to return" (Ebrahimi 19). By joining the Iranian diaspora, they create a critical and intimate space from which to articulate the ongoing trauma and speak candidly about the state's violations of human rights. In this regard, they are able to renegotiate their position within the vulnerability-resistance dialectic and escape its worst effects, if not evade it altogether. But dislocation is not an option for everyone living under similar warscape conditions. What if one is permanently stuck in a warscape, unable to turn a new page in a new country? The next chapter considers comics creators and protagonists who not only identify with a regional identity now transformed into a warscape but understand themselves as products of that warscape and their artistic agency as linked to their presence within it.

CHAPTER 4

Shaheed and Border Witnesses

The previous chapter focused on the Muslim homeland, exploring the ways in which the Islamist state turned a nation into a warscape. Both Amir and Khalil's *Zahra's Paradise* and Mana Neyestani's *An Iranian Metamorphosis* illustrated how repressive state apparatuses had transformed a nation into a theocratic penal colony. The emphasis on institutional warscapes, specifically the prison, provided a glimpse into the ghettoization as well as the criminalization of secular Muslims who refused to bear false witness to state-sponsored atrocities. This chapter shifts its focus from the fully controlled and clearly demarcated nation as a whole to a region within a nation: the liminal border zone. Here we will define borders broadly, as "territorial dividing lines as well as sociocultural boundaries," implicated both in the codification of citizenship and the parameters of belonging (Mendez and Naples 2). Simultaneously a symbolic concept "inherent to logics of inside and outside, practices of inclusion and exclusion, and questions about identity and difference" and a practical state institution, borders are highly complex imaginary legal constructs (Vaughan-Williams 1). In much academic work, borders are treated as ambiguous sites of hegemony and resistance, signaling both the reach and the limits of nationalism: They are portals to free movement in between territories on the one hand and fortified entry

115

points notable for heavy policing and surveillance on the other. This tension between movement and stagnation, inclusion and exclusion, homogeneity and alterity is at the heart of border studies, a growing field dedicated to the investigation of the border subjectivities situated in contact zones.

The US-Mexico border, often referred to as the birthplace of border studies, has inspired invaluable critical work that understands the frontier as a site of reinvention and resignification, pregnant with productive entanglements. Perhaps the most prominent theorist associated with such ideas is Gloria Anzaldúa.[1] For Anzaldúa, the US-Mexico border itself—what she describes as a "1,950 mile-long open wound" (24)—is a hegemonic site that stretches the mechanisms of the state to their limit; the broader, and more broadly understood "borderland," on the other hand, is a more nebulous and elusive concept, one that disrupts the centrifugal forces of the state by nurturing cultural impurity and cross-contamination. She suggests that the "contradictions" of this peripheral site, "where people of different races occupy the same territory, where under, lower, middle and upper classes touch, where the space between two individuals shrinks with intimacy," facilitate new and antihegemonic interactions (Preface). As a locus of departure and loss as well as arrival and recovery, the border begets the marginalized space of the borderland:

> Borders are set up to define the places that are safe and unsafe, to distinguish *us* from *them*. A border is a dividing line, a narrow strip along a steep edge. A borderland is a vague and undetermined place created by the emotional residue of an unnatural boundary. It is in a constant state of transition. The prohibited and forbidden are its inhabitants. Los *atravesados* live here: the squint-eyed, the perverse, the queer, the troublesome, the mongrel, the mulato, the half-breed, the half dead; in short, those who cross over, pass over, or go through the confines of the "normal." (3)

The ultimate legacy of the borderland, in this theory, is the development of *mestizaje* consciousness, "an 'alien' consciousness" that springs from "racial, ideological, cultural and biological crosspollenization" (77). In her thinking, crossing the border allows for and encourages self-reinvention and paves

---

1. As Michaelsen and Johnson observe, the US Southwest "has been privileged as the site of production of border discourses" (29). Indeed, border theory has been disproportionately plotted by scholars focused on the American southwest. Gloria Anzaldúa's groundbreaking work, *Borderlands / La Frontera*, for one, successfully illustrates the physical and psychological ramifications of the border as an "unnatural boundary" that induces an ontological crisis for the disaffected *pueblo*.

the way for hybridity, helping to heal the "wounds" of the racially mixed, culturally fragmented border subject (140).

Anzaldúa's theories have been widely influential and have been applied to frontier zones around the world. "Borderland" has become a highly positive, almost utopian concept in many areas of humanistic scholarship. In *Culture and Truth*, Renato Rosaldo writes about "people between cultures" (198) and makes the case that ethnographers should "look less for homogeneous communities than for the border zones within and between them" (217). Drawing on Anzaldúa's "tolerance for ambiguity" (30), Rosaldo discusses the borderland as the site of creativity that can usher in a "renewed concept of culture" vis-à-vis the Other (217).[2] In a similar vein, José David Saldívar advocates for a "regionally focused and broadly cosmopolitan" (84) analysis of borderlands, defining them as places of "hybridity and *betweenness*" (153). For Emily Hicks, borders are instrumental in generating "perception informed by two different sets of referential codes" (xxiii). But are any and all borderland contacts always productive and beneficial? Does life in a border zone always privilege intimacy and hybridization? What happens if the frontier becomes a warscape? How does a disputed border complicate border existence, and what happens to "moral possibility" once the borderland transforms into a "topography of cruelty" (Mbembe 92)? Finally, how does such a transformation affect the border subject, particularly in terms of bearing witness to suffering and trauma?

The two Muslim Comics discussed in this chapter, namely Naseer Ahmed and Saurabh Singh's *Kashmir Pending* and Malik Sajad's *Munnu: A Boy from Kashmir*, offer a new model of witnessing—what I call "border witnessing"—that directly challenges the idea of border subjectivity as an inherently intuitive and productive negotiation between two or more cultures. Set in the disputed territory of Kashmir, often described as "the most heavily militarised region in the world," the two comics highlight the difficulties of navigating everyday life in a warscape (Kazi 85). According to Aroosa Kanwal, an environment of unrelenting violence, indefinite detentions, and extrajudicial killings has turned Jammu and Kashmir into a labyrinthine prison camp "monitored and controlled by more than seven hundred thousand Indian paramilitary soldiers" (3). The militarization of the borderland is indicative of New Delhi's ruthless approach to containing the Kashmiri insurgence, including the denial of a UN-supported plebiscite for a diplo-

---

2. Rosaldo further argues that "all of us inhabit an interdependent late-twentieth-century-world marked by borrowing and lending across porous national and cultural boundaries that are saturated with inequality, power, and domination" (217).

matic solution.³ As Partha Chatterjee explains, the Indian government has "come to believe that Kashmir is a property of India—a valuable piece of real estate that Pakistan wants to grab—and that Kashmiris are a nuisance who must be taught to behave." Yet since the parliament's vote to repeal Article 370 in 2019, the popular call for a separate state of Kashmir, historically known as "Azadi" (independence), has helped to reconfigure the borderland as a counter-hegemonic site of resistance and political dissent.⁴ As these two comics illustrate, the converging vectors of violence shaped by various constituents—the Indian army, the Pakistani-backed insurgence, various factions of the Azadi movement—have created a state of warscape exception, where individual rights are suspended and civilians are exposed to extreme conditions of abuse and degradation.⁵ From the graphic representation of deadly combat and spontaneous protests in *Kashmir Pending* to the repeated use of tombstones in *Munnu*, Kashmir is consistently depicted as a habitat for "killable Kashmiri bodies," where the everyday lives of Muslims become testaments to the challenges of navigating a taxing border existence (Kanwal 2). Indeed, as we will see in this chapter, in the Kashmiri warscape, the Muslim corpse itself becomes a kind of symbolic witness, its mute power battled over by various factions and its message used to further or counter the necropolitical power of the state. Both *Kashmir Pending* and *Munnu* speak against precisely this kind of idealization of the martyr-as-witness by creating the figure of the border witness—one who, by reaffirming the vision of

---

3. Kashmir's vexed relationship with the union government in New Delhi dates back to the partition of India. India's despotic handling of the region as an occupying force has led to countless human rights violations. Since 1954, Jummu and Kashmir enjoyed the special provisions guaranteed under Article 370 of the Indian constitution, which included a "certain amount of autonomy—its own constitution, a separate flag and freedom to make laws" (BBC News). The most recent episode of India's power grab in 2019, which culminated with the repeal of Article 370 that gave limited autonomy and special provisions to states, confirmed that the conflict is far from over.

4. Kabir explains that the term "Azadi," a borrowed word from Urdu that translates to "freedom," signifies various things in the Kashmiri context:

> The word can signal complete independence—political freedom from both India and Pakistan, or freedom from India in order to integrate into the nation-state of Pakistan; or greater federal autonomy within the Indian Union (Article 370). In everyday speech, its precise meaning is often left undefined, and a general sense of "freedom to choose" signified. (10)

5. Hogan maintains that in this region, "violence is not only a matter of state versus militant or state versus Kashmiri sympathizer (or putative sympathizer) but also militant versus Kashmiri civilians with different political views or cultural practices, foreign or Islamist militant versus Kashmiri and semisecular militant, and so on" (*Imagining Kashmir* 5).

Kashmiri unity known as Kashmiriyat, uses the act of witnessing as an antidote to radicalization rather than an accelerant for it.

KASHMIR PENDING tells the story of Mushtaq Miyan, "a reformed ex-terrorist," presently an inmate, reflecting back on his life as he converses with Ali, the twenty-two-year-old prisoner in the neighboring cell (Bharat 106).[6] The opening lines reveal the prison as an isolating space but also a space that, through self-discipline, can lead to spiritual fulfillment: "There is no place like prison if one wishes to get closer to God. It sounds funny when I say it so, but it's true. Solitary confinement can do that to a man. But it's not a very pleasant experience, and I do not recommend it. [. . .] Here in Srinagar jail, all is routine" (5). With this statement, Miyan depicts Islam as a mechanism that can offset the abject conditions of his confinement. In the full-page spread, Mushtaq sits alone in his cell, preparing to pray. In this particular moment, Islam is depoliticized and presented solely as a personal matter of faith. The shading in the panel gives the impression that he is seated on a prayer rug; the white, sunlit square against the dark background transforms the cell into a place of worship. His devoutness is further emphasized by his larger shadow, barely visible in the dark frame, reflected on the wall, implying that through prayer he is able to grow, stretch out, and transcend his small existence. Across the following pages, the motions of prayer are interspersed with images of the landmarks of Srinagar, providing the reader with a visual tour of the city (see figure 4.1): The river, the temple, the fort are all parts of the social and cultural fabric of Kashmiri identity. Later, his white silhouette with hands raised in prayer position appears adjacent to the illustration of his family's house—as if to suggest that he is able to find his way home through meditation and communion with Allah. Islam

---

6. Meenakshi Bharat positions *Kashmir Pending* as a post-terrorist graphic novel emerging from India, similar to *The Believers* written by Abdul Sultan and illustrated by Partha Sengupta. Bharat observes that

> both the narratives delve into the conditions that breed terror, particularly the global alienation of the Muslim community. Both highlight the daily travails of the marginalized Muslim, and the violent fallout of terrorist activity. The publishing house also seems to be making a statement about the spread of terrorism in the country, by siting one novel in Kerala, one of the southernmost Indian states, and another novel in the horrors and brutality that have overtaken strife-torn Kashmir on the northern border. At the same time, Phantomville seems to be making a case for the suitability of the graphic genre for addressing the somber issue of terrorism. (117)

FIGURE 4.1. Mushtaq prays in his prison cell.

gives him an avenue to feel momentarily free of the coercive mechanisms of prison resubjectification. The movement in these pages, reuniting Mushtaq with his community and linking spirituality with Kashmiri identity, establishes *Kashmir Pending* as a fictional memoir that transcends the story of the individual and extends to the story of the region.

Sajad's *Munnu* similarly creates a triangulation between the self, the Kashmiri identity, and Islam as it offers the coming-of-age story of the protagonist growing up under Indian occupation alongside an increasing number of Pakistani-backed insurgents.[7] As mentioned earlier, Sajad employs a "visual grammar" that echoes Spiegelman's anthropomorphic use of animals in *Maus*, but rather than Spiegelman's allusion to extermination, Sajad invokes the idea of extinction—the elimination of a species through the invasive resettlement and repurposing of a native environment.[8] By illustrating the members of the Indian army as humans while depicting Kashmiris as hanguls, an endangered species of deer, he emphasizes the lack of state protection available for the warscape inhabitants. Sajad is careful not to present religion as a precondition to being a Kashmiri; as the reader quickly discovers, hanguls do not represent Muslims only, but all Kashmiris regardless of their religious affiliations. The humanoid hanguls are not personalized; they appear as indistinguishable figures with no facial expression, "frozen in [a] non-emotive and unindividualized woodcut style" to stress their stagnation and entrapment in a perpetual state of mourning (Rajendran 159).[9] The hanguls, in other words, visually reinforce the idea of dehumanization experienced by those excluded from traditional human rights as their constitutional privileges are violated by crackdowns, illegal detentions, unjustified violence, and killings.

Both comics combine life writing with witness accounts. Mushtaq's confessional description of his militant past initially starts as a conversa-

---

7. As C. Christine Fair explains:

> Pakistan's use of Islamist militancy as a tool of foreign policy is not new and in fact dates back to the early beginning of statehood. Pakistan's ability to field sustained militant campaigns with significant degrees of public support is likely tied to the historical and social milieus of jihad, which has long been understood as a legitimate mode of militarized conflict in the areas that now make up Pakistan. (136)

We see this vicious cycle play out in Kashmir; according to Jonah Blank, "The longer Kashmir is held by brute force, the more convincing the rationale of Partition will seem. For this reason, Pakistan cannot sever its ties to the insurgents. And for this reason, India cannot simply crush the insurgency by military means" (51).

8. As Punnya Rajendran explains, "Hanguls and mice offer a contrasting interrogation of humanity. While the hanguls are picturesque creatures of beauty, mice scuttle down sewage lines. A rhetoric of conservation and exclusionism, as opposed to extermination and abjectness, dominates the figure of the hangul" (159).

9. By contrast, the members of the Indian army appear as humans, who can hunt and kill the native fauna with impunity. The human status of the Indians, argues Amit Baishya, "is an ironic visual/narrative device as it underscores their 'bestial' brutality against an occupied population portrayed as an alter-species" (51). Through this animal-human juxtaposition, Sajad interrogates the boundaries of humanity within the everyday life of one living a warscape existence, "torn between his or her aspiration for 'humanity' and the actual socio-historical experience of being treated as sub-human" (JanMohamed 115).

tion with Ali, formally marking their roles as the witness and the audience. Looking back, Mushtaq regrets his fervent attachment to political Islam and details the evolution of his activism—from throwing stones to armed struggle—as a warning meant first for Ali and then for the broader audience of at-risk Kashmiri youth.[10] In a similar vein, Sajad's subversive use of the bildungsroman enhances the testimonial thrust of the graphic narrative: The first part of the book focuses on the personal experiences of the seven-year-old Munnu, whereas the second half more closely documents the collective trauma experienced by "a persecuted people" in the region (Chandra 26).[11] This meshing allows Sajad to build a complex web of stories to testify for those who can no longer speak for themselves. As Mushtaq and Sajad shed light on the everyday lives of the Kashmiri Muslims trapped in a vicious cycle of political Islam, radical ideologies, religious extremism, and ethnocentric nationalism, they simultaneously meditate upon the construction of border consciousness in a warscape, where border crossing is not an emancipatory or a transformative act but a form of trauma. In this regard, their accounts deviate from Anzaldúa's characterization of the borderland as a positive site of cultural production and instead raise questions about different "manner[s] of border-crossing," as Abdul JanMohamed puts it, as well as the "intents" for crossing borders (98). Both Muslim Comics move away from the singular understanding of border consciousness as a productive process of re-creation, pointing out that this understanding ignores the restricted reality of those stranded by warscape borders. In the case of

---

10. For Patrick C. Hogan, the question of audience in *Kashmir Pending* is a complicated one and is built upon layers. He contends that, while the primary reader seems to be "potential militants," the actual audience is mostly English-speaking liberal humanists ("*Kashmir Pending*" 109):

> It is important for liberal humanists reading the work to think of its primary audience not as liberal humanists, but as "at risk" Kashmiri youths. Put differently, we may say that there is what might be called a rhetorical audience for the work. The *rhetorical audience* is a group assumed to be the main implied audience by the *actual* implied audience. (109)

Sajad, on the other hand, identifies his immediate audience as Kashmiris and urges them to learn about the rich history of the land.

11. Nandini Chandra describes the tension between the first and the second halves of the comic: "There are two contradictory aspects to the story: the unapologetic narrative of growth of the seven-year-old Munnu amidst political turmoil (the *bildungs*), and the need to downplay that growth as a reminder that the story is about a persecuted people (the counter-*bildungs*)" (26). Furthermore, Sajad's use of the third-person narration strategically employs defamiliarization that separates the author from the protagonist, suggesting that their witnessing is implicated in a narrative posture that rests on the threshold of perspectives.

Kashmir, the artists note, the "reinvention" offered by borders more often signifies the transformation of the individual into a political-religious martyr and a symbol for the cult of the *shaheed*, the Muslim martyr-witness. Ultimately, both comics critique the celebration of border hybridity by depicting the warscape borderland as a zone of necropolitical entrapment that regularly leads to radicalization and (self-)destruction. Instead, they promote a different kind of witnessing—border witnessing—embedded in pluralist regionalism. Finally, the border witness works against the necropolitical conditions that valorize self-sacrifice and toward a different understanding of the borderland—not as a space of hybridity but one of empathetic solidarity.

Shaheed: Terrorism and Horrorism

In both comics, the shaheed is presented as a magnetic necropolitical emblem, a figure whose heroic death brings together "nationalist-religious motivations" (Hasso 31). Derived from Arabic, *shaheed* literally translates to "seeing" and "giving evidence"; the shaheed's self-sacrifice in the service of Allah attests to the power of faith at the moment of his death. By testifying without speaking, the shaheed emerges as the ideal witness, forever unanswerable and unquestionable—much like Levi's idea of the mute Muselmann as the "true witness" (*The Drowned* 84).[12] However, unlike the Muselmann, the abject figure of the eternal quasi-death of the concentration camp, the shaheed actively embraces death as the culmination of his militancy.[13] The heroism of the shaheed, his resolve to "take power over [his] death by approaching it head-on," marks him as a particularly powerful and desirable warscape commodity (Mbembe 90). Gradually, however, the popularity of the shaheed in Kashmir transforms the region into one in which the dominant voice is the voice of the dead: Kashmir becomes a place where living

---

12. By disavowing his worldly existence, the shaheed becomes God's chosen to "testify with the prophets on the day of Judgement" (Haleem 51). Drawing on Islamic scholars, Nadia Taysir Dabbagh explains that in death, the martyr "is not judged as an ordinary human, but all his sins are forgiven by the very act of martyrdom" (30).

13. Masood Ashraf Raja explains that the shaheed "achieves a special status through his corporeal death, for he is, as the verses state, not dead. [. . .] The Shaheed earns special favors through his sacrifice both for himself and also for his family, including freedom from fear and humiliation" (13). Mbembe draws on this belief to argue that "self-sacrificers proceed to take power over their death by approaching it head-on. This power may be derived from the belief that destroying one's own body does not affect the continuity of being" (90).

witnesses are silenced or ignored as a way of privileging those who sacrificed their lives. According to Nayar, this marks Kashmir as a necropolitical habitat "peopled with the dead, [where] narratives are framed by the dead, [and where the] stories are stories of the dead" ("Postcolonial Gothic" 6).

The protagonists of the two comics position themselves against this figure and turn a critical eye on the glorification of the shaheed, and particularly the shaheed's funeral, the ultimate necropolitical site of public mourning as well as political ground for recruitment for the Azadi movement. In *Kashmir Pending,* Mushtaq attributes his escalating involvement with the insurgency to his witnessing of a shaheed's funeral. He recalls how the burial rites were carefully orchestrated, peppered with Azadi mantras, and how the entire ritual gradually shifted from religious ceremony into political theater. While the slain body is a physical indicator of the Indian's state necropolitical reach, its ability to kill Kashmiris with impunity, the resistance slogans of the mourners point to the limits of India's hegemony. For young Kashmiris like Mushtaq, forced to occupy a state of exception, the funeral provides an outlet to express anger and frustration as well as an opportunity to temporarily escape the realities of warscape existence. In joining in the ceremonial mourning and glorification of martyrdom, Mushtaq experiences a shift in consciousness, not because he crosses a geographical border but because he ritually joins in the crossing of the border between life and death, entering into a space where acknowledgment of that crossing becomes a collective expression of dissent.[14] The funeral he recalls was for a street vendor named Jabbar, caught in crossfire and then cynically elevated to shaheed status, an innocent pseudo-witness co-opted by the Azadi movement. Mourners gather from all corners of the region to pay their respects:

> The news of Jabbar's death spread like wildfire. People started pouring in from every nook and corner in the city. It seemed as if all of Srinagar turned up to witness this moment of grief. Eyes brimmed with tears and anger. His body taken in a procession through the narrow lanes of downtown Srinagar. His widow was beside herself with grief. The husband she just lost was now a martyr. And she was the martyr's wife. (37–38)

The choreographed rituals sustain a feeling of solidarity: The shrouded body is carried over the crowd as the attendees put up their hands to touch him. Visually, this solidarity quickly turns into deindividualization.

---

14. As Stephen Morton observes, "postcolonial narratives of mourning offer an important counterpoint to the necropolitical logic of India's performance of sovereignty over the contested space of Kashmir" (21).

The large congregation stands shoulder to shoulder as the body makes its way to the burial ground; eventually, they perform the Namazi Jenaza in unison, repeating words and movements in concert. Suhaan Mehta draws attention to the way facial expressions blur into "extreme close-ups, pronounced lines on foreheads, dark, narrowed eyes, and partially concealed faces" (179). Jabbar's widow remains on her knees as family and friends surround her, wailing together, everyone dressed in black: The panels contain minimum narrative, but the visualization of the shaheed's widow with her mouth open, in particular, suggests raw sounds emanating from her, sounds beyond human language. The upward movement within the panels, the men carrying the deceased on their shoulders as well as the women lifting their heads up, suggests a heavenward gaze but also reflects the way the crowd is encouraged to look away from earth and the concerns of humankind. A religious ritual becomes necropolitical rhetoric.

The "normative crisis" produced by the necropolitical logic of the funeral, deftly summarized by Foucault's statement "Go get slaughtered and we promise you a long and pleasant life," takes the two comics in different directions (S. Murray, "Thanatopolitics: On the Use" 195). The immediate effect of the shaheed's funeral on Mushtaq is a resolve to act—a decision that pushes him toward radicalism.[15] He heeds the words of Qasim, one of the Hurriyat leaders, as he advocates for "askari tehreek" ("armed action"): "The valley is drenched in words and political slogans. Now is the time for action" (34). Gradually, the Azadi call for action resonates with Mushtaq: "This overwhelming response to his death strengthened my resolve and hardened my belief. I would follow Qasim's way. I would fight for a free Kashmir. [. . .] Jabbar's funeral played an important part in our decision-making. We thought we couldn't be silent spectators to this injustice anymore" (39). By moving away from the world of individuals controlled and

---

15. Cavarero writes:

> Within a theoretical framework created to justify war—and even the highly anomalous concepts of "preventative war" and "humanitarian war"—terrorism is, in substance, accused of differing from it as regards both subjects and methods, of being a criminal form of violence, given that both its actors and its acts are incompatible with the conventional system of destruction. [. . .] It tends to repeat, in line with the tradition, that the gular combatant directs his fire against other combatants or the enemy's strategic sites, hitting civilians only by mistake. The terrorist not only does not follow this rule, he most often does aim to kill civilians. This renders him doubly criminal and makes his violence distinct from that of regular troops who have a legitimate government and a state behind them. (70)

segregated by borders and warscape infrastructure, Mushtaq embraces the idea of self-sacrifice. His ideological realignment is an expression of his desire to break out of the role of "silent spectator" and to embark on the radical path to become a shaheed, crossing the border to Pakistan to receive training as an armed fighter.

Even though scholars working on Kashmir are careful not to conflate the Kashmiri insurgence with jihadi terrorism—typically, insurgence is understood as a localized struggle for nationhood, and jihadism as a movement more invested in a unifying vision of God—there are similarities in the manner of violence and the ideological postures exhibited in both (Sharma 126).[16] Mushtaq, although religious, is not, strictly speaking, a jihadi terrorist. But in the warscape borderland, the categories are blurred as religious and political motivations become interlaced. The different phases of his militant evolution—from emigration, to mental preparation, to physical training—closely resemble those of the jihadi. Scholarship on jihadism helps us recognize Mushtaq's illegal passage to Pakistan over the heavily militarized Line of Control (LOC), a border created by the United Nations at the end of the 1972 cease-fire between Indian Hindus and Pakistani Muslims, as the first and the most significant phase of his conversion into extremism. The border, which Mushtaq describes as "a line of finality that is religiously patrolled by forces from both sides," is hardly a site of hybrid consciousness or progressive cultural cross-pollination; his "emigration" (a term adopted by jihadist scholars) shows his commitment to inflicting violence on the

---

16. It is important to heed to Alpana Sharma's assertion that the two categories should be evaluated "on their own terms and not automatically conflated with global terrorism and the war on global extremism" (126). Sharma further elucidates the difference between the two categories:

> Indeed, the global terrorists and the local insurgents are two distinct entities. The former envisions a single world, won by might, ruled by a single faith with a single god and no defining national boundaries; it is the theocratic co-optation of globalization, whose ordinary processes were thus far confined to the economic and cultural realms of free market capitalism. The latter appears, by contrast, smaller in aim and aspiration; while not itself infused with the benign secular spirit of Kashmiriyat—this group promotes and wreaks violence, after all—it has been co-opted by the impersonal machinery of global terrorism. (128)

Still, despite the significant nuances between the global structure of jihadists and the limited scope of the anticolonial struggles of Kashmiris, the motivation behind crossing borders bears semblance.

Other (51).¹⁷ Thus where some scholars characterize border crossing as a generative experience that allows the crosser to navigate oppressive ideologies and coercive apparatuses in an effort to subvert them, *Kashmir Pending* depicts crossing as neither an individually empowering nor a curative act but rather an initial expression of one's "willingness to commit savagery and mass casualty" (Lia 537). Mushtaq and his friend are escorted through the frontier by operatives familiar with the terrain; to evade the border patrol, they walk for miles under cover of night, picking up other recruits along the way.¹⁸ Already the passage is presented as a necropolitical ensnarement, a movement through a zone of terror in which different warscape constituents "exert [. . .] control over mortality [. . .] to define life" (Mbembe 66). Borderland existence, and border crossing, does not remake the individual as newly creative and independent of state hegemony but rather into a pawn of a different sort—no longer a subject of Indian military control but now, instead, an object of Pakistani extremism.

When Mushtaq's group safely reaches its destination in Muzzafarabad (known as the "capital of Pakistan's Azad Kashmir"), the recruits gather to pray (Blank 51). Prayer in this context is not only a spiritual performance of devotion but a political bonding ritual that unifies strangers under a com-

---

17. In *Munnu*, Sajad makes numerous visual references to the Line of Control. Guarded by the Border Security Force, this arbitrary dividing line not only fails to keep Indian and Pakistani ambitions in check, but it also appears as a visual sore to keep people apart, discouraging travel, interaction, and exchange: "The L.O.C. blocked traditional routes and people from both sides of the fence were cut off from each other" (208). In one panel, Sajad draws an area map that separates the two countries with a dark chasm; he shows the border areas heavily militarized with multiple watchtowers, barbwire, and even tanks facing each other; he places the national flags prominently at opposite sides as symbols of land ownership. In another editorial, he places skulls along the LOC to signify the countless number of dead people due to the ongoing conflict (205).

18. Brynjar Lia elucidates that Abdallah Azzam, the ideologue of the Egyptian Islamic Jihad, describes the four phases as follows: "Azzam divides jihad into four stages: emigration (al-hijra), preparation (al-i'dad), garrison (al-rabat), and combat (al-qital). All three preparatory stages are indispensable for the participation in combat. Together, the four stages encompass the jihad as understood by Azzam" (520). Lia further explains that "emigration" is the most significant sign of one's dedication:

> In Azzam's doctrine, the "emigration" is perhaps the most important stage for a jihadi recruit since it demonstrates his willingness to sacrifice. The willingness to give up every worldly pleasure, even life, lies at the core of Azzam's message, and already in the initial paragraph, this emphasis is very clear. "Emigration" implies leaving behind home, family, work, and disengaging from many of the daily bonds linking an individual to this world. (521)

mon ideology. It is also a ceremonial gesture to recognize Pakistan's role as the protector of the Azadi movement—an idea that has been hammered into Kashmiri Muslims from a young age.[19] As he settles into camp life, Mushtaq realizes that the few rules that exist there are meant to keep the trainees in line by discouraging them from entering into political discussions or behaving in individualized ways:

> On our first day, we settled in the camp with our belongings. Each tent was shared by ten other youths like us. We were provided beds and given a few pamphlets to read: the rules of the camp . . . Be punctual. Keep yourself clean. Keep a low profile; do not step out of the compound without permission. Keep your surroundings clean. Refrain from political discussions and arguments. Wake up and sleep on time. (43)

Where for Anzaldúa and others, crossing borders to a new environment is supposed to initiate meaningful exchange and stimulate a "double vision" by straddling "two or more cultures," the trans-border camp here seeks to replace dialogue with silence and double vision with mono-vision (Anzaldúa 80). The fact that Mushtaq is training with a transnational cohort in Pakistan to become a part of a multinational network in Afghanistan does not afford him a global view, nor does it allow him to rise above his ideological entrenchment. In retrospect, Mushtaq recognizes border crossing not as an opportunity for the kind of cultural hybridity implicated in oppositional consciousness but rather as an act that ossifies his ideological positions, reaffirms his entrenched convictions, and accelerates radicalization.

Mushtaq's testimony about the camp includes descriptions of the physical training, which overlap with typical representations of the "active" jihadi abundantly referenced (negatively) in Western comics; as discussed in previous chapters, the vigorous, animated Muslim militant preparing for violent

---

19. Mushtaq recalls how the imam's Friday sermons would contain political propaganda to establish a kinship between Kashmiri Muslims and Pakistan:

> The mosque holds an important position in the political history of Jammu and Kashmir. It has been at the center stage of political dissent. [. . .] In present times it is a symbol of Kashmiri nationalist sentiment. [. . .] Every Friday prayer would be followed by fiery speeches against the government. Political messages were expressed freely. The consequence of such instigations was often felt on the streets. (12)

The Pakistani flag looms large in the background of the panel to glue Islam with nationhood (13). The mosque's portrayal of Pakistan as a "holy" site is meant to establish a "deep love" for the neighboring country and to recognize its role within the global *ummah* (13).

FIGURE 4.2. Mushtaq receives training at camp.

action is a familiar trope. We might recall, for example, the transformation of an American convert recruited by Jamaat ul-Fuqra from an aimless idler to brainwashed jihadi in Inzana's *Johnny Jihad*: In that work, the protagonist joins a training camp in upstate New York complete with obstacle course, shooting range, and "silhouetted targets" riddled with bullets; as he becomes absorbed in camp life, he loses his individuality ("The immature boy I was when I entered the camp had become a machine" [Inzana]). This image of the physically vital, "machine"-like jihadi is carefully and deliberately deployed in *Kashmir Pending* as well: In this series of panels, the recruits are reduced to mere bodies as they run from station to station (obstacle course, close combat techniques, target practice, etc.). Each panel progressively expunges the distinct features of the individuals, transforming them into mere figurines and, ultimately, into red lumps, barely recognizable as humans (see figure 4.2). The erosion of the self suggests the diminishing of agency—the bodies are mere commodities to be traded in the warscape economy. As they become a faceless mass, it becomes clear that they have lost the ability to think and act independently, fully entrenched in an extremist ideology that normalizes self-sacrifice and sacrifice of self.

Whereas Mushtaq presents his border crossing as an overture to terrorism, Sajad invokes something closer to the idea of what Adriana Cavarero calls "horrorism," a strategic manipulation of the subject into intimidated powerlessness. Cavarero argues that

> in contrast to what occurs with terror, in horror there is no instinctive movement of flight in order to survive, much less the contagious turmoil of panic. Rather, movement is blocked in total paralysis, and each victim is affected on its own. Gripped by revulsion in the face of a form of violence that appears more inadmissible than death, the body reacts as if nailed to the spot, hairs standing on end. (8)

An example of the turn to horrorism comes when Munnu attends the funeral of Mustafa, a suspected militant killed by the Indian army. A full-page spread illustrates the funeral procession, showing a massive herd of hanguls walking behind the corpse (see figure 4.3):

> Papa, Bilal, Adil and Akhtar rushed back into the street and merged with the river of people. Mamma also disappeared to join the wailing women. [. . .] As the funeral prayers were offered, it got darker and Mustafa was taken to the sacred mound, and laid in the earth, under the mulberry tree, where the descendent of the prophet Mohammed was buried. As if the small mound of loose soil over Mustafa's grave was a groom on his wedding day, people showered it with flowers, toffees and dried fruits. (35–36)

They pull the weeds from "the sacred mound" as the shrouded bodies of the dead are carried over the shoulders of mourners. As Munnu reveals,

FIGURE 4.3. Munnu describes Mustafa's funeral.

the shrouds mask the mutilated corpses, which the Indian army had previously "dragged through the streets of Batmaloo until there was no skin left on their faces" (38). The disfigurement and towing of Mustafa's body by the Indian army serve as a warning to Kashmiri youth and invoke what François Debrix describes as radical recruitment's "pulverization of the human," a process that aims to strip the human qualities from the body (qtd. in Kanwal 4). Drawing on Debrix, Kanwal further suggests that "the violence inflicted on Kashmiri bodies not only erases their uniqueness and individuality, but also leaves them unrecognizable as human bodies, so that they fail to elicit any empathy in spectators" (4). The scale and the tenor of the funeral are meant to offset the brutal dehumanizing of the Kashmiri militant: If the Indian army defaces the bodies of suspected militants to further "traumatize the civilian through horroristic violence so that they offer no opposition," the funeral rites not only restore the humanity of the dead but elevate the deceased beyond the average human to martyr status (Kanwal 5). But Munnu finds himself unconvinced about the supposed humanizing aspect of the spectacle, which, with its ominous swarms of frenzied, wailing mourners, itself seems to him like something out of "a horror movie" (35); he recalls that he "shivered and buried his face" in his sister's arms to avert his eyes from the dreadful display (35). He spends the following nights racked by nightmares: First, he sees the corpse floating out of the grave in a beam of light, and then he starts having visions about his older brother, Bilal, being buried alive in a coffin. Thus, the horrors of the Indian army's mutilations are compounded, not diminished, by the horroristic spectacle of the funeral glorifying the dead.

Cavarero suggests that horrorism is not only an intimidation tactic but a petrifying experience: "The physics of horror is often linked to another, equally well-known symptom, that of feeling frozen" (7). Along these lines, Munnu describes a newfound incapacity to act at an *ijtima* (gathering) to commemorate Ajaz, a young Kashmiri man gunned down for trying to protect his sister from harassment by Indian soldiers. The gathering starts with the offering of prayers and chanting the name of Mohammed, but eventually, the mood of the crowd shifts and slogans fill the air, blending sacred rituals with political activism: "Don't fool yourself by thinking that martyrs die. No. Never! They live forever" (66). After Munnu volunteers to read a poem, the bereaved father offers him a piece of bread to thank him. Shocked and repulsed by the father's spectral appearance and ashen hands, Munnu feels frozen, unable to react or move. He gradually reaches for the piece of bread, but chewing it feels like consuming "a chunk of raw flesh," which he associates with cannibalism (70). He imagines the father's veiny hands reaching toward him from a whirlwind to pull him into the abyss; the father's shrouded body in the next panel fractures into multiple, amoebalike beings, trying to capture him and making the tent feel like "a morgue full of breathing corpses" (70). The father's metamorphosed body becomes a synecdoche of the region, representing a "death-world" in which the living consume the dead by mythologizing them (Mbembe 92). Unlike Mushtaq, whose experiences at a shaheed's funeral push him to active terrorism, Munnu's reaction to the necropolitical conditions that create the cult of the shaheed is pure, paralytic horrorism.

For Sajad, then, border crossing provides a political education in exploitation: He realizes that insurgents "took advantage of the faith of the majority in Kashmir and established Islam in a divine marriage with Pakistan," using young Kashmiris as pawns (281). He reiterates the suggestion that in warscapes, border crossing can be a trap that leads to the zombification of the Muslim. He notes how his brother's friends volunteer to cross the border and then cross back again, now converted into militants: "Most of [Bilal's classmates] crossed the border to receive armed training in Pakistan's portion of Kashmir and had come back to fight against the Indian portion of Kashmir" (4). He shows a group of hanguls actively training, climbing rope ladders, and practicing with their automatic weapons; adjacent to this illustration, he places a number of unmarked tombstones to signify the inevitable death of these trainees (5). The sheer number of graves that appear throughout the graphic narrative provides a poignant criticism of the shaheed's mute incorporation into "an encompassing heroic structure" (Hogan, *Imagining Kashmir* 26). Consequently, these tombstones become the "cultural frame through which we read Kashmir" as a topography of silenced witnessing, dishonesty, and death (Nayar, "Postcolonial Gothic" 5).

The various forms of terrorism and horrorism triggered by border crossing therefore accord less with visions of creative reclamation of agency through hybridity and more with JanMohamed's suggestion that the border often becomes a quagmire based on "the 'identity' and 'homogeneity' of the group that has constituted it" (103). The two Muslim Comics demonstrate exactly how the resolute singularity of culture emblematized by the figure of the shaheed cannot be reconciled with the notion of a self-affirming border existence that privileges and empowers contradiction and ambiguity over the shaheed's certainty and inflexibility. Both comics argue that in warscapes, border crossing is commonly an overture to radicalization, brainwashing, and silencing. As the muted witness, the shaheed represents the ultimate warscape irony: Despite his embodied experience of war, he cannot testify to and warn of the trap represented by the border crossing. Instead, the use of the muted shaheed, and the speaking of propaganda through him, accelerates the transformation of the entire region into a morgue. The border witness emerges as a life-affirming speaker capable of countering this transformation.

Border Witness

Thus far, Mushtaq's and Sajad's criticism of the glorification of the shaheed, and their condemnation of Kashmir's metamorphosis into a death world, has been relatively clear and straightforward. Speaking of the martyrs, Sajad's teacher states: "I had many bright students who sacrificed their lives for Kashmir. If they were to rise from their graves, they'd regret giving so much"

(176). Mushtaq, similarly, rejects the celebration of the death of his friend Aziz: "My comrades hailed him as a martyr. They said [. . .] Aziz had gone to paradise; he was definitely having a good time, therefore there was nothing to despair. [. . .] Try telling that to his parents" (69). The repeated images of massive graveyards, unmarked tombstones, and public spaces turned into makeshift morgues act as unsubtle visual reminders of the precarity of life in warscapes. More subtle is the way that, in denouncing the cult of the shaheed, Mushtaq and Sajad reinvent themselves, participating in a distinct form of witnessing that allows them to capture—without participating in warscape propaganda—the collective trauma that pervades the region.

As they position themselves as skeptic storytellers who push against the typical teleological arc of border tales, Mushtaq and Sajad emerge as examples of "border witnesses."[20] By abandoning the traditional narrative of escape and empowerment in favor of more accurate and cynical tales of border existence in warscapes, they create counter-archives that challenge the political status quo in the region as well as push back at the theoretical orientation of a great deal of academic border studies. For Ross Castronovo, complicating the representation of the borderland as an irresistible source of inspiration and growth is an invaluable activity: "'Border theory' narrativizes a history in which culturally transgressive texts, actions, and bodies circumvent traditional structures of power, but this emplotment of resistance can mute another narrative in which power can and does reassert itself" (199). Making room for alternative accounts, he argues, can also spotlight other types of border experiences that do not fall in line with narratives of hybridity, multiculturalism, or global citizenship:

> This [optimistic] narrativization obscures other ways of thinking about the border that must be recognized if negotiations involving nations, hybrid identities, and cultural liberation are to acknowledge not simply the celebratory potential of the contact zone, but also the ineradicable trappings of power that patrol the boundaries of any area of culture. This thinking [. . .] suggests the need to create cautionary tales about the border. (203)

Mushtaq and Sajad's portrayals of border consciousness as prone to radicalization, and border existence as a source of trauma, fit nicely into this alternative way of thinking. If the funeral functioned as a way of celebrating the shaheed despite his muted status as a religious witness, the stories that Mushtaq and Sajad uncover and relay as border witnesses are invested in

---

20. Castronovo further explains: "A text overcomes the impediments of being marginal to two or more cultures, and indeed subversively benefits from these limitations and prejudices to undermine the oppressive structures" (195).

unmuting the dead and enfolding them into a different sort of history that refuses to glorify them in any bombastic or simplistic way. Through their guarded storytelling, the two border witnesses replace propagandistic tales of heroism with more troubled and cautionary narratives, clearing space for Kashmiris to take ownership of their narratives and acknowledge their accountability. And, by directly speaking to Kashmiris, they also position themselves as facilitators: Mushtaq, for example, dedicates himself to community building by opening a restaurant after his release, which becomes a space where he can share his personal experiences with his patrons: "Sometimes I share my stories with my clients . . . the bloodshed, the body count, the passion, the losses . . . I narrate as best as I can remember and every time I do, I sense the recklessness of that violent journey. My past makes it difficult for me to make peace with my conscience" (93). Sajad becomes a cartoonist in a Kashmiri newspaper, offering sharp criticism of India's repressive regime as well as pointed censure of local leaders benefiting from war. In a chapter titled "Footnotes," he writes: "It's the ordinary people of Kashmir who need to know about Kashmir" (221). In this way, both Mushtaq and Sajad speak of death without romanticizing it, depict the shaheed without valorizing him, and capture the victimization of Kashmiris without reducing them to victims.

Fundamentally, border witnessing is about collectivity. If the figure of the shaheed is about separating the self from the community, and then sacrificing that self to attain external recognition, the border witness is about holding on to the self while imagining its place within a collective trauma. Mushtaq and Sajad achieve this by suturing together disjointed individual histories into a cohesive narrative of the region. In decentering the self, they create what Nayar describes as a "composite I witness," a symbolic linking of an individual's story of suffering to that of a community: "These are testimonial bodies, so to speak, populating the panel, corroborating the eyewitness narrative, even when only one eye/I is doing the speaking" (*Human Rights* 127). Therefore, the inner journey of the border witness, the act of "travelling within himself," is implicated in a larger regional struggle of becoming (Gasset 140). The inward, self-reflective turn is coupled with outward communication to a warscape constituent—be it the random listeners in Mushtaq's restaurant or the traumatized interviewees in Sajad's reportage.[21] Such interweaving of private and community stories is consis-

---

21. Drawing on Richard Rorty, Paul Lauritzen writes that "we must turn inward, because in the unconscious one finds alternative descriptions of one's self and one's past. The turn inward thus helps us to see moral deliberation as a matter of self-creation rather than self-knowledge, and morality as a matter of self-enlargement rather than self-purification" (194).

tent with the Islamic understanding of *nafs,* which translates to "the self" but also refers to "brother" or "fellow Muslim." As Dabbagh explains, "the Islamic concept of the self is more collective and has more connection with the group or community than the Western individualistic, separated sense of self" (25–26). As they become border witnesses, the obscuring of the boundary between the self, the community, and the Other allows these protagonists to dislocate the primacy of the "I" and incorporate multiple voices from the region.

This decentering is best exemplified through the use of genre in the construction of the self in the two comics. Both in the title and the first half of the book, Sajad uses the nickname "Munnu" to refer to himself. An affectionate appellation that exists in a number of South Asian languages, "Munnu" literally translates as "the youngest" (Sarkar 106). This nickname, along with the subtitular epithet "A Boy from Kashmir," hints at Sajad's subversive use of the bildungsroman form: His insistence on third-person narration disconnects him from the particularity of his own history and places him amid the multiple, contested visions of the region—one childhood enfolded within innumerable others, all compromised by necropolitical manipulation and military domination. The second half of the comic builds an archival "evidentiary base" that includes "devices of documentary, ethnography, and reportage" as a way of keeping intact "the consciousness of communities" (Chandra 26). As the personal arc of the story fades, making room for communal and regional stories, Sajad's witnessing becomes bolder and more pronounced. He starts to refer to his brush as a "weapon" that allows him to testify for those who cannot speak for themselves. As a cartoonist, he takes it upon himself to use his platform to shed light on "events that are considered outside the pale of official history" and to link life stories rather than push one personal narrative forward while burying others (Chandra 26). In one instance, he interviews a mother whose son never returned from work sixteen years ago. Hoping for a miraculous homecoming, the mother remains stuck in a permanent state of desperation that has partially robbed her of her sanity. Sajad inserts himself into the story, both as a journalist on a fact-finding mission but also as an empathetic listener. His role as a journalist gives him the opportunity to excavate vividly traumatic stories—and in this case to confirm details of the son's death that would have provided him with the status of a shaheed. However, Sajad refuses to focus on the potential martyr and turns his gaze instead on the survivor to witness *her* loss—no matter how inarticulate the survivor might be. Sajad the journalist is obligated to tell the story of the mute, dead witness; Sajad the empathetic listener is obligated to hear and represent the mother's pain in a way that she cannot.

Kashmir Pending is also less interested in centering the voice of a single narrator or growing the fame of one individual subject than it is in drawing attention to the warscape existence of the average, anonymous individual and then showing how that individual subjectivity is inevitably linked to and created by the life experiences of others. In the "prelude," a boy watches a dinghy carrying two Indian soldiers across the river. He picks up a stone and throws it toward the slow-moving vessel, fully knowing that he will not be able to harm them. There is no narrative; nor is there any identification of the boy. The pacing of the panels is slow and deliberate. Ahmed and Sigh capture the symbolism of this defiant gesture by focusing on various body parts to show the purposeful movements. The feet dangle casually from the dock, and the eyes watch the approaching dinghy like a hawk; the easy, effective momentum of the throw, carried through the whiplike extension of the elbow, illustrates how resistance, however pointless, is engrained in each Kashmiri from youth. The boy is fully aware of the futility of his action, but the act is illustrative of his connection to the land and the impulse to defend his territory. The soldiers attentively watch the harmless performance as they hold on to their machine guns. They do not respond or retaliate, but they remain alert, keeping the boy in focus as he flees the scene. One of them thinks aloud: "Kid's going to run into trouble someday"—the only speech bubble in the prelude (4). The fact that the boy is unidentified marks him as a generic Kashmiri youth, just another anonymous warscape denizen who grew up practicing stone-pelting (*sang-baz*) as part of his everyday life. He could be anyone. The cinematic sequence of the prelude, heavy with picture and lacking dialogue, hints at the silence surrounding the Kashmiri plight. But through this silent narration, the border witness emerges: The wordless prologue, with its nameless boy (who we find out is Mushtaq's younger self), establishes Mushtaq as a decentered storyteller, the unmuted borderline witness, who can narrate without speaking and tell his story even when Kashmiris are rendered voiceless on the global stage. Prajna Desai's analysis of the sparse use of narrativization in *Kashmir Pending* draws attention to the menacing presence of silence: "In Mushtaq's narrative, encounters between protestors and police are portrayed as silent iconic scuffles devoid of speech and sound effect." But this use of silence is a strategic method of moving the borderland narrative away from being the simple story of one hero who finds his creative voice.

Another important characteristic of the border witness is his or her disavowal of a "ritualized move into liminality" and his or her choice to embrace instead an existence more firmly grounded in their specific communities (Turner 28). In border studies (as well as in postcolonial studies more broadly), liminality has come to designate a sought-after position that can produce "double vision." Described as "a processual state or border zone mediating between cultures, races, or nations," liminality allows for the "blurring and merging of distinctions" eventually creating a condition of in-betweenness that favors transitional and shifting subjectivities in lieu of fixed identity positions (Henderson 5). Sajad and Mushtaq question the validity of liminality as a performative gesture and a precondition of deterritorialized subjectivity.[22] As the two Muslim Comics illustrate, liminality can trigger a sense of false consciousness that fosters destructive tribalism: Kashmiri Muslims are on a political level naturally liminal, but because of this liminality they are easily swayed into identifying with Pakistan on the basis of religion, for example. Instead of fetishizing hybridity or promoting a hollowed-out globalism as the inevitable outcome of crossing borders, both Mushtaq and Sajad show the protective value of being firmly rooted in their communities, advocating for a consciousness embedded in the idea of Kashmiriyat, a regionally shared identity. Both protagonists invoke Kashmiriyat—"Kashmir's longstanding secular spirit of community and tolerance"—at different points in their narratives (Sharma 127).[23] Kashmiriyat upholds the idea of a stable relationship between the rival Muslim and (Hindu) Pandit communities, one based on "reconciliation and rehabilitation" that can lessen hostility and animosity (Bhan et al. 290). In *Munnu*, Sajad laments the hounding of Pandit communities ("They'd pelt stones at their houses and call them infidels" [281]); similarly, *Kashmir Pending* includes Mushtaq's confessions about his "innate dislike for the Pandit families" as something engrained in him as a child and something he much regrets (14). Their projection for an independent Kashmir, therefore, entails a more inclusive regionalist perspective originating from a sense of territorial belonging that supersedes religious tribalism and ethnocentric nationalism.[24]

---

22. The relationship between the territorial and deterritorial has been at the heart of Arjun Appadurai's project of redefining modernity; he asks: "What is the nature of locality as a lived experience in a globalized, deterritorialized world?" (52).

23. Kashmiriyat, far from being an ideal solution, represents a nostalgic desire to reestablish harmony among various cultural and religious groups in the valley; as Sharma and Giggoo note, "Kashmiriyat, if it ever existed, is a term given to the mutual and peaceful coexistence of Pandits and Muslims in Kashmir much before insurgency erupted. Kashmiriyat ceased to exist when the ethnic cleansing of Kashmiri Pandits took place" (255).

24. Mona Bhan, Deepti Misri, and Ather Zia explain that Kashmiriyat is not immune from complications: "The notion of Kashmiriyat has been widely problematized by both Kashmiri Pandits and Muslims. One Pandit writer notes in a recent collection that 'reconciliation between Kashmiri Muslims has been widely debated under the ambit of Kashmiriyat'" (293).

Sajad's emphasis on regional identity is expressed when he contemplates producing a graphic novel about the 2010 uprising in Kashmir. When consulting with a friend, he is advised to change the title of the comic from *Endangered Species* to *Kashmiri Intifada*, thereby connecting the Kashmir uprising to the Palestinian rebellion (334). Marketing is the main motivation behind this suggestion—especially considering Joe Sacco's success with *Palestine*. But Sajad refuses to conflate Kashmir with Palestine as two Muslim spaces under occupation; rather, he is determined to characterize the Kashmiri warscape as unique: "We aren't Arabs, and it isn't spring here either. I am writing about an 8-year-old boy and he wouldn't be aware of such a term. [. . .] My story's about Kashmir. They should know Kashmir as it is, not through a generalizing lens of intifada" (334). Sajad's resistance to this conflation stems from his desire to avoid the homogenization of Muslims around the globe; he fears that linking Kashmir with other Muslim geographies would actually "collapse, reduce, and effectively exoticize the complex history of the Kashmiri political struggle into a generic 'Islamic rebellion'" (Sarkar 108).

Clearly Sajad's emphasis on regionalism and regional difference is meant to give Kashmiriyat, specifically, "a new lease of life" and its own voice and vision (Bharat 159). Therefore, it is unsurprising that Kashmiriyat helps shape a climactic section of *Kashmir Pending*, where Mushtaq is trapped at a checkpoint; he can either reach for his bag of grenades to attempt an escape or turn himself in in order to prevent bloodshed. At this pivotal moment, he notes the presence of a Kashmiri man walking toward the checkpoint and a Kashmiri woman sitting on the side of the road with her infant, as well as two Indian soldiers nearby. Mushtaq's reflections are in line with the spirit of Kashmiriyat: "A simple pulling of the pin would buy me out of the situation . . . but it would be at the cost of many innocent lives. They had done nothing to deserve this, the sight of their faces made it easier for me to decide" (78). This narrative is spread across a series of panels that show Mushtaq considering various inhabitants of the region, refusing to exclude any of them from the community, or from humanity; by choosing not to pull the grenade pin, he prevents them from becoming the latest entrants into the cycle of violence. This is a key moment, in which inclusive regional identity triumphs over necropolitics, and the value of individuals is preferred to the power of the shaheed.

Sajad, Ahmed, and Singh allude to Kashmiriyat as a regional aspiration that needs to be resuscitated to bring peace and harmony to warscape occupants. Such a plea has become a staple of recent Kashmiri writing that seeks to use literature as a tool in nation-building. As Kabir explains, for Kashmiris, kashmiriyat is invoked usually in the context of its perceived erosion, in conformation of the "community-in-neglect." The psychological repercussions of political conflict are attributed to the suspension of kashmiriyat, and aazadi relied upon to ensure its restoration; when the Kashmiris will have obtained aazadi, kashmiriyat will have returned to them. (20)

The authors are not naive about Kashmiriyat as a political solution, but their vision for the future certainly includes a regional ethos that promotes the cohabitation of Muslims and Hindus.[25] As border witnesses, they use Kashmiriyat not only as a way to erase "the masculinist zeal of Islamic fundamentalism with which the state has come to be associated" but as a call for communal healing (Sharma 127).

Kashmiri Future in Question

If the shaheed's death is commonly presented as a "happy ending" within the logic of radicalized Islamist resistance, the border witness remains skeptical of optimistic resolutions of warscape existence. The artists' narrativization does not automatically lead to empowerment or progress; rather, the recurring appearances and celebrations of shaheeds remind the reader of the ongoing debilitating impact of border crossing in warscape zones. By the end of *Kashmir Pending,* we find out that Ali, the inmate in the neighboring cell, has embarked on a cross-border suicide mission that kills a number of people, including two Border Security Force soldiers. If Ali represents the comic's immediate audience (at-risk Kashmiri youth), his indifference and unresponsiveness to Mushtaq's cautionary tale express a level of pessimism about the short-term prospects for the success of the border witness. Laub contends that in testimonies, it is imperative to have an empathetic listener: "The absence of an empathetic listener, or more radically, the absence of an addressable other, an other who can hear the anguish of one's memories and thus affirm and recognize their realness, annihilates the story" (69).[26] Ali's

---

25. As Sharma rightly points out, "what already lies in ruin is Kashmiriyat, Kashmir's longstanding secular spirit of community and tolerance; even its mystical, Sufi-inspired Islamic faith is at odds with the masculinist zeal of Islamic fundamentalism with which the state has come to be associated" (127).

26. In a similar fashion, Susan Spearey argues that "listening to accounts of trauma [. . .] becomes a profoundly ethical and dialogic act, and not merely a means of facilitating the victim's psychic healing. How these stories reshape the listeners' worlds is every bit as important as how they begin to reshape those of the victim and teller, and this is even more urgently the case when the trauma in question is collective" (71).

refusal or inability to "hear" Mushtaq shows the limits of the border witness in preventing future violence. This sense of failure is reiterated in the subnarrative that describes Mushtaq's dream of building a community via the restaurant—a dream that remains half-realized. His final statement conveys a wish rather than a clear conclusion: "I do not want any more innocent lives to be lost in the cross fires of my war" (95). Mushtaq utters these words as he sits in the restaurant all alone—with no immediate audience or community surrounding him. More importantly, he blends in with the dark shading of the panel, his face only partially visible, implying a melancholic decay that threatens his physical integrity. He is barely perceptible, as if he is dissolving into the story he narrated.

In a similar vein, *Munnu* ends with Sajad's failure as a "hero," or even as a positive protagonist: When he stumbles upon the gang rape of a disabled woman by hanguls (representing Kashmiri men), not only does he refuse to interfere (instead fleeing the scene), but he becomes complicit in the abuse by remaining silent about what he has seen.[27] Baishya describes the way the scene identifies the cyclic nature of the toxic elements of Kashmiri masculinity: "The male hanguls may be animalized and terrorized themselves, but [they] are equally capable of inflicting immense pain and injury upon others. The brutal violence of the state seems to find its noxious reflection in the masculinist violence that pervades quotidian life in necropolitical locales" (66). Sajad is incapable of disrupting this cycle: His intrusion initially forces the men to stop—they push the homeless woman out of the car, as if she is "unwanted filth" (Sajad 347)—but the threat continues to linger as Sajad leaves the men unchallenged, enabling them to resume their abusive behavior at a later point.[28] As one scholar argues, Sajad's own refusal

---

27. Ng writes that "it is notable that all the actors in this episode are Kashmiris; this directly confronts the protagonist (and the reader) with the realization that Kashmiris are not always the victims, but can be victimizers as well in given circumstances" (170).

28. Even at the moment of trauma, the victim's words emphasize kinship: "They're my brothers . . . I didn't have a firepot . . . cold outside . . . my brothers" (Sajad 348). Baishya's brilliant reading of this scene illustrates the familial roots of nation-building and its collapse due to existing social and gendered fissures:

> Conversely, her indictment—"They are my brothers . . ."—poignantly vocalizes how the men tipple over into the realms of nonrelation when they force themselves on her and reduce her to an object. "Brother" has a specific relational connotation in situations of anticolonial rebellion as in Kashmir. To be called brother is both a signifier of comradeship in an imagined national community and simultaneously an inscription into the patriarchal semiotics of what McClintock called the "national family of man" (McClintock 1993, 63). As her "brothers" rape and throw her away as "filth," they actively make her into a nonrelational object that is ejected outside. (66)

to bear witness, and his inability to call out the perpetrators, is not simply gross negligence but is suggestive of the protagonist's "ambiguous ethics"—ethics that occasionally "border on the criminal" (Ng 170). As Ng further explicates:

> Using a moment-to-moment panel transition to stretch every second of Munnu's involvement in the episode, and consistently framing characters illuminated by a backlight against an otherwise dark background to inversely mimic the spotlighting of convicts (a strategy possibly inspired by Maus as well), the episode's noir-ish implication is clearly predisposed towards incriminating Munnu in the incident, not exonerating him from blame. (170)

The book ends with a final panel featuring the abusers under a lamppost against a dark background. Sajad is absent; he inserts no commentary, no final word, but rather lets the perpetrators cast a shadow on the future of Kashmir. Ironically, like the shaheed, he has gone mute.

But where Mushtaq and Munnu fail as protagonists, they triumph as border witnesses by holding themselves accountable, refusing to end their narratives with misleadingly simplistic closure, to wrap up their individual stories with neat, discrete, happy endings. Both Mushtaq and Sajad admit to their failure to change their environment and conclude by showing their stories subsumed back into the complexities and trauma of the other lives of the warscape. Sajad envisions his own "healing" not as a quick, final culmination but as a long process that starts with self-reflection, which later extends to and involves the whole community; Mushtaq is similarly invested in communal self-examination. If he gradually fades into the background in the final frame of the book, it is because he resists the idea that his story must be the single dominating narrative of the region.

In theorizing border writing, Emily Hicks employs holography as a metaphor to describe the "multilayered semiotic matrix" that undermines cultural hierarchies and disrupts "the one-way flow of information" (xxiv, xxvii).[29] She identifies three common features of border writing: It is "(1) deterritorialized, (2) political, and (3) a product of collective enunciation"

---

29. According to Hicks, "Border writing emphasizes the differences in reference codes between two or more cultures. It depicts, therefore, a kind of realism that approaches the experience of border crossers, those who live in a bilingual, bicultural, biconceptual reality" (xxv).

(12).³⁰ Sajad, Ahmed, and Singh present an alternative to Hick's categories and reimagine border writing as a regionally conceived narrative that is territorialized, depoliticized, and silently, if collaboratively, implied. Clearly, they are skeptical about the general optimism associated with border writing as well as universalizing claims about border crossing as an act of self-affirmation and self-avowal. If the legacy of the border witness is to push back against the certainty of the shaheed by acknowledging the debilitating and harming effects of border crossing, the legacy of border writing promoted by these artists is to rekindle regionalism as a different kind of plurality that can restore Muslim-Hindu relations for a politically viable Kashmir by prioritizing collective healing over "heroic" harming.

---

30. Focusing on Latin American literature, Hicks characterizes border writing as a realist narrative that "re-presents and translates from a multiplicity of perspectives" (8). Similar to Anzaldúa, she proposes to capture the fragmentary nature of reality by crossing borders. She concludes her study by emphasizing repetition and by underscoring the ability to move back and forth: "The destination of the border writer is to cross the border as many times as possible" (123).

CHAPTER 5

Surrogate Witnesses and Memory

The blending of individual and collective memory is a central feature of the testimony offered by border witnesses. This chapter continues to analyze the way this sort of blurring marks the everyday existence of Muslims in contested zones but shifts its focus from the Kashmiri border to the Israeli-Palestinian conflict. This shift is not meant to suggest that the warscape conditions in Kashmir and Palestine are identical or interchangeable. Certainly, the two spaces are politically linked as Muslim spaces under siege and are rhetorically coupled as sites of suffering; as Ather Zia contends, "strong overlaps [between Kashmir and Palestine] exist in having been midwifed by the waning British Empire in 1947, UN intervention and internationalisation, and in their resistance movements constantly battling being subsumed under what the current global politics brands erroneously as 'Islamic terrorism'" (367–68). But it is equally important to recognize the dramatic differences between the two forms of oppression. We may recall Sajad's objections to promoting his work as an extension of the intifada or Arab Spring, asserting that the Kashmiri warscape cannot be portrayed "through a generalizing lens of intifada" (Sajad 334). In this chapter, I connect (rather than conflate) Palestine with Kashmir symbolically as unrelenting warscapes in which necropolitical conditions render Muslims as disposable bodies and tolerable casualties. However, rather than concentrating on the warscape experiences of border subjects, I focus now on the warscape *memories* emanating from and relating to refugee camps—the memories of "stateless" people who are hardly subjects at all.

THE MODERN iteration of the Israeli-Palestinian conflict was sparked by the drawing of borders. The establishment of an independent Israel following the 1947 partition plan and the expulsion of Palestinians to make room for Israeli settlers following the 1948 Nakba (referred to as the "catastrophe") both deepened a long-standing rift between the two communities.[1] Israel's clearing of Palestinian villages, which directly violated the provisions of the Geneva Convention, displaced millions of Palestinians from their homes.[2] Those who remained, writes Cheurfa, faced "the impact of the violent division of the land and [were] subjected to the discriminatory and military machinations of occupation" (362). Israel's resettlement programs in the West Bank and portions of Jerusalem ignited decades of unrest and inspired the First Intifada in 1987. The following year, Yasser Arafat issued the Palestinian Declaration of Independence, at which point Palestine became a de facto sovereign state under an independent administrative body (the Palestinian National Authority)—although it was offered only observer status in the United Nations. Negotiations throughout the 1990s for a two-state solution culminated in the Camp David Summit brokered by Bill Clinton in 2000, which ended without an agreement. That diplomatic collapse led to the Second Intifada, which gradually petered out with Israel's disengagement from Gaza. Today, dozens of refugee camps set up by the United Nations Relief and Works Agency spread across Syria, Jordan, and Lebanon—as well as Gaza and the West Bank—to aid "persons whose normal place of residence was Palestine during the period 1 June 1946 to 15 May 1948, and who lost both home and means of livelihood as a result of the 1948 conflict" (UNRWA). These camps, meant to be temporary settlements, continue to expand as the prospect of a Palestinian "right to return" remains dim.

---

1. Sa'di and Abu-Lughod explain that "for Palestinians, the Nakba was mostly about fear, helplessness, violent uprooting, and humiliation. It embodies the unexpected and unstoppable destruction that left them in disarray, politically, economically, and psychologically" (9).
2. Article 53 of the Convention provides protections for civilian populations in occupied territories: "Any destruction by the Occupying Power of real or personal property belonging individually or collectively to private persons, or to the State, or to other public authorities, or to social or cooperative organizations, is prohibited, except where such destruction is rendered absolutely necessary by military operations" (United Nations).

This chapter focuses on Palestinian refugee camps located in Lebanon, imagining them as extended warscapes created by the Israeli-Palestinian conflict. Pairing Leila Abdelrazaq's *Baddawi* (2015) with Ari Folman's *Waltz with Bashir* (2009), I explore how memory and postmemory contribute to the development of different forms of witnessing and how those modes of witnessing interact with (and often challenge) nationalist propaganda. The coupling of these two memoirs—one a reimagining of the life of a Muslim refugee boy, the other a collection of testimonies collected by a Jewish ex-serviceman—diverges from the strategy of previous chapters, which focused solely on Muslim Comics. I suggest that pairing a Muslim Comic with a non-Muslim one in this specific context offers an opportunity to analyze the representation of Muslim refugees from diverse perspectives and examine how different manifestations of warscape witnessing might complement or contradict each other. In his comparative analysis of historical trauma, Michael Rothberg sees memory as an "ongoing negotiation, cross-referencing, and borrowing" between cultures (7), an interactive involvement with shared experiences. He coins the term "multidirectional memory," which he envisions as a methodological tool to study the history of oppression, occupation, and violence on the global stage (20). My intent is to acknowledge connections and correlations between separate but related narrativizations of memory without erasing the uniqueness of each traumatic event or succumbing to the "contest of comparative victimization" (Rothberg 7).[3] Reading Abdelrazaq in tandem with Folman, I argue, uncovers connections and contradictions that can inspire future dialogue and recognition between Muslim Comics and other traditions and genres.

MEMORY AND POSTMEMORY are at the heart of Abdelrazaq's *Baddawi* as she reconstructs her father's childhood in a northern Lebanon camp—the titular "Baddawi"—in the post-Nakba period. The name of the camp, derived from the word "bedouin" (literally, "nomad"), connects Ahmad to a history

---

3. Multidirectionality reconfigures the relationship between memory and identity in two distinct ways: First, it challenges the belief that memory can only be "competitive," with multiple rival groups antagonistically seeking recognition by erasing others. Rothberg instead treats memory as a multitude of concomitant discourses embedded in the same public sphere. He writes: "Debates about collective memory and group identity are primarily struggles over injustices of recognition, over whose history and culture will be recognized. Such injustices are real, but the rethinking of the relation between memory and identity can contribute to a rethinking of cultural recognition beyond zero-sum logic" (20). Second, rather than drawing a direct link between memory and identity, multidirectionality connects them dialogically, treating history not as a series of isolated events but as interwoven relationships.

of "desert dwellers," comparing that history to his statelessness as a refugee. Ahmad's liminality and marginalization as a displaced subject stranded in a warscape has a direct impact on his ability to construct a sense of self. The father's recollection of his childhood is a way of giving meaning to his precarious existence, while also shedding light on the condition of millions of refugees going through similar experiences. *Waltz with Bashir*, originally an animated film later turned into a graphic memoir, approaches memory more clinically by framing remembering as a form of therapy intended to cure the protagonist's trauma-induced amnesia.[4] Twenty years after his discharge from the Israeli army, Ari Folman reaches out to his friends to record their testimonies about the military operations of the First Lebanon War—a campaign that was initially planned as a quick strike to secure Israel's northern settlements but turned into a three-year occupation (Yosef 311). His excavation of the past, which starts as a personal quest, quickly attains a political tenor and becomes a meditation on the legitimacy of Israeli military campaigns conducted outside its legal borders.

Throughout this chapter, I argue that the yoking of memory with postmemory creates a new witness figure, one I call the "surrogate witness." Unlike the eyewitness, one who directly observes events and speaks up to give evidence, the surrogate witness relies on the testimonies of others to reproduce the past. Abdelrazaq and Folman maintain a distance, acting as surrogate witnesses as they record, document, and recontextualize the past by using various focalization techniques. Yet if lack of access to direct and personal memory separates them from traumatic events, their engagement with postmemory, what Marianne Hirsch defines as transgenerational "acts of transfer," becomes a way that both they and the reader can relive the emotional effects of the original trauma (31). In this way, both creators insert themselves into the graphic narratives—explicitly, as a real character, in the case of Folman, and implicitly, as a veiled character, in the case of Abdelrazaq—to amend the inscription of past and ongoing trauma onto public memory.

Baddawi

Abdelrazaq's *Baddawi*, which initially started as a webcomic series, illustrates her father's childhood memories as a refugee. Like Sajad's *Munnu*, it contains two intertwined narratives: One is a private story that follows

---

4. The film won the 2009 Golden Globe and was nominated for the Best Foreign Language Film category for the Academy Awards.

Ahmad's maturation into adulthood, centering on his life in Baddawi and Beirut and ending with his departure from Lebanon to pursue an education in the US; the other is a general depiction of the Palestinian experience within the necropolitical conditions of warscape. Abdelrazaq frames Ahmad as an emblem of millions of people "born into a life of exile and persecution, indefinitely suspended in statelessness" (12). Thus, the narrative arc quickly shifts from a tight, bildungsromanesque focus on individual hardship to a larger documentation of the loss and suffering of warscape inhabitants with no civil and legal protections. The collaborative enterprise between the father and daughter illustrates the way different forms of witnessing can work together: Young Ahmad is a direct and immediate witness, while the older father is a recollecting (and often hesitant) witness, looking back on his life to speak about his warscape experiences. In addition, Abdelrazaq's subtle interventions throughout the comic position her as a surrogate witness, recording the testimony of her father while tapping into her own postmemory to complement the factual with the emotional.

Ahmad's role as a direct witness is emphasized from the onset: The cover of the comic features him with his back turned to the audience with clasped hands behind him, mirroring Handala, the beloved cartoon figure of a ten-year-old boy created by Naji Al-Ali that became a national Palestinian symbol in the 1970s.[5] The larger-than-life icon of "Palestinian defiance," Handala represents the ultimate witness of a relentless humanitarian crisis. His characteristic pose (with his concealed visage, placed slightly off-center) is meant to be a commentary on the victimization and exile of countless Palestinians.[6] For Joe Sacco, Handala was a symbol of "knowing": "His arms are not by his side as in surprise or shock. They are behind his back, hands together, as if inspecting. [His] stance says, Don't mind me. I'm off to the side. Watching. Recording. And I know exactly what you are doing" (viii). By invoking Handala, Abdelrazaq not only pays homage to Al-Ali but also takes the symbolic baton from him. She states: "Handala is a symbol of the Palestinian refugee child. [. . .] Making that connection to Handala was asserting that this was not just my dad's story, it's also bigger than that. But

---

5. Al-Ali writes: "I drew him as a child who is not beautiful; his hair is like the hair of a hedgehog who uses his thorns as a weapon. Handala is not a fat, happy, relaxed, or pampered child. He is barefooted like the refugee camp children, and he is an icon that protects me from making mistakes. Even though he is rough, he smells of amber. His hands are clasped behind his back as a sign of rejection at a time when solutions are presented to us the American way" (Handala.org).

6. Al-Ali states: "My job was to speak up for the people, my people who are in the camps, in Egypt, in Algeria, the simple Arabs all over the region who have very few outlets to express their points of view" (qtd. in Sacco viii).

I wasn't saying, 'This is the story of every Palestinian.' I wasn't trying to be reductive. I was just trying to emphasize that it's not a standalone story" (Herwees). Abdelrazaq therefore consciously places Ahmad in an ambiguous space: deeply personal and meditative, but part of an artistic oeuvre invested in articulating the Palestinian plight to a global audience.

Despite the strong intertextual connection, however, there are significant differences between Ahmad and Handala in terms of their witnessing: While Handala is the passive observer of momentous events—a voyeur standing apart from the scene—Ahmad epitomizes what Youval Noah Harari calls "flesh witnessing," embodying the kind of witness experiences derived from "sensory miseries" (Harari 235). Harari explains that while eyewitnessing is associated with the objective transmission of facts, flesh witnessing emphasizes the elusively subjective nature of certain kinds of traumatic sensory experiences: "A witness in a murder trial tells what she saw to the judge, and once her story is told, the judge knows everything the witness knows. [. . .] In contrast, a flesh-witness can never really transmit her knowledge to other people—she cannot really describe what she witnessed, and the audience cannot really understand" (7). When Ahmad moves to Beirut with his family, for example, it becomes clear that although he is no longer confined in a refugee camp, he cannot "outrun the war" just by changing his address (Abdelrazaq 101). Indeed, the complex nature of the fighting in divided Beirut—with Phalangist militants attacking Palestinian refugees, or Islamist conservatives threatening Maronite Christians—marks that larger urban space as itself a warscape, one just as potent and ominous as the refugee camp, one where everyday chores can easily turn into life-threatening ordeals. One day, as Ahmad goes grocery shopping, he becomes the target of a random attack. Across a series of mostly silent panels, arranged in a semicircle around the word "BOOM," Abdelrazaq records his narrow escape, not as a calm, objective eyewitness, but as someone who experiences the events in a visceral and physical way. The sequence depicts the different phases of his reaction: He freezes in apprehension; he ducks and yells to warn others; he braces for impact by squatting on the ground, lowering his head, and covering his ears; after the explosion, he cautiously stands up to assess the danger; and finally, he dusts himself off and walks away calmly (111). The scene reveals the primacy of the body in warscape existence: The physical survival instinct pushes reason and reflection aside and automatically performs the appropriate behaviors. As Harari puts it: "When war puts humans to the test, it reveals to them that it is really their material flesh who is in control, rather than their cherished, conscious, mental 'I'" (18). Ahmad's intuitive reaction to random and sudden violence cannot be conveyed effectively through language alone: His instinctive bodily reactions point to the immediate and purely physical existence of the warscape, an existence that lends itself to flesh witnessing.

Acting as a recollecting witness, the older Ahmad does not limit his witnessing to harrowing events only but also includes scenes from everyday refugee life. By weaving the traumatic with the mundane—from the distribution of meager school supplies among students at the beginning of each term to the daily dispensation of "fish oil pills and powdered milk"; from soccer games with other kids on the streets to making za'atar with his mother and neighbors—Ahmad's recollection offers an alternative picture of humble and humdrum existence that complicates academic discussions of the refugee/militarized camp as a permanent state of trauma and exception. Agamben, for example, envisions the camp as a site in which individuals are reduced to bare life, existing outside the civic and political order: "Insofar as its inhabitants were stripped of every political status and wholly reduced to bare life, the camp was [. . .] the most absolute biopolitical space ever to have been realized, in which power confronts nothing but pure life, without any mediation" (*Homo Sacer* 171). In Agamben's view, the state of exception gradually becomes a new normality, where "temporary suspension" turns into "a permanent spatial arrangement," and the everyday only reappears in diminished form, diminished by countless interruptions, from extrajudicial detentions to night raids to state-orchestrated assassinations (*Homo Sacer* 168).[7] While *Baddawi* affirms Agamben's theorization of acclimation to a new arrangement of reality—and even embraces Mbembe's characterization of the necropolitical conditions that transform the camp into a death world—it also offers the alternative and more optimistic notion that the camp can act as an "affective space[ ] of diasporic belonging" where new identities can be forged and old traditions upheld (Banerjee 14).[8] The older Ahmad's emphasis on shared communal rituals is especially profound and illustrates a vision of the camp that deviates from Agamben's ghastly descriptions. It becomes clear, for example, that where law and politics fail, religion takes over, bringing some sense of stability and harmony to a broken population. Ramadan, in particular, gains special significance, becoming a time of self-

---

7. Agamben contends that "in the camp, the state of exception, which was essentially a temporary suspension of the rule of law on the basis of a factual state of danger, is now given a permanent spatial arrangement, which as such nevertheless remains outside the normal order" (*Homo Sacer* 168).

8. The ambivalent depiction of the camp as a site in which "the ordinariness of everyday life [. . .] coexists with the constant presence of danger" attests to the difficulties of navigating the warscape (Banerjee 14).

reflection and unanimity. Ahmad recalls that his "favorite tradition was getting up early to wake up the camp for suhoor along with the other kids in the neighborhood" (Abdelrazaq 36). The panel shows a group of kids roaming the street as they bang on kitchen pots and pans to wake up the neighborhood for the early meal. In this instance, the camaraderie fostered and sustained through Islamic traditions strengthens their sense of Palestinian identity, reminding us that the refugees are not always hollowed out, "abject and disempowered," but are capable of forging social relations and cultural bonds (Banerjee 17).[9] As Banerjee points out, these interactions illustrate a sense of human belonging as well as a sense of being human (as opposed to being reduced to the status of a victim).

Ahmad's witnessing—both as a flesh witness and a recollecting witness—is obviously central to the overall narrative. I argue, however, that the power of witnessing is not restricted to Ahmad: Abdelrazaq inserts herself as a hidden witness of sorts, manipulating the testimonial thrust of the narrative. In embracing the position of a surrogate witness, I further argue, Abdelrazaq interjects herself into Ahmad's testimony to capture what he misses, overlooks, or underemphasizes. If the child protagonist brings a degree of innocence and naiveté to the storyworld, Abdelrazaq ushers in a more mature and somber commentary that contextualizes, reimagines, and reinterprets the young Ahmad's testimony. She achieves this in two ways: First, through focalization ("the filtering of a story through a consciousness prior to and/or embedded within its narratorial mediation"), Abdelrazaq adds her own perspective, using the visual structure of the panel to elaborate and embellish her father's witnessing (Horstkotte and Pedri 330). Second, her proximity to her father as a listener renders her the "co-owner of the traumatic event," allowing her to blend memory with postmemory (Laub 57).[10] In an interview, Abdelrazaq explained that her creative process allowed her to lay claim to her father's trauma: "I was operating with that understanding and my own interruption of [Ahmad's memory], looking at which events am I going to put in and which ones am I going to leave out. [. . .] So even though I don't write myself into the story, I see the graphic novelist as a character in the story" (4). As a surrogate witness, then, Abdel-

---

9. The solidarity of the community becomes more evident when Ahmad's parents move to Beirut, leaving him behind to finish the school year. In the absence of the parents, the community pulls together to help Ahmad: The butcher gives him "kafta" free of charge; his aunt hosts him for dinner regularly; his friend Manal invites him to study while her mother prepares snacks.

10. According to Laub, "The listener [. . .] is party to the creation of knowledge de novo. The testimony to the trauma thus includes its hearer, who is, so to speak, the blank screen on which the event comes to be inscribed for the first time" (57).

razaq is conscious of her arbitration of the narrative and witnessing as an interdependent partnership that extends beyond the roles of flesh witness or recollecting witness. The end result of including various forms of witnessing in a collaborative manner is a narrative bricolage, a multiperspectival patchwork that complicates the representation of warscape existence.

The collaborative aspect of witnessing in *Baddawi* is best exemplified in a chapter titled "The Cluster Bombs." The two parallel, vertically laid-out stories emphasize the complementary nature of the two witnesses (see figure 5.1). In the right-hand column, Ahmad watches the skyline from the rooftop of his apartment, gazing at two fighter jets approaching the camp. The third panel is a close-up of his eyes, highlighting his puzzlement and alarm at the aircraft "flying so low" (62). In the left-hand column is Ahmad's cousin, Zuheir's wife, making bread in her kitchen, ostensibly set apart from the warscape outside and safe in the domestic sphere. Zuheir's wife puts the dough in the oven just as the jets drop their bombs. The reader is told that "the blast sent her headfirst into the oven"—though this moment is not visualized (64). By creating parallel narratives that share "spatiotemporal simultaneity," Abdelrazaq imagines what Ahmad does not see (Cheurfa 374). The reconstructed visualization of the wife's final moments is clearly Abdelrazaq's way of commenting on the retrospective prevalence of danger as the necropolitical conditions of warscape intrude on areas of everyday life that feel safe in the moment, including the domestic sphere. Ahmad wonders how the news will reach their children: "He realized Zuheir's children were not home from school yet. As far as they knew, their mother was still busy baking bread" (64). Dead and alive at once, Zuheir's wife's body represents the simultaneity of incompatible states of existence in camps, where necropolitics "condemns lives to be erased and eradicated," reducing Palestinian civilians to dispensable bodies who can be killed with impunity (Debrix 11).

Abdelrazaq's role as a surrogate witness extends to highlighting particular aspects of Ahmad's testimony to clarify his disorienting experiences with death. Her focus on the precarity of life, for example, leads her to depict Ahmad joining a group of scavengers on the street to collect undetonated bombs in buckets. Here, Ahmad's flesh witnessing—his careful touching and tentative handling of the bombs, feeling their weight—is complemented by Abdelrazaq's surrogate witnessing as she stays in the scene after Ahmad is shooed off by adults fearing he might accidentally set off a bomb. Abdelrazaq adds a panel that depicts an undetonated bomb bearing the inscription "Made in USA" (64). This detail is not a part of Ahmad's recollection, nor is it something anyone else notices while collecting the bombs. Rather, it is a detail imagined and added by Abdelrazaq to illustrate her own criti-

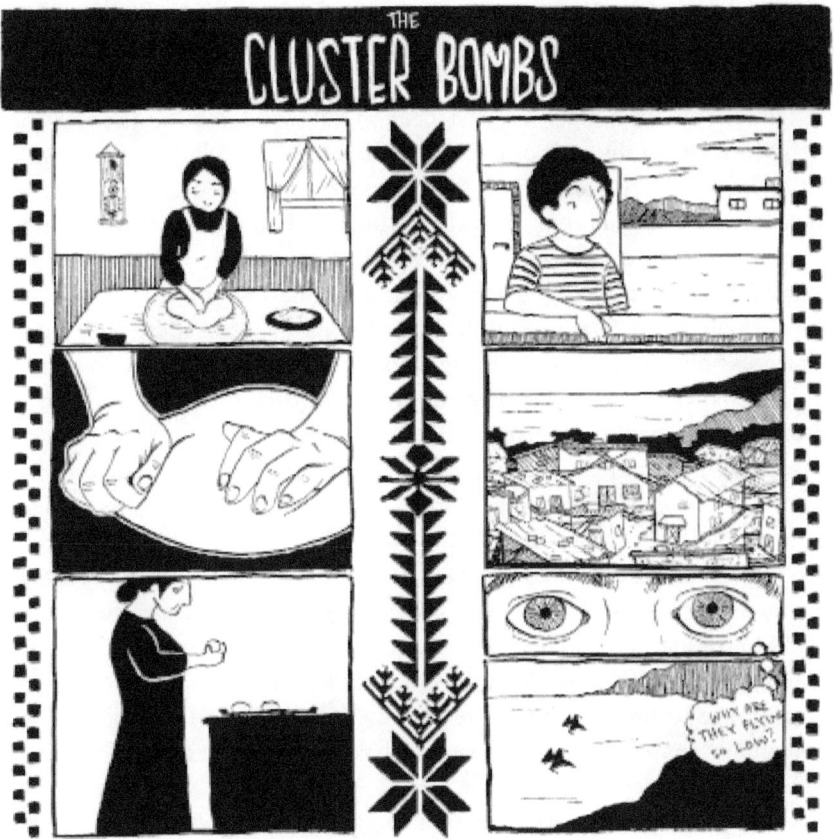

FIGURE 5.1. "The Cluster Bombs" in *Baddawi*.

cism of global weapons trafficking, her introduction of new information and her filtering of that information through her own point of view rather than the character's. Such positioning sets her as a different, active kind of a witness, not merely a stenographer or amanuensis.[11] In this particular instance, her visualization deploys what we might describe as the "lingering gaze," a staying behind to offer visual details that enhance Ahmad's flesh witnessing; the collaborative nature of their narration helps develop a larger framework and critical context for life in the warscape.

---

11. As Uri Margolin explains, "focalization in narrative involves the textual representation of specific (pre)existing sensory elements of the text's story world as perceived and registered (recorded, represented, encoded, modeled and stored) by some mind or recording device which is a member of this world. In other words, focalization involves at least the internal inscription of external data" (42).

Abdelrazaq uses the lingering gaze not only to offer political critique but also to bring out the abnormality of Ahmad's everyday life. In the previously discussed scene in which Ahmad escapes from a street bomb in Beirut, Abdelrazaq shows him leaving the location but moves him off to the side as her gaze shifts to the trail of destruction behind him: While Ahmad walks out of the frame, the reader's eyes are drawn to the blasted windows, collapsed trees, and numerous fires, all of which take up the central space in the panel. By forcing the reader to gaze upon the devastation left behind, and by showing Ahmad walking away from it to continue his day, she stresses the normalization of necropolitical conditions in warscapes, and indeed their occasional invisibility to those who must live among them. In another instance, her lingering gaze becomes a way of diving deeper into history, reaching back in time to provide historical context. For example, she discusses the impact of the Nakba, which happened before Ahmad was born (18). Much later, she references a Phalangist attack on a bus—miles away from Ahmad's dwelling—that left twenty-seven refugees killed and nineteen injured (80). Neither of these events are directly witnessed by Ahmad, but this does not minimize their importance to Abdelrazaq. Indeed, her visual narration here changes from sequential frames to full-page spreads; in making this shift, she freezes time and allows the single large representational image to sink in with the reader. By presenting and expanding these momentary snapshots, Abdelrazaq teaches the reader about the longevity and scale of violence in the region.

Clearly, being a witness without actually witnessing can be knotty, ethically speaking. Hirsch reveals the complicated nature of secondhand witnessing as she asks: "How are we implicated in the aftermath of crimes we did not ourselves witness?" (2).[12] In her view, postmemory provides that

---

12. For some scholars and writers, fictional elements of a testimony greatly compromise the ethos of the speaker; by deviating from facts, the speaker yields to fabrication. Especially in the case of second-generation storytellers, who are temporally and spatially removed from the scene of trauma, the value of their testimony is questioned as they are accused of indulging themselves in "fantasies of witnessing" (Gary Weissman qtd. in Hirsch 20). Others believe that slips and flaws in memory do not impugn the facts; indeed, facts alone without interpretation fail to generate meaning. James E. Young, for one, argues that "once we recognize that the 'facts' of history are not distinct from their reflexive interpretation in narrative, and that the 'facts' of [. . .] their interpretation may even have been fatally interdependent, we are able to look beyond both the facts and the poetics of literary testimony to their consequences" (421). For Hirsch, the question is less about the dilution of facts and more about the way memory can be transferred intergenerationally.

bridge, as it connects generations on the basis of suffering—even when the original affliction no longer exists. She writes:

> "Postmemory" describes the relationship that the "generation after" bears to the personal, collective, and cultural trauma of those who came before—to experiences they "remember" only by means of the stories, images, and behaviors among which they grew up. But these experiences were transmitted to them so deeply and affectively as to seem to constitute memories in their own right. Postmemory's connection to the past is thus actually mediated not by recall but by imaginative investment, projection, and creation. (5)

The "temporal delay" (5) associated with postmemory reveals "an uneasy oscillation between continuity and rupture" (6), making it possible for younger generations to sustain the trauma endured by the older ones. This is precisely where Abdelrazaq's surrogacy becomes more evident: If listening to her father gives her co-ownership of trauma, the intensity of that ownership equips her with postmemory and a means of investing the material scraps of history with emotions. An excellent example of this is the illustration that features Ahmad going to sleep after a deadly Israeli air raid. Ahmad visits his butcher, Abu Muhammad, just before the incident and enjoys the "kafta" sandwich he purchases from him. A few minutes after their interaction, bombs fall, flattening the butcher's shop and taking his life. The documentation of this horrific event is followed by a more surreal illustration of Ahmad; feeling terrified and unsettled, he hides a "knife under his pillow" before going to sleep that night (100). In the full-page spread, he appears motionless in a fetal position, lying down in front of a tank about to flatten a pile of dead bodies (see figure 5.2). Behind the tank is a depiction of a city being bombarded by fighter jets—a city also infiltrated by dark shadows that metamorphose into otherworldly monsters, enveloping Ahmad from the margins of the frame. Marguerite Dabaie explains that the use of silhouettes "serves multiple purposes in the story—to portray anonymity, silence and violence in a non-gratuitous way. The silhouettes are also used to suggest, but never actually show, aggressive forces like the Israeli and Lebanese armies, who are spectral in nature or are only witnessed through the aftermath of their destruction." This complicated focalization helps convey the emotively charged scene in visual terms as Abdelrazaq inserts her own subjective interpretation of Ahmad's experiences—experiences he has described to her but that she is conveying in her own way—and also

FIGURE 5.2. Ahmad has a nightmare.

his dreams, which she can never have witnessed. Her role as a surrogate witness, then, enhances the reader's cognizance of Ahmad's interiority by creating not a factual but an affective image. Her visual coding, blending Ahmad's fear with her own rendition of what his horror may look like, allows her to tap into her postmemory to link his feelings with her own sense of dread.

Waltz with Bashir

Braiding memory with postmemory is equally significant in defining Folman's role as a witness in *Waltz with Bashir*. Clearly, *Waltz with Bashir* is not a Muslim Comic in the technical sense; however, as a visual documentation of the Israel-Palestine conflict, it offers its own insight into the warscape existence of Muslims, complicating both the ethics of seeing and the politics of testifying by presenting a position other than the victim's. Folman's retrospective gaze diverges from Ahmad's nostalgic gaze: Unlike Ahmad, he conveys neither a melancholic longing for home nor an interest in the preservation of a culture under siege. Rather, he is motivated by the desire to cure his trauma-induced amnesia by collecting testimonies about the Phalangist attack in refugee camps during the First Lebanon War. Two decades after his discharge from the Israel Defense Forces (IDF), Folman's missing memories surface in the form of vague images and nebulous dreams triggered by his meeting with a fellow soldier, Boaz. Folman reveals: "For the first time, after more than 20 years, I had a terrible flashback from the war in Lebanon. Not just Lebanon, but West-Beirut; and not just West-Beirut but from the massacre in Sabra and Shatila refugee camps" (10–12). This incentive sends him on a fact-finding mission, impelled in part by a yearning for self-discovery and in part by the desire to amend propaganda-saturated public memory.

Unlike Abdelrazaq's relatively subtle insertion of her creator/illustrator self into the narrative, Folman places himself center stage: Younger Ari appears as the subaltern IDF soldier, older Ari is the inquisitive investigator, and Folman the creator is the arbitrator who reproduces the collected testimonies in his storyworld. This wide range of self-representation not only blurs the boundary between the subject and the object of investigation but also points to a messy entanglement of perspectives. Additionally, Folman's self-referential narrative raises questions about the ethos of the speaker. His vantage point, as someone participating in the victimization of refugees, complicates his moral standing. As Ari's investigation gradually reveals, he and his regiment were charged with shooting flares in the sky "a hundred yards away from the massacre" to provide light for the Phalangists in their mission to avenge Bashir Gemayel's assassination (Folman 8). Critics have reacted to Folman's involvement in the very acts he criticizes in various ways. According to Shmulik Duvdevani and Raz Yosef, Folman's complicity as a soldier following orders during the massacre impacts his credibility; they contend that the "narrowing of perspective" between Folman the creator and Folman the protagonist operates as "a narrative and ideological device that is meant to portray the Israeli soldier as victim, thus removing any accountability of the national apparatus which he serves" (202). Such positioning, they maintain, essentially negates the text's potential to recuperate the victim's voice and capture the true extent of human suffering

(201). In contrast, Claire Launchbury regards Folman's ambiguous witness status as a commentary on the nebulous nature of testifying: "Testimonial perspectives are negotiated by witnesses who are simultaneously (if sometimes passively) perpetrators, victims, and bystanders" (195). She coins the term "disavowed witness-perpetrator" to describe Folman's vexed position:

> It is precisely this confusion of conflicting witnessing positions created by the separation of conscripted duty and its subsequent actions and individual trauma which lies at the root of the crisis of memory that Folman's work tries to expose. Such a crisis is signaled through the attempt the project makes to search for both personal responsibility—it is Folman's autobiographical quest in one sense—and confronting contentious collective responsibility by positioning the exposition of recovering memory in the public arena. (195)

My own position is closer to Launchbury's. Folman is clearly conscious of his own role in a larger injustice, but he is also clear that he and his fellow soldiers did not possess the wider view that would have allowed them to witness their actions in proper moral context; furthermore, he is also alert to the idea that the horror of the events in which he is engaged interferes with his ability to recollect them in a neutral and objective way. While it would be shortsighted to equate Ahmad's position as a displaced Palestinian with Folman's experiences as an IDF soldier, they can still be understood as characters whose interests in bearing witness are complicated by trauma—regardless of the differences in scale and intensity.[13]

To his credit, rather than collapsing witnessing positions, Folman keeps them neatly separated as a way to assert his credibility; in doing so, he also delays his witnessing. The three iterations of Folman throughout the narrative illustrate the inadequacy of each subject position, and it ultimately becomes clear that the crisis of fragmentation can only be resolved through

---

13. Dominic LaCapra discusses the dangers of conflating these categories:

> The distinction between victims, perpetrators, and bystanders is crucial. "Victim" is not a psychological category. It is, in variable ways, a social, political and ethical category. Victims of certain events will in all likelihood be traumatized by them, and not being traumatized would itself call for explanation. But not everyone traumatized by events is a victim. There is the possibility of perpetrator trauma which must itself be acknowledged and in some sense worked through if perpetrators are to distance themselves from an earlier implication in deadly ideologies and practices. Such trauma does not, however, entail the equation or identification of the perpetrator and the victim. (723)

a collaborative effort. For example, while younger Ari is the flesh witness, directly experiencing the "sensory miseries" of war, his exposure to trauma impairs his ability to contextualize or morally evaluate his own actions. Older Ari, experiencing amnesia, is unable to recall his role in the massacres with precision. At one point he asks: "Is it possible that I evacuated some of your guys?"; in another exchange, Ari asks outright: "Was I there?" (57). The inability to locate himself is indicative of self-estrangement; looking at a picture of himself as a young soldier, he pleads: "Do you recognize me here? [. . .] I don't recognize myself either" (34). Only as he reminisces with his friends can he start piecing together the past, creating what Launchbury describes as a "polyphony of witnessing positions" (194). As he forages for information from friends, reporters, and trauma experts, he carefully and dutifully assembles a web of testimonies—even if that means discovering "things about [himself] that [he does] not want to know" (Folman 17). His deferred witnessing gradually comes to fruition as he puts together a subjective narrative intended to account for his actions—without presuming to speak for the victims.[14] His silence—what some critics view as a failure to create space for direct testimony from Palestinians—signals a restrained approach to witnessing that acknowledges and engages with the speaker's limited capacity to capture the horror. Here, we see how "first-degree source memories, which serve as a trigger or as 'indexical' raw material, converge with second or third-degree narrative practices that incorporate autobiographical affects or drives" (Fajardo and Laffond 65).

Thus, surrogate witnessing becomes a way to avoid the endless deferring of bearing witness. As a surrogate witness, Folman (the older creator) records and contextualizes what Ari (the young character) cannot remember and articulate on his own. This collaborative effort is similar to that seen in *Baddawi*; as with Abdelrazaq, Folman catalyzes the testimonies of others and inserts his own perspective, through various visual tactics. His ambivalent position—simultaneously visible and invisible, present and absent, forgetful and mindful, informative and critical—paves the way for a polyphony of testimonies. And, again similarly to Abdelrazaq, his surrogacy allows him to manipulate various points of view through "variable focalization"

---

14. Many critics question Folman's presentation of Palestinian characters as props, reduced to lifeless bodies or stereotypical aggressors. Similarly, his depiction of Lebanon as an unstable warscape has been viewed as a justification of the Israeli intervention. Duvdevani and Yosef contend that "Folman could have traced Palestinian witnesses to the massacre, those whose family members and relatives have been murdered, or they themselves saved from the mass killing, so that they will testify in their own words to the tragedy" (203). In a similar vein, they argue that Lebanon "has no function other than to serve the tormented Zionist soul, nor does it have any history of its own" (199).

(accessing the perception of a number of characters) as well as "internal ocularization" (shifting directly to the character's visual field) that create a "perspectival mismatch."[15] As the surrogate witness Folman illustrates Ari's flesh witnessing, he uses various focalization tactics to recreate Ari's memory. For example, Folman illustrates a memory from a time when he and his men were ordered to "load up the dead and the wounded on [his] vehicle and dump them" (30). Stunned by the command, Ari sheepishly asks where he should go. The response: "Look for a bright light. That's where they usually dump the bodies" (12). Ari complies, but Folman intervenes in a voice-over to explain and emphasize the confusion and horror of the experience: "Me, who in my whole life has hardly seen a drop of blood, let alone an open wound, suddenly I'm commanding an APC full of injured soldiers and dead men, looking for a bright light" (31). When Ari's men ask what they should do, a farcical exchange takes place:

ARI: Shoot.
SOLDIER: At what?
ARI: I don't know. Just shoot.
SOLDIER: Isn't it better to pray?
ARI: You can shoot and pray. (31)

The last frame on the page shows the company's tank in the thick of night, as the soldiers shoot aimlessly into the dark. As a surrogate witness, Folman is able to capture and comment upon both the futility and the absurdity of the situation, in a way that those who actually experienced it could not.

Folman also uses abrupt perspectival shifts in his recounting of the past, adopting several different ocularizing positions throughout the narrative. For instance, when older Ari finds out from his friend, Frenkel, that he had been part of a group deployed to "go hunt for terrorists" in the countryside, a flashback shows a group of Israeli soldiers including the younger Ari and Frenkel combing the terrain (53). As they walk silently, a silhouette of a combatant carrying an RPG appears. Hiding among the trees, a young Palestinian fighter steals quietly toward the Israelis and aims his weapon at the tank behind them. The reader sees the rocket leaving the nuzzle (pointed straight at them, as if the reader were being attacked); a close-up of the warhead is featured in the next panel, dwarfing other objects (see figure 5.3). The explosion sends the soldiers to the ground; they start shooting even though they

---

15. According to Pedri, especially in memoirs, "visuals are for the most part externally ocularized (i.e., they show the focalizing character from outside), [but] they are also oftentimes internally focalized (i.e., they betray what the character feels)" (11).

FIGURE 5.3. A Palestinian boy opens fire.

cannot identify a specific target. The flashback concludes with Frenkel being alerted by another soldier about the boy getting ready to launch another rocket. Frenkel fires at him. This panel is now flipped around, perspective-wise, arranged so that the reader is put in the position of the Palestinian boy, directly facing Frenkel's bullets; the last panel of the flashback depicts the bloodstained corpse of the young boy lying on the ground (57). There is hardly any commentary, hardly any verbal description, no voice-over to make sense of the events; that is to say, if Folman is guilty of silencing the Palestinian boy, it is part of a general silencing strategy that also includes the Israeli soldiers. What commentary we do get comes through the visuals, which emphasize the fluidity of the victim/perpetrator in warscapes. The Palestinian boy simultaneously occupies both positions—Folman neither vilifies nor apologizes for him. More importantly, his use of the ocularized panels, where "the framing may correspond exactly to what can be seen by a character," is clearly meant to put the reader in the position of the seeing subject (A. Miller 91). Switching the gaze of the seeing subject—first presenting the Israeli soldier's perspective as the boy fires the rocket, and then placing the reader in the position of the Palestinian boy as Frenkel discharges his machine gun—allows Folman to create the sense of an imminent threat in both directions and reinforces the text's focus on the inescapable necropolitical conditions of the warscape.

Through his use of ocularization, Folman continues to manipulate the reader's perspective. In a separate interview with Dror Harazi, also a war veteran, Folman finally gets an accurate account of the Phalangist forces raiding the refugee camps. The night-long attack ends in the morning with refugees forced into trucks as bulldozers move in. When Folman asks Harazi whether he suspected this was a prelude to a massacre, he replies: "Yes, of course. But that only happened at the point when my men said 'we saw it'" (99). Observing the scene from the top of a tank, the Israeli soldiers look

FIGURE 5.4. Israeli soldiers surveil the scene from afar with binoculars.

through binoculars to witness two Phalangists lining up a group of civilians, including women and children, in front of a wall (see figure 5.4). The next panel, also drawn as if looking through binoculars, shows the two Phalangists with their weapons directed at the people as dead bodies pile on top of each other. This kind of "seeing," having the reader become one with the witness by placing him or her directly behind the binoculars, emphasizes the complexity of the witnessing at work: The soldier is the direct witness, who sees and speaks about the horror unfolding before his eyes, but he is also the bystander witness, not only because he is physically removed from the actual atrocities and visually separated from them with binoculars, but also because his subaltern position in the army does not allow him to intervene. The reader, too, is implicated: The act of reading is both an exposure to and an acknowledgment of the trauma but also a passive and ultimately voyeuristic processing of events. Ironically, only Folman (the creator), the surrogate witness with hindsight, is able to interject himself into the events themselves with a critical gaze.

Perhaps the most agonizing moment of Folman's surrogate witnessing comes when he visualizes Ron Ben-Yisha's account of the "final day of the massacre" in Sabra and Shatilla (108). In this sequence, Folman sustains the "perspectival mismatch" established earlier: Some panels are externally ocularized (showing Ben-Yisha from outside as he moves along the camp); in others, he remains the focalizing character, allowing the reader to see what he sees. Folman's reproduction of Ben-Yisha's memories resembles a series of snapshots rather than a flowing, uninterrupted sequence of actions. He first observes a group of refugees walking out of the camp with their hands in the air—a scene he compares to a famous photograph of the Warsaw ghetto that shows a boy with his hands up followed by a "long train of women, old people and children" (108). But once Brigadier Amos shows up to order a cease-fire, telling the refugees to return to their homes, they turn around limply, almost lifelessly. Ben-Yisha's team follows the crowd into the camp, now mostly reduced to "a huge amount of rubble" (110). The aerial perspective, showing the refugees staggering back into the camp under the watch of a tank, suggests stupor and exhaustion: The silhouettes of the survivors convey the numbed, hollowed-out existence of a death world rather than brave persistence. Indeed, as Ben-Yisha drifts among the rubble, he sees "a small hand [. . .] sticking out of the rubble" with a "curly head covered with dust" (111). The next panel is a close-up of the lifeless body of the young victim: "My daughter was about the same age as that girl. She had curly hair, too" (111). As Ben-Yisha continues to walk through the houses into open courtyards, he sees piles of dead bodies. The sparse narration enhances the stillness and horror of the images, as does Folman's use of chiaroscuro, creating a contrast between the dark surrounding and the rays of light that reveal the dead bodies. Ben-Yisha's final words encapsulate the unavoidable reality of the necropolitical trap: "And then it came over me: what I was looking at was a massacre" (113).

Similar to Abdelrazaq's, Folman's witnessing blends memory with postmemory; as Ori explains, Ari's various acts of witnessing connect with and trigger trauma inherited from his parents, who are Holocaust survivors: "For you, the significance of the massacre was set long before the actual event. It comes from a different massacre. It's about what happened in the other camps, those camps" (91). Ori helps Folman process trauma not as an isolated incident but as something occurring within a larger historical frame of reference. Postmemory received from his parents, in other words, becomes the lens through which to process his own traumatic memory of his military engagement; in this regard, the massacres in Beirut "exist in an awkward constellation of identity formation" (Launchbury 200).[16] Such historical reference is not a welcome inclusion for Duvdevani and Yosef, who argue that the allusion to the Holocaust diminishes the Palestinian plight, in that the "interest in Palestinian victimhood is possible only through its linkage to Jewish victimhood" (203–04). But Folman does not engage with postmemory simply to create a hierarchy of victimization; he does it to offer a dialogic vision of history, to demonstrate the commonality and cyclic repetition of "human-perpetrated horrors" (Rothberg 6). In one section, he interrupts the plot to introduce a story he heard from his father about World War II. The black-and-white representation of the anecdote, depicting a group of Russian soldiers coming home to see their loved ones at the train station only to turn around and immediately return to the battlefields, is meant to evoke the Israeli military's investment in a similar system of permanent war. In this way, Folman contextualizes human suffering as a common condition of war zones and warscapes across time and space, locating trauma as a transgenerational injury.

The repetitive cycle of violence is reiterated at the end of the book, as the comic ends with a re-creation of Folman's recurrent dream/flashback. Ari sees himself walking toward a group of wailing women, throwing their hands in the air, pleading with God, pain written all over their faces. In this series of silent panels, the facial expressions—conveying anguish and loss—reflect the everlasting effects of trauma for survivors. The last illustration of the comic focuses on Folman's face, his eyes directly gazing at the reader, almost expressionless, as if he is sleepwalking. This final emphasis on himself is a sort of reckoning about his deferred position as a witness. He keeps his eyes open—as if to say that he is trying, or at least willing, to see and

---

16. In a similar fashion, Claire Launchbury argues that "while Folman overtly acknowledges his descent from parents who had survived the camps, the inclusion of this fact in a film that seeks to use personal narratives as mediating collective ones legitimizes, in my view, Laub's concept in relation to a complex confrontation between the concentrationary trope of conscription and perpetration and the function of intergenerational Holocaust memory" (200).

take responsibility for his past. He is both part of the trauma he witnessed (as someone who feels its heavy burden), but also outside of its most direct effects. This is the last illustration in the book—though not the last image: The four photographs included at the end of the comic officially validate the account of the massacre and bring the book into the world of reality. Both in the film and the book, Folman makes a conscious decision to give the last word to a Palestinian survivor: an old woman, moaning with her eyes closed, as her hands rest on her face, who becomes the embodied representation of pain and loss. Duvdevani and Yosef see the ending as a kind of abdication, arguing that Folman "does not take accountability. He does not address the victims, through their families, and ask for forgiveness. To be exact, he doesn't speak at all" (203). I find not a lack of agency in Folman's silence but a recognition of the limits of agency. It is a gesture toward the inadequacy of language. He simply lets the images do the talking.

Surrogacy and the Aesthetics of Violence

Throughout this book, I have considered Muslim Comics as an emerging genre made up of diverse texts linked by various common interests (a focus on the everyday, a move away from traditional stereotyping, an emphasis on bearing witness, etc.). As we begin to draw to a close, it is perhaps worth pointing out that these common interests can be and generally are pursued according to very different visual strategies. Muslim Comics do not share a visual grammar. Said argues that remembering "raise[s] the question not only of what is remembered but how and in what form. It is an issue about the very fraught nature of representation, not just about content" ("Invention" 176). *How* the surrogate witness remembers and represents violence is an important issue in these comics. Abdelrazaq and Folman in particular make strikingly different aesthetic choices in terms of how to depict the necropolitical conditions of warscape. We might recall that the tombstone was the dominant motif in *Munnu*, a blunt image conveying not just the precarity of warscape borderland existence, but the monolithic silence of the dead recruits. For Abdelrazaq, too, loss and destruction are conveyed through absence. Going back to the "Cluster Bombs" chapter, for example, we note that she represents Zuhair's wife's death by way of suggestion: In one frame, we see the silhouette of her putting bread in the oven; in the following frame, we see jets dropping bombs. The reader is able to make the logical connection between the two frames without Abdelrazaq having to show it. The news of the butcher's death is also divulged indirectly: Onlookers beside the debris inform Ahmad of the man's fate; there is no direct view of a corpse or any funeral scene. In other instances, Abdelrazaq manipulates time by superimposing different time frames onto a single panel—a tactic that not only strengthens her position as a surrogate witness but also lets her avoid offering a realistic depiction of death. In these panels, Ahmad occupies one temporality while Abdelrazaq "interrupts" the scene to reproduce a past incident that Ahmad did not witness directly. For example, in the aftermath of the Israeli and Lebanese armies raiding the camp, Ahmad and his friends retrace the steps of the intruders: The children look in on a raided apartment and run down the street where militant and civilian Palestinians were killed indiscriminately. Abdelrazaq compresses time in these panels by sketching two timelines: The realistic representation of the present is overlaid with more abstract and symbolic silhouettes of victims and the perpetrators from the previous night (41). The black figures representing the army are designated by the machine guns they hold as extensions of their bodies, while the victims, shown with their hands up, are covered with multiple bullet holes. Abdelrazaq repeats this temporal and visual maneuver in other episodes: When Ahmad is delivering groceries, he sneaks into a "deserted and unlocked building" that has been raided by the army. Looking at the bullet holes and bloodstains, he speculates about the violence that had taken place. Abdelrazaq complements his inference by drawing white silhouettes of victims with dark bullet holes (74). The image of the perforated body comes to represent a visual map of violence, but the abstraction of violence also draws attention to the absence of victims.

Such a strategy serves a variety of purposes: First, the abstract simulation of violence anonymizes the victims and perpetrators just enough to protect Abdelrazaq from historical inaccuracy; she captures the general effect of violence inscribed on the bodies without having to individualize the victims. This also connects neatly with the thematic anonymity of Palestinian victims in the comic book: They remain faceless casualties of the warscape. Second, this tactic allows Abdelrazaq to release Ahmad from the burden of representation—since Ahmad is not a direct eyewitness or a flesh witness, it is Abdelrazaq who assumes the role of recording the traumatic events in her capacity as the surrogate witness. The abstraction of death is also consistent with a child's naiveté: The fact that children do not appear to be especially or permanently bothered by the horrific onslaught, that they do not see it as particularly "real," is a reminder of the normalization of death in refugee camps. Finally, the absence of actual dead bodies reveals a refusal to turn death into a spectacle and to inadvertently contribute to "the deadening of feeling" that cultural representations of warscape can create (Sontag 106).[17] In this way, Abdelrazaq's avoids turning the deceased into commodities to profit from—a concern that Spiegelman admitted to while writing *Maus*.

Unlike Abdelrazaq, Folman does not shy away from depicting death in a realistic manner: His journalistic gaze becomes a form of reportage. Carmi, for example, recalls an assault on a fast-moving car during a night raid. He remembers "shooting like maniacs," motivated by "pressure and fear": "There's nothing but uncontrollable fear. And then silence, the horrific silence of death. When it's fully light, you see the havoc you've caused" (25). In the morning, they find the car covered with bullet holes, dead bodies hanging from the open driver's-side door, and slumped cadavers in the back seat with their heads tilted unnaturally behind the broken windows. Carmi bluntly declares: "And lying in the car . . . are the bodies of a family" (25). Elsewhere, as we discussed, Folman concludes Frenkel's recollection of the assault by a young Palestinian boy with a vivid illustration of the boy's lifeless body, a few inches from his weapon, with red blood oozing from his wounds. The placement of the body at the center of the panel participates in what Allen Feldman has called the "trauma-aesthetic," "a visual genealogy of witnessing and testimony-giving that sorts victim and witness into positions of hierarchical observation, compulsory visibility, and non-reciprocal appropriation of the body in pain" (186). Folman's visual documentation is accompanied by a simple caption that states, "He was a young boy": The stark contrast between the rhetorical construction of the perpetrator's youth and the stylized realism of the dead body reasserts the idea of the camp as death world. His normalization of death is consistent with the attitudes of warscape constituents, who live with violence on a day-to-day basis, "a perennial source of inner torment" (Sontag 96).

Folman's investment in realism reaches its apogee in the comic's photographic conclusion. On the one hand, Folman's desire to give the last word to photographs might be a way for him to acknowledge the limit of comics—suggesting that comics can go only so far in capturing the topography

---

17. Brad Evans and Henry A. Giroux argue that

> the spectacle of violence represents more than the public enactment and witnessing of human violation. It points to a highly mediated regime of suffering and misery, which brings together the discursive and the aesthetic such that the performative nature of the imagery functions in a politically contrived way. In the process of occluding and depoliticizing complex narratives of any given situation, it assaults our senses in order to hide things in plain sight. (32)

of warscape. In his discussion of the animated version of *Waltz with Bashir*, Yosef alludes to a pivotal exchange between Ari and Carmi; when Ari asks whether he can draw Carmi, Carmi responds: "As long as you only draw me and don't photograph, it's OK." Yosef contends that

> the film sees the photographic image, in contrast to animation, as overly threatening and as dangerously close to the reality that Carmi is struggling, or refusing, to remember. Only at the end of the film, after Folman's deferred acknowledgment of his memory of the massacre, does an archival photographic documentary sequence of events at Sabra and Shatila appear on the screen. This footage exposes us to shocking images of the slaughtered bodies of Palestinian men, women and children. The documentary footage represents Folman's repressed memory. In contrast to the iconic animation, the photographic archival sequence is an indexical sign—that is, a sign that results from a causal relation with the object in reality. (321–22)

Donato Loia draws on another exchange between Folman and Zahava Solomon in which they talk about an amateur photographer's habit of seeing the harrowing images around him as if viewing them through an "imaginary camera" and approve of this as a kind of coping mechanism. Loia argues that "Solomon and the movie itself testify that a representative apparatus, such as an 'imaginary camera,' can shield a subject from a traumatic experience" (96). At the same time, as Susan Sontag suggests, while photography "implies instant access to the real," in actuality "the results of this practice of instant access are another way of creating distance. To possess the world in the form of images is, precisely, to reexperience the unreality and remoteness of the real" (164). I argue that Folman's decision to end with photographic evidence—realistic images that convey impersonal, objective facts in a detached fashion—is consistent with his desire to create a counter-archive. This is not an admission of failure but a reinforcement of the visual aesthetics employed throughout the graphic narrative, his final acknowledgment of his (as well as our) distance along with our ability to feel empathy.

GIVEN THE CONSPICUOUS DIFFERENCE between the two comics' visual palettes, and indeed between their creators' general political positions and priorities, we might finally ask why both choose to focus on the idea of surrogate witnessing. Why is the surrogate witness important? The surrogate witness has the license to substitute, embellish, and reenact the past by tapping into his or her postmemory. Unlike the border witness, who is invested in an inward journey, the surrogate witness starts his or her reinscription of memory externally by leaning on the testimony of others. Both Mushtaq and Sajad, we recall, shed light on the contested border region by centering on their own personal stories. In contrast, the surrogate witness starts in the void, in an absence of memory, and reaches out to other sources to reconstruct the past; postmemory becomes one tool to help in this reconstruction, a way of connecting with generational experiences to contextualize the present self. Memory and postmemory blend what is present and knowable with what is absent or elusive to create a usable past.

Despite their investment in memory, both Abdelrazaq's and Folman's projects are also forward-looking, creating counter-histories that attend to the absence, silence, and erasure of victims. For them, storytelling is a form of activism, a way to employ the past to inform the future. *Waltz with Bashir*'s subversive tone can be attributed to the "memory law" passed by the Israeli legislature, in which strict restrictions were placed on the presentation and interpretation of history. This restrictive decree was intended to control the circulation of information in the public domain and regulate the tenor of public debates:

> By classifying certain interpretations of the past as deviant and stigmatizing, regulating and punishing the groups that express them, memory laws exert social control. [. . .] We call these forms of social control "forced forgetting" and the "balancing of atrocities." The first form makes official the memory of one group in order to actively exclude other groups' memories from public debate on their shared past. The second creates analogies that equate victim groups, pitting the suffering of one group against the suffering of another for the purpose of dismissing the former group's claims for recognition and redress. (Gutman and Tirosh 705–06)

Folman's retrospective reconstruction of the past is a highly political one that attempts to connect memory with nationalism in a nonpropagandist way: By documenting his own complicity in the Palestinian massacres, he holds his superiors in the Israeli state accountable.[18] For this reason, Folman's intended audience, similar to Sajad's, is his fellow Israelis first and

---

18. Matt Reingold observes that the First Lebanon War "marked the first time in Israel's history in which many Israeli citizens believed that their country engaged in an unnecessary war and one in which it played the role of aggressor, as opposed to the role of defender" (324).

foremost.[19] Folman's reclamation of memory as a surrogate witness thus represents an interventionist stance against the state-imposed demand for forgetting and a plea for national remembering and self-reflection.

If *Waltz with Bashir* speaks directly to the national audience, *Baddawi* identifies the Palestinian diaspora as an important constituent tasked with the preservation of Palestinian culture away from home. To this end, Abdelrazaq complements her surrogacy by creating a visual grammar that emphasizes Palestinian identity throughout the comic in the form of *tatreez*—a regionally popular pattern of cross-stich embroidery, aiming to ground the reader within a visual coding of Palestinian culture. The panels, gutters, and grids are laden with motifs, functioning as a "language native to the community" (Priyadarshini and Sigroha 414). One could even frame Ahmad's story as "a tatreez in itself, an intricate and personalized pattern of home and memory in the face of displacement and forgetting: a textured document of survival" (Mangles). Such visual components reinforce the idea of a stateless people, seeking to safeguard their regional roots by sustaining traditions. Abdelrazaq is able to fill that gap. In this way, she similarly pushes for an "activist and interventionist" platform from which to address the Palestinian plight (Hirsch 6).

Reading Abdelrazaq side by side with Folman allows for a dialogic, humanistic inquiry into questions of memory, into how memories can be used to construct and preserve home—even in the aftermath of displacement, dispossession, and disavowal. As surrogate witnesses, Abdelrazaq and Folman complement each other's perspective, creating a complex web of testimonies. The way they weave the personal together with the political in their representations of warscape echoes the narrative techniques utilized by other Muslim Comics creators in previous chapters. Compared to the Kashmiri border witnesses who express dread over the future, however, the surrogate witnesses here convey a cautious sense of optimism—not because the experiences of Muslims in refugee camps are less horrific but because there is a belief that the ongoing trauma can usher in a sense of activism that might change the rhetoric about the refugee Other. At the same time, both *Baddawi* and *Waltz with Bashir* can be viewed as a commentary on the notion of the homeland: Abdelrazaq, despite her desire to emphasize human connection and belonging as part of camp life, does not surrender to nostalgia for warscape existence; Folman is also guarded in his treatment of national

---

19. Comparing *Waltz with Bashir* with Galit and Gilad Seliktar's "Houses," Reingold argues that "these two works are designed by Israelis and for Israelis, and present a portrait of the Israeli soldier in his or her most vulnerable and weak way as either a perpetrator or bystander to excessive violence towards Palestinians" (327).

belonging and does not shy away from overtly criticizing the state to offset nationalistic propaganda. In this sense, both comics creators echo each other in their creation of forward-looking eulogies for lost, unrecoverable homes subsumed by an ominous, unrelenting warscape. In their eulogy, I argue, is a shared enthusiasm for "new forms of solidarity and new visions of justice" (Rothberg 5).

CONCLUSION

The Future of Muslim Comics

The comic book series *The Boys,* by Garth Ennis and Darick Robertson, features a memorable flashback in which we see a group of superheroes ("The Seven") attempt and fail to rescue a hijacked plane. The hijackers themselves appear in one panel, but they do not speak before they are killed by Homelander, the leader of The Seven. They are the only Muslim characters in the series. In the TV adaptation of *The Boys,* several speaking Muslim characters are introduced, mainly villains (including the hijackers in the heavily altered plane scene), but also one hero: Silver Kincaid, the self-described "first superhero in a hijab" (the character exists in the comic but is not a Muslim). Kincaid is a finalist in a reality show designed to choose the next member of The Seven, and the superhero judge of the competition, Starlight, advocates for her, calling Kincaid "the most qualified" superhero candidate. It feels like progress, an evolution away from the traditional trope of the silent Muslim jihadi to an articulate, qualified, admirable Muslim superhero. But any hopes one might have for Kincaid are quickly checked when the producers of the competition express nervousness about her background ("She's from Afghanistan," objects one producer, about the English-born Kincaid) and, later, when the tyrannical Homelander overrules her as a potential winner of the competition: "Do you really think I'm going to let a fucking Muslim in The Seven? Captain Al Qaeda? We're Americans!" *The Boys* effectively parodies the push for inclusivity within the comics industry, along with, in language that echoes some of the backlash against new superheroes like Ms. Marvel, the hostility toward that new inclusivity from many comics readers.

So what is the future for Muslim Comics and their attempt to foreground Muslim experiences that move beyond the familiar, two-dimensional depictions of faith-based subjectivities? On the most basic level, Muslim Comics will continue to fight against the deep-seated stereotypes ("Captain Al Qaeda") that still echo throughout the industry and cause a certain number of readers to resist more human and complex Muslim characters. Speaking more generally of Muslim writing, Laila Lalami argues that undoing Islamophobic clichés is an ongoing battle: "To write from the point of view of a Muslim character at this particular moment in history is in some sense to be at war constantly. [. . .] The Muslim writer, perhaps more than another writer, is at war with cliché, perpetually in search of what Martin Amis called 'freshness, energy and reverberation of voice'" (147–48).

Combating clichés is and will continue to be at the heart of Muslim Comics for the immediate future as they create complex, credible, and forward-thinking Muslim characters that resist the homogenization of this faith group. This is why, while they continue to attend to questions of violence, conflict, and unrest, they keep shifting the focus from the predictable Muslim perpetrator (defined by unvarying fanaticism and inevitable extremism) to the disaffected and uncertain Muslim situated in unstable warscapes—spaces of sporadic violence that shape the everyday lives of their inhabitants in unpredictable ways. The shift to warscapes has brought and will continue to bring with it a move away from another stereotype: the tongue-tied Muslim, only acting and never conversing in any genuine way (the unspeaking hijackers in *The Boys* are a classic example—what would such clichéd characters even have to say, if they did talk?). In Muslim Comics set in warscapes, silent characters are replaced by witnesses. Warscape witnessing documents the trauma of everyday existence without reducing the Muslim to a victim. By testifying to the physical and emotional anguish of the vulnerable, Muslim warscape comics explore how witnessing can offer ways to write absence into presence and erasure into resilience. And while witnessing itself may look different in each comic—ranging from legitimate to illegitimate, secular to religious, public to private—the motivation behind testimony remains the same: Speaking up becomes a way of showing resistance to oppressive power structures, opposing the traction of warscape conditions, and asserting one's right to exist as a human being in a space where the Muslim has become a disposable object. In effect, the testimonial arc of Muslim Comics reinforces the humanization of this faith group and empowers the Muslim as a free and autonomous agent (as opposed to the brainwashed, self-sacrificing radical).

Perhaps the ideal outcome of Muslim Comics (as well as a study such as this) is the normalization of Muslim subjectivities to such an extent that this oeuvre of comics ceases to exist as an oppositional, interventionist category. However, that endpoint is still far from reach—there are a great many Homelanders out there, and persistent xenophobia, fearmongering, and anti-immigrant rhetoric continues to sustain the us/them binary. I started this book with a close examination of the US comics market; let me end on a similar note as I speculate on the possible future of Muslim Comics. As this book has shown, a substantial number of Muslim Comics are set in warscapes—a setting that presumably comes across as exotic and unfamiliar to the American audience. But what if the focus on warscape turns out to be a prescient one for American readers? The political climate in the US has shown an uptick in domestic extremism—from the Unite the Right violence to the January 6 insurrection to the mass shooting in Buffalo to the thwarted plot of the Proud Boys targeting an LGBTQ parade in Idaho—and the deepening of racial and ideological rifts within the US society points to the fact that warscape is increasingly not something that exists elsewhere but an environment that can materialize anywhere, unexpectedly. What if, ironically, Muslim Comics begin to be read as a warning of what could happen here, or as an example of resistance? During the Trump presidency, for example, images of Muslims began to appear at anti-Trump rallies (most notably, perhaps, a poster of Munira Ahmed, a Bangladeshi American with a veil made of stripes and stars, with the slogan, "We the people are greater than fear" written underneath). Similarly, posters of Muslim American Kamala Khan punching the former president appeared in antifascist and anti-MAGA rallies (see figure 6.1).[1] Other images of Kamala popped up on buses after Trump's "Muslim Travel Ban" and his controversial statements about Muslim countries. As one journalist noted, "Ms. Marvel has been drafted in by culture jammers in San Francisco to protest against Islamophobic adverts—it's the latest chapter in comic book diversity" (Letamendi).

The increasing visibility of Muslim Comics, I argue, brings us to an intriguing moment. Muslim Comics, like Black Comics, have perhaps

---

1. Illustrator Matt Stefani explains: "After Trump made those comments about requiring all Muslims to wear ID cards and be heavily monitored, there were a lot of comic fans asking specifically for Kamala Khan v. Trump in the style of Kirby's *Captain America* no. 1. Not my original idea, but when I saw the outcry for it, I knew I could take a decent crack at realizing the image" (Baker-Whitelaw).

FIGURE 6.1. Kamala Khan punching President Trump.

reached a place where they can push back against the universalization and fetishization of American whiteness and redefine what heroism is or what heroes look like. Taking their cue from Black Comics, which "emphasize and represent the composite Black experience," Muslim Comics, too, have "the powerful potential to weave imaginary narratives that offer possibilities" for defining Muslim heroism (Howard and Jackson). Muslim Comics not only contest the residual logic of colonialism that turns Black and Brown bodies into raw commodities but also challenge the Orientalist fantasies of the gendered Muslim as an object of fantasy—as exemplified by Kamala Khan as well as other hijabi superheroes such as Qahera from Egypt or the crime-fighting Burqa Avenger from Pakistan, among others. And as these examples suggest, Muslim Comics also have the potential to redefine identity on a truly global scale. Thus, one aspect of future work in Muslim Comics might be a notably globalist and internationalist approach. We might consider, as an early example of this approach, Naif Al-Mutawa's *The 99* comic series. The series tells the story of ninety-nine young people who attain various powers when they come into possession of magical "Noor" stones. Many of the ninety-nine (a number alluding to the ninety-nine names of God in Islam) are Muslims from Muslim countries; one, Batina the Hidden, wears a burqa. But some are not, including Mumita the Destroyer (originally Catarina Barbosa from Portugal) and Darr the Afflicter (John Weller from America). Al-Mutawa has been vocal about his desire to create a more globally minded comic, while still using the familiar American superhero model: "I knew from the beginning that I wanted the 99 to look like an American comic book. I didn't want the language or the art to be anything different or unusual. I didn't want to use a Middle Eastern style, or try to invent one. I wanted to use something that existed. The only thing that would be different would be the Islamic archetypes" (qtd. in Santo 687). By creating a "superhero league" comic where Muslims are the majority and an "exotic" Westerner or two are recruited to fill out the team, Al-Mutawa inverts a standard American subgenre to make something more globally minded.

Perhaps more ambitiously, and radically, Muslim Comics in the near future may pivot from a focus on overcoming the past—on "correcting" or fighting the old stereotypes of the Muslim as radical Other—and toward a focus on a future where Muslimness is no longer an obstacle, or indeed even remarkable. In this sense, Muslim Comics have the potential to pave the way for Muslim futurism. Muslim futurism itself is a complex enough idea that we can only gesture at one or two possible manifestations of it here. Perhaps the most familiar discussion of the idea is Thorsten Botz-Bornstein's "ISIS and Futurist Terrorism versus Cyberpunk," which offers a futuristic reading of the religiously dogmatic worldview. According to Botz-Bornstein, extremism propagated by ISIS is not actually invested in a dystopian nihilism but in a future-oriented hope for a new global order/caliphate: "It is not backwardness that determines the actions of ISIS, but rather a firm belief in the future, which is a modernist tendency" (7).[2] Of course, this particular theorization has the unfortunate effect of continuing the tradition of linking Muslim thought with jihadism and anti-Western extremism, now and in the future. A more positive and less limiting model of Muslim futurism might more closely resemble Afrofuturism—itself a highly complex notion, which Isiah Lavender defines broadly as "a narrative practice that enables users to communicate the interconnection between science, technology, and race across centuries, continents, and cultures" (2). Although Afrofuturism is often regarded as a subcategory of science fiction (SF) that emphasizes Black

---

2. Botz-Bornstein further suggests:

> Marinetti, the father-figure of futurism, speaks of the "deafening din of the motor, bone shaking reverberations of the chassis, [and the] cheek-coloring massage of a frenzied wind." Similarly, when Raqqa and Mosul became again accessible to outsiders, the world was fascinated by what the press would soon dub "Mad-Max-style" armored cars and bulldozers. Those civilian vehicles with steel plates bolted to their bodies and other strange weapons of war often required remarkable engineering skills. ISIS could attract talents able to tamper with "heavy metal." Lacking its own sophisticated weapons factories and cut off from the international market, ISIS depended on improvisation. (8–9)

experience, it can also be applied, Lavender argues, to texts that are not necessarily SF but can be read "as if" they were written in this genre. Applying Afrofuturism as an interpretive tool to study Black literature in general, he further writes, allows the critic to underscore the way the Black experience "has always been an experience of spatial and temporal dislocation and disorientation, not unlike the events experienced by the protagonists of the genre SF" (2). Might we apply this model to Muslim Comics as a way of connecting their interventionist roots with futurist thinking—even when they do not operate within the SF genre? What would it be like, for example, to read Riad Satouff's *The Arab of the Future* series (which is not SF) through a futurist-bildungsroman lens? Or could Willow Wilson's use of magic realism in *Cairo* with shape-shifting djinns be interpreted as an example of the "spatial and temporal dislocation" that ensues when a work re-centers itself around Muslim culture?

Finally, another form of futurism in Muslim Comics might investigate how a Muslim consciousness could become not a hallmark of antimodern isolation but rather a locus of "communal memories and traditions, which link the past, present, and future," as Lavender says of Afrofuturism (7). I would imagine two elements as vital to this potential manifestation of Muslim futurism: One is the global Muslim network that includes various Islamic communities under the larger umbrella of the Muslim *ummah*; the other is global connectivity via technology. The *ummah*, "a flexible rather than static" signifier of "Muslim collective identity," alludes to the multiethnic, multinational composition of the congregate (Cooke and Lawrence 2). As Miriam Cooke and Bruce B. Lawrence argue, "Precisely because Islam is not homogeneous, it is only through the prism of Muslim networks—whether they be academic or aesthetic, historical or commercial—that one can gain a perspective on how diverse groups of Muslims contest and rearticulate what it means to be Muslim" (2). The plurality of this assemblage, however, would become an engine for a Muslim futurism invested in empowerment, equality, respect, and social justice. Just as significantly, the modern connectivity of the Muslim *ummah* through various virtual platforms could connect with the presence of Muslim Comics on these same platforms to realize a solidarity and camaraderie that transcends national inclusion and belonging within the single Muslim homeland.

The idea that Muslim Comics might both emblematize and facilitate virtual connectivity between Muslims is exemplified by Amir and Khalil's *Zahra's Paradise*, which started as a web project. As Ivor Tossell explains, soon after it was launched, the webcomic attracted twenty-four thousand visitors and was read in fifteen cities in Iran, "attracting commentary from mem-

FIGURE 6.2. Political advertisement featuring Zahra.

bers of the Iranian diaspora and outsiders alike." More strikingly, Zahra herself came to be an emblem of defiance and anticorruption in unofficial communication between dissidents and protesters, ultimately declaring her virtual candidacy for president in 2013 (see figure 6.2). Launching a website, Vote4Zahra, Amir and Khalil started a movement that found a global audience; people taking pictures of themselves with Zahra's image started to post them online to show their support for an imaginary candidate, alluding to the sham elections. The momentum behind the campaign shows the potential for Muslim Comics in accelerating the virtual coalescing of Muslims as activists. In one poster, Zahra's friend Miriam states: "If a fruit peddler in Tunisia can change the destiny of nations and wake people across the Arab world, why can't we do the same?" Connecting Iran with developments in the larger Muslim world, Miriam not only invokes the idea of a Muslim network but also alludes to the alternative future projected by the Arab Spring.

Whatever form it may take, the afterlife of Muslim Comics will undoubtedly continue its ongoing engagement with Muslim community, suffering, and hope. From Neyestani's graphic novels produced in France to Sajad's editorial cartoons portraying the power struggle between India and Pakistan in the Kashmir region, there is a unified sense of the urgent need to fix the present and enable a viable Muslim future that moves beyond violence, suffering, and trauma. Ultimately, Muslim Comics are their own community, and the artists within them are working together in hopes that the larger world will witness their stories.

WORKS CITED

Abdelrazaq, Leila. *Baddawi*. Just World Books, 2015.

Abirached, Zeina. *A Game for Swallows: To Die, to Leave, to Return*. Translated by Edward Gauvin, Graphic Universe, 2012.

Abu-Lughod, Lila. "Do Muslim Women Need Saving?: Anthropological Reflections on Cultural Relativism and Its Others." *American Anthropologist*, vol. 104, no. 3, 2002, pp. 783–90.

Ackerman, Spencer. "Frank Miller's *Holy Terror* Is Fodder for Anti-Islam Set." *Wired*, 28 Sept. 2011, https://www.wired.com/2011/09/holy-terror-frank-miller/.

Agamben, Giorgio. *Homo Sacer: Sovereign Power and Bare Life*. Translated by Daniel Heller-Roazen, Stanford UP, 1998.

———. *Remnants of Auschwitz: The Witness and the Archive*. Translated by Daniel Heller-Roazen, Zone Books, 1999.

———. *State of Exception*. Translated by Kevin Attell, U of Chicago P, 2005.

Akash, Munir, and Khaled Mattawa, editors. *Post Gibran: Anthology of New Arab American Writing*. Syracuse UP, 2000.

Ahmed, Naseer, and Saurabh Singh. *Kashmir Pending*. Phantomville, 2007.

Akhtar, Zainab. "Graphic Novel 'Steeped in Islamophobia' Pulled after Protests." *The Guardian*, 26 Nov. 2018, https://www.theguardian.com/books/2018/nov/26/a-suicide-bomber-sits-in-the-library-comic-pulled-protests-jack-gantos-dave-mckean.

Aldama, Frederick Luis, editor. *Multicultural Comics: From Zap to Blue Beetle*. U of Texas P, 2010.

Ali, Eashan, and Nirban Manna. "Cartography of Terrorism: America's Cultural Imperialism and Geopolitical Anxiety in Frank Miller's Holy Terror." *IUP: Journal of International Relations,* vol. 10, no. 4, 2016, pp. 32–50.

Al-Mutawa, Naif. *The 99.* Teshkeel Comics, 2007.

Amir and Khalil. *Zahra's Paradise.* First Second Books, 2011.

Anzaldúa, Gloria. *Borderlands / La Frontera: The New Mestiza.* Aunt Lute Books, 1987.

Appadurai, Arjun. *Modernity at Large: Cultural Dimensions of Globalization.* U of Minnesota P, 1996.

Appadurai, Arjun, and Carol A. Breckenridge. "Public Modernities in India." *Consuming Modernity: Public Culture in a South Asian World,* edited by Carol A. Breckenridge, U of Minnesota P, 1995, pp. 1–19.

Arendt, Hannah. *The Human Condition.* U of Chicago P, 1958.

Arjana, Sophia Rose. *Veiled Superheroes: Islam, Feminism, and Popular Culture.* Lexington Books, 2018.

Asad, Talal. *Formations of the Secular: Christianity, Islam, Modernity.* Stanford UP, 2003.

Backus, Madeline, and Ken Koltun-Fromm. "Writing the Sacred in Craig Thompson's *Habibi.*" *Comics and Sacred Texts: Reimagining Religion and Graphic Narratives,* edited by Assaf Gamzou and Ken Koltun-Fromm, UP of Mississippi, 2018, pp. 5–24.

Baishya, Amit. "Endangered (and Endangering) Species: Exploring the Animacy Hierarchy in Malik Sajad's *Munnu.*" *South Asian Review,* vol. 39, no. 1–2, 2018, pp. 50–69.

Baker-Whitelaw, Gavia. "Fanart Shows Muslim Superhero Ms. Marvel Punching Donald Trump in the Face." *Daily Dot,* 15 Dec. 2015, https://www.dailydot.com/parsec/kamala-khan-marvel-donald-trump-fanart/.

Banerjee, Bidisha. "Picturing Precarity: Diasporic Belonging and Camp Life in Leila Abdelrazaq's *Baddawi.*" *Journal of Postcolonial Writing,* vol. 57, no. 1, pp. 13–30.

Bartley, Aryn. "Staging Cosmopolitanism: The Transnational Encounter in Joe Sacco's *Footnotes in Gaza.*" *Transnational Perspectives on Graphic Narratives,* edited by Daniel Stein et al., Bloomsbury, 2013, pp. 67–82.

Bayoumi, Moustafa. "A Bloody Stupid War." *Middle East Report,* no. 231, 2004, pp. 36–45.

———. "Racing Religion." *CR: The New Centennial Review,* vol. 6, no. 2, 2006, pp. 267–93.

———. *This Muslim American Life: Dispatches from the War on Terror.* NYU P, 2015.

BBC News. "Article 370: What Happened with Kashmir and Why It Matters." 6 Aug. 2019. https://www.bbc.com/news/world-asia-india-49234708.

Beaty, Bart. "Some Classics." *The Cambridge Companion to the Graphic Novel,* edited by Stephen E. Tabachnick, Cambridge UP, 2017, pp. 175–91.

Bennett, Andy. *Culture and Everyday Life.* Sage Publications, 2005.

Beverley, John. *Testimonio: On the Politics of Truth.* U of Minnesota P, 2004.

Bhan, Mona, et al. "Relating Otherwise: Forging Critical Solidarities across the Kashmiri Pandit-Muslim Divide." *Biography,* vol. 43, no. 2, 2020, pp. 285–305.

Bharat, Meenakshi. *Troubled Testimonies: Terrorism and the English Novel in India.* Routledge, 2016.

Biddle, Craig. "Bosch Fawstin on Combating the Evil of Islam." *The Objective Standard,* 1 Jan. 2020, https://theobjectivestandard.com/2020/01/bosch-fawstin-on-combating-the-evil-of-islam/.

Blank, Jonah. "Kashmir: Fundamentalism Takes Root." *Foreign Affairs*, vol. 78, no. 6, 1999, pp. 36–53.

Bornstein-Gómez, Miriam. "Gloria Anzaldúa: Borders of Knowledge and (Re) Signification." *Confluencia*, vol. 26, no. 1, 2010, pp. 46–55.

Botz-Bornstein, Thorsten. "ISIS and Futurist Terrorism Versus Cyberpunk." *Contemporary Aesthetics*, vol. 7, 2019, pp. 1–18.

Brothers, David. "Frank Miller's 'Holy Terror': A Propaganda Comic That Fights Faith Instead of Evil." 26 Sept. 2011, *Comics Alliance*, https://comicsalliance.com/frank-millers-holy-terror-review/.

Butler, Judith. "Guantanamo Limbo: International Law Offers Too Little Protection for Prisoners of the New War." *The Nation*, vol. 274, no. 12, 2002, https://www.thenation.com/article/archive/guantanamo-limbo/.

———. *Precarious Life: The Powers of Mourning and Violence.* Verso, 2004.

———. "Rethinking Vulnerability and Resistance." *Vulnerability in Resistance*, edited by Judith Butler et al., Duke UP, 2016, pp. 12–27.

Cantor, Jay, et al. *Aaron & Ahmed: A Love Story.* DC Comics, 2011.

Castronovo, Ross. "Compromised Narratives along the Border: The Mason-Dixon Line, Resistance, and Hegemony." *Border Theory: The Limits of Cultural Politics*, edited by Scott Michaelsen and David E. Johnson, U of Minnesota P, 1997, pp. 195–220.

Cavarero, Adriana. *Horrorism: Naming Contemporary Violence.* Translated by William McCuaig, Columbia UP, 2011.

Celermajer, Danielle. "The Tick-Tick-Ticking Time Bomb and Erosion of Human Rights Institutions." *Angelaki*, vol. 24, no. 4, 2019, pp. 87–102.

Chandra, Nandini. "The Fear of Iconoclasm: Genre and Medium Transformations from Comics to Graphic Novels in Amar Chitra Katha, Bhimayana, and Munnu." *Graphic Narratives about South Asia and South Asian America*, 2 Nov. 2018, pp. 11–33.

Chatterjee, Partha. "Kashmir Is the Test Bed for a New Model of Internal Colonialism." *The Wire*, 28 Aug. 2019, thewire.in/government/kashmir-is-the-test-bed-for-a-new-model-of-internal-colonialism.

Cheurfa, Hiyem. "Testifying Graphically: Bearing Witness to a Palestinian Childhood in Leila Abdelrazaq's Baddawi." *a/b: Auto/Biography Studies*, vol. 35, no. 2, 2020, pp. 359–82.

Chute, Hillary. *Disaster Drawn: Visual Witness, Comics, and Documentary Form.* Belknap Press, 2016.

ComicBookWire. "Review: Green Lantern Vol. 3—The End." 12 Dec. 2019, https://www.comicbookwire.com/review-green-lantern-vol-3-the-end/.

Consonni, Manuela. "Primo Levi, Robert Antelme, and the Body of the Muselmann." *Partial Answers: Journal of Literature and the History of Ideas*, vol. 7, no. 2, 2009, pp. 243–59.

"Convention against Torture and Other Cruel, Inhuman or Degrading Treatment or Punishment." *OHCHR*, https://www.ohchr.org/en/instruments-mechanisms/instruments/convention-against-torture-and-other-cruel-inhuman-or-degrading.

Cooke, Miriam, and Bruce B. Lawrence. Introduction. *Muslim Networks from Hajj to Hip Hop*, edited by Miriam Cooke and Bruce B. Lawrence, U of North Carolina P, 2005, pp. 1–28.

Coundouriotis, Eleni. "Torture and Textuality: Guantánamo Diary as Postcolonial Text." *Textual Practice*, vol. 34, no. 7, 2020, pp. 1061–80.

Dabaie, Marguerite. "Palestinian Refugee Boy Comes of Age in Graphic Novel 'Baddawi.'" *The Electronic Intifada*, 6 Apr. 2015, https://electronicintifada.net/content/palestinian-refugee-boy-comes-age-graphic-novel-baddawi/14284.

Dabashi, Hamid. "The End of Islamic Ideology." *Social Research*, vol. 67, no. 2, 2000, p. 475–518.

———. *Islamic Liberation Theology: Resisting the Empire*. Routledge, 2008.

———. "A Persian Letter to Arab Revolutionaries." *Aljazeera*, 18 Sept. 2012, https://www.aljazeera.com/opinions/2012/9/18/a-persian-letter-to-arab-revolutionaries.

Dabbagh, Nadia Taysir. *Suicide in Palestine: Narratives of Despair*. Hurst & Company, 2005.

Damluji, Nadim. "The Spectre of Orientalism in Craig Thompson's Habibi." *Medium*, 20 Feb. 2017, https://medium.com/@ndamluji/the-spectre-of-orientalism-in-craig-thompsons-habibi-dde9d499f403.

Dar, Jehanzeb. "Holy Islamophobia, Batman! Demonization of Muslims and Arabs in Mainstream American Comic Books." *Counterpoints*, vol. 346, 2010, pp. 99–110.

Darraj, Susan M. *Scheherazade's Legacy: Arab and Arab American Women on Writing*. Westport: Praeger, 2004.

Davies, Dominic. "Introduction: Documenting Trauma in Comics." *Documenting Trauma in Comics: Traumatic Pasts, Embodied Histories, and Graphic Reportage*, edited by Dominic Davies and Candida Rifkind, Palgrave Macmillan: 2020, pp. 1–26.

Debrix, Francois. Introduction. *Beyond Biopolitics: Theory, Violence, and Horror in World Politics*, by Debrix and Alexander D. Barder, Routledge, 2013, pp. 1–25.

de Certeau, Michel. *The Practice of Everyday Life*. 2nd ed., translated by S. Rendall, U of California P, 2002.

Desai, Prajna. "Kashmir Pending." *The Comics Journal*, 18 Nov. 2011, https://www.tcj.com/reviews/kashmir-pending/.

Díaz, Wendy. *The Secret of My Hijab*. Illustrated by Uthman Guadalupe, independently published, 2020.

Dittmer, Jason. "Captain America's Empire: Reflections on Identity, Popular Culture, and Post-9/11 Geopolitics." *Annals of the Association of American Geographers*, vol. 95, no. 3, 2005, pp. 626–43.

Dokterman, Eliana. "Everyone's a Superhero." *Time*, 7 Sept. 2014, 77–80. http://time.com/4012852/everyones-a-superhero-at-marvel/.

Duvdevani, Shmulik, and Raz Yosef. "Witnessing the Perpetrator: Testimony and Accountability in Current Israeli Documentary Film." *Continuum*, vol. 34, no. 2, 2020, pp. 197–209.

Ebrahimi, Mehraneh. *Women, Art, and Literature in the Iranian Diaspora*. Syracuse UP, 2019.

Eisner, Will. *Comics and Sequential Art: Principles and Practices from the Legendary Cartoonist*. W. W. Norton, 2008.

El Rassi, Toufic. *Arab in America*. Last Gasp, 2008.

Engdahl, Horace. "Philomela's Tongue: Introductory Remarks on Witness Literature." Translated by Tim Crosfield, *Witness Literature: Proceedings of the Nobel Centennial Symposium*, edited by Engdahl, World Scientific, 2002, pp. 1–14.

Ennis, Garth. *The Boys*. Illustrated by Darick Robertson, Dynamite Entertainment, 2008.

Evans, Brad, and Henry A. Giroux. *Disposable Futures: The Seduction of Violence in the Age of Spectacle*. City Lights Publishers, 2015.

Fadda-Conrey, Carol. *Contemporary Arab-American Literature: Transnational Reconfigurations of Citizenship and Belonging.* NYU P, 2014.

Fahmy, Huda. *Huda F Are You?* Dial Books, 2021.

———. *That Can Be Arranged: A Muslim Love Story.* Andrews McMeel Publishing, 2020.

———. *Yes, I'm Hot in This: The Hilarious Truth about Life in a Hijab.* Adams Media, 2018.

Fair, Christine C. "The Militant Challenge in Pakistan." *Asia Policy,* vol. 11, no. 1, 2011, pp. 105–38.

Fajardo, Elena Galán, and José Carlos Rueda Laffond. "Those Wars Are Also My War: An Approach to Practices of Postmemory in the Contemporary Spanish Comic." *Catalan Journal of Communication & Cultural Studies,* vol. 8, no. 1, 2016, pp. 63–77.

Fawaz, Ramzi. *The New Mutants: Superheroes and the Radical Imagination of American Comics.* NYU P, 2016.

Fawstin. *Infidel: Featuring Pigman.* O'Ink Comics, 2011.

Featherstone, Mike. "The Heroic Life and Everyday Life." *Theory, Culture & Society,* vol. 9, no. 1, 1992, pp. 159–82.

Feldman, Allen. "Memory Theaters, Virtual Witnessing, and the Trauma-Aesthetic." *Biography,* vol. 27, no. 1, 2004, pp. 163–202.

Fitzgerald, Ali. *Drawn to Berlin: Comic Workshops in Refugee Shelters and Other Stories from a New Europe.* Fantagraphics, 2018.

Folman, Ari. *Waltz with Bashir: A Lebanon War Story.* Metropolitan Books, 2009.

Forna, Aminatta. "Nadine Gordimer Helped Me See How Fiction Writing Can Illuminate Reality." *The Guardian,* 20 Aug. 2013, https://www.theguardian.com/commentisfree/2013/aug/20/aminatta-forna-witness-inward-testimony-gordimer.

Foucault, Michel. "The Subject and Power." *Critical* Inquiry, vol. 8, no. 4, 1982, pp. 777–95.

Freidman, Susan Stanford. "Cosmopolitanism, Religion, Diaspora: Kwame Anthony Appiah and Contemporary Muslim Women's Writing." *New Literary History,* vol. 49, no. 2, 2018, pp. 199–225.

Gallaher, Valerie. "'Zahra's Paradise'—Using Webcomics as a Force for Human Rights." *MTV News,* 12 Oct. 2010, http://www.mtv.com/news/2620045/zahras-paradise-using-webcomics-as-a-force-for-human-rights/.

Gana, Nouri. "Introduction: Race, Islam, and the Task of Muslim and Arab American Writing." *PMLA,* vol. 23, no. 5, 2008, pp. 1573–80.

Ganteau, Jean-Michel. *The Ethics and Aesthetics of Vulnerability in Contemporary British Fiction.* Routledge, 2015.

Gardiner, Michael E. *Critiques of Everyday Life.* Routledge, 2000.

Gardner, Jared. "Same Difference: Graphic Alterity in the Work of Gene Yuan Lang, Adrian Tomine, and Derek Kirk Kim." *Multicultural Comics: From Zap to Blue Beetle,* edited by Frederick Luis Aldama, U of Texas P, 2010, pp. 132–47.

Gasset, Jose Ortega y. *Meditations on Hunting.* Translated by Howard B. Wescott, Wilderness Adventures Press, 1995.

Giroux, Haney A. *The Violence of Organized Forgetting: Thinking beyond America's Disimagination Machine.* City Lights Open Media, 2014.

Glidden, Sarah. *Rolling Blackouts: Dispatches from Turkey, Syria, and Iraq.* Drawn and Quarterly, 2016.

Gregory, Derek. "The Black Flag: Guantánamo Bay and the Space of Exception." *Geografiska Annaler,* vol. 88, no. 4, 2006, pp. 405–27.

Groensteen, Thierry. *The Expanding Art of Comics: Ten Modern Masterpieces.* UP of Mississippi, 2019.

Gutman, Yifat, and Noam Tirosh. "Balancing Atrocities and Forced Forgetting: Memory Laws as a Means of Social Control in Israel." *Law & Social Inquiry,* vol. 46, no. 3, 2021, pp. 705–30.

Haleem, Harfiya. "What Is Martyrdom?" *Witness to Faith?: Martyrdom in Christianity and Islam,* edited by Brian Wicker, Ashgate Publishing, 2006, pp. 49–78.

Halpern, Jake, and Michael Sloan. *Welcome to the New World.* Metropolitan Books, 2020.

Handala.org. "Who Is Handala?" http://www.handala.org/handala/.

Harari, Youval Noah. *The Ultimate Experience: Battlefield Revelations and the Making of Modern War Culture, 1450–2000.* Palgrave Macmillan, 2018.

Hasso, Frances S. "Discursive and Political Deployments by/of the 2002 Palestinian Women Suicide Bombers/Martyrs." *Feminist Review,* vol. 81, no. 1, 2005, pp. 23–51.

Hatfield, Charles. *Alternative Comics: An Emerging Literature.* UP of Mississippi, 2005.

Hayman, Greg, and Henry John Pratt. "What Are Comics?" *A Reader in Philosophy of the Arts,* edited by David Goldblatt and Lee Brown, Pearson Education, 2005, pp. 419–24.

Henderson, Mae G. "Introduction: Borders, Boundaries, and Frame(work)s." *Borders, Boundaries, and Frames: Essays in Cultural Criticism and Cultural Studies,* edited by Mae G. Henderson, Routledge, 1995, pp. 1–30.

Herman, Judith. *Trauma and Recovery: The Aftermath of Violence—From Domestic Abuse to Political Terror.* Basic Books, 1992.

Hersh, Seymour M. "Torture at Abu Ghraib: American Soldiers Brutalized Iraqis. How Far up Does the Responsibility Go?" *The New Yorker,* 10 May 2004, https://www.newyorker.com/magazine/2004/05/10/torture-at-abu-ghraib.

Herwees, Tasbeeh. "The Graphic Novel 'Baddawi' Looks Back at Life in a Palestinian Refugee Camp." *Vice,* 5 Dec. 2015, https://www.vice.com/en/article/9bg8g3/the-graphic-novel-baddawi-is-like-a-palestinian-persepolis-111.

Hescher, Achim. *Reading Graphic Novels: Genre and Narration.* De Gruyter, 2016.

———. "Transgressing Borders in and with Comics: Mana Neyestani's Graphic Novel *Une Métamorphose Iranienne* (2012)." *PhiN,* vol. 70, 2014, pp. 54–73.

Hicks, D. Emily. *Border Writing: The Multidimensional Text.* U of Minnesota P, 1991.

Hirsch, Marianne. *The Generation of Postmemory: Writing and Visual Culture after the Holocaust.* Columbia UP, 2012.

Hitchens, Christopher. "Londonistan Calling." *Vanity Fair,* June 2007, https://www.vanityfair.com/news/2007/06/hitchens200706.

Hoffman, Danny, and Stephen Lubkemann. "Introduction: West-African Warscapes: Warscape Ethnography in West Africa and the Anthropology of 'Events.'" *Anthropological Quarterly,* vol. 78, no. 2, 2005, pp. 315–27.

Hogan, Patrick C. *Imagining Kashmir: Emplotment and Colonialism.* U of Nebraska P, 2016.

———. "*Kashmir Pending*: Narrative and Ideology in a Graphic Novel." *Narrative Works,* vol. 4, no. 2, 2019, pp. 108–29.

Horstkotte, Silke, and Nancy Pedri. "Focalization in Graphic Narrative." *Narrative,* vol. 19, no. 3, 2011, pp. 330–57.

Howard, Sheena C., and Ronald L. Jackson II. *Black Comics: Politics of Race and Representation.* Bloomsbury, 2013.

Human Rights Watch. "Getting Away with Torture." 11 July 2011, https://www.hrw.org/report/2011/07/12/getting-away-torture/bush-administration-and-mistreatment-detainees.

———. "'Like the Dead in Their Coffins': Torture, Detention, and the Crushing of Dissent in Iran." 7 June 2004, https://www.hrw.org/reports/2004/iran0604/index.htm.

Inzana, Ryan. *Johnny Jihad*. Nantier, Beall, Minoustchine Publishing, 2003.

Isin, Engin F. "Citizenship in Flux: The Figure of the Activist Citizen." *Citizenship Rights*, no. 29, 2017, pp. 367–88.

Islam, Inaash. "Muslim American Double Consciousness." *Du Bois Review: Social Science Research on Race*, vol. 17, no. 2, 2020, pp. 429–48.

JanMohamed, Abdul. "Worldliness-without-World, Homelessness-as-Home: Towards a Definition of the Specular Border Intellectual." *Edward Said: A Critical Reader*, edited by Michael Sprinker, Wiley, 1993, pp. 96–120.

John, Eileen, and Dominic McIver Lopes, editors. *Philosophy of Literature: Contemporary and Classic Readings*. Blackwell, 2004.

Johnston, Rich. *Iron Muslim*. BOOM! Studios, 2012.

Jolly, Margaretta. "Introduction: Life/Rights Narrative in Action." *We Shall Bear Witness: Life Narratives and Human Rights*, edited by Meg Jensen and Margaretta Jolly, U of Wisconsin P, 2014, pp. 3–22.

Kabir, Ananya Jahanara. *Territory of Desire: Representing the Valley of Kashmir*. U of Minnesota P, 2009.

Kahf, Mohja. "Teaching Diaspora Literature: Muslim American Literature as an Emerging Field." *The Journal of Pan African Studies*, vol. 4, no. 2, 2010, pp. 163–67.

Kahn, Paul W. *Sacred Violence: Torture, Terror, and Sovereignty*. U of Michigan P, 2009.

Kanwal, Aroosa. "'No Bodies.'" *Interventions*, 2021, pp. 1–17.

Kaplan, Amy. "Where Is Guantánamo?" *American Quarterly*, vol. 57, no. 3, 2005, pp. 831–58.

Karim, Persis. "A Cartoonist's Metamorphosis: An Interview with Mana Neyestani." *World Literature Today*, vol. 89, no. 2, 2015, pp. 38–41.

Kaufmann, Michael. "Locating the Postsecular." *Religion and Literature*, vol. 41, no. 3, 2009, pp. 68–73.

Kazi, Seema. *In Kashmir: Gender, Militarization, and the Modern Nation State*. South End, 2010.

Kent, Miriam. "Unveiling Marvels: Ms. Marvel and the Reception of the New Muslim Superheroine." *Feminist Media Studies*, vol. 15, no. 3, 2015, pp. 522–38.

Khadem, Amir. "Framed Memories: The Politics of Recollection in Mana Neyestani's *An Iranian Metamorphosis*." *Iranian Studies*, vol. 51, no. 3, 2017, pp. 479–97.

Khan, Mahvish. *My Guantanamo Diary: The Detainees and the Stories They Told Me*. PublicAffairs, 2009.

Kugler, Olivier. *Escaping Wars and Waves: Encounters with Syrian Refugees*. Penn State UP, 2018.

Kuhlman, Martha. "The Autobiographical and Biographical Graphic Novel." *The Cambridge Companion to the Graphic Novel*, edited by Stephen E. Tabachnick, Cambridge UP, 2017, pp. 113–29.

Kunzle, David. *The Early Comic Strip: Narrative Strips and Picture Stories in the European Broadsheet from c. 1450 to 1825*. U of California P, 1973.

Kurnaz, Murat. *Five Years of My Life: An Innocent Man in Guantanamo.* Palgrave MacMillan, 2008.

LaCapra, Dominic. "Trauma, Absence, Loss." *Critical Inquiry,* vol. 25, no. 4, 1999, pp. 696–727.

Lalami, Laila. "Writing Muslims." *Religion and Literature,* vol. 43, no. 1, 2011, pp. 144–48.

Landis, Winona. "*Ms Marvel, Qahera,* and Superheroism in the Muslim Diaspora." *Continuum: Journal of Media & Cultural Studies,* vol. 33, no. 2, 2019, pp. 185–200.

Larson, Doran. "Toward a Prison Poetics." *College Literature,* vol. 37, no. 3, 2010, pp. 143–66.

Laub, Dori. "Bearing Witness, or the Vicissitudes of Listening." *Testimony: Crises of Witnessing in Literature, Psychoanalysis, and History,* by Shoshana Felman and Laub, Routledge, 1992, pp. 221–26.

Launchbury, Claire. "Animated Memory: Ari Folman's Waltz with Bashir." *Concentrationary Memories: Totalitarian Terror and Cultural Resistance,* edited by Griselda Pollock and Max Silverman, Bloomsbury, 2015, pp. 193–201.

Lauritzen, Paul. "The Self and Its Discontents: Recent Work on Morality and the Self." *The Journal of Religious Ethics,* vol. 22, no. 1, 1994, pp. 187–210.

Lavender, Isiah III. *Afrofuturism Rising: The Literary Prehistory of a Movement.* The Ohio State UP, 2019.

Letamendi, Andrea. "Meet the Muslim Superhero Fighting Bigotry on San Francisco Buses." *The Guardian,* 1 Feb. 2015, https://www.theguardian.com/books/2015/feb/01/meet-the-muslim-superhero-fighting-bigotry-on-san-francisco-buses.

Levi, Primo. *The Drowned and the Saved.* Vintage Books, 1989.

———. *The Periodic Table.* 1975. Translated by Raymond Rosenthal, Schocken Books, 1984.

———. *Survival in Auschwitz: The Nazi Assault on Humanity.* Translated by S. J. Woolf, Simon & Schuster, 1996.

Lewis, A. David. *Kismet, Man of Fate.* Bomber Comics #1, 1944.

Lia, Brynjar. "Doctrines for Jihadi Terrorist Training." *Terrorism and Political Violence,* vol. 20, no. 4, 2008, pp. 518–42.

Logan, Katie M. "Why Donald Trump's America Needs Marvel Superhero Kamala Khan Now More Than Ever." *Independent,* 20 Feb. 2017, http://www.independent.co.uk/arts-entertainment/books/features/marvel-superhero-kamala-khan-america-muslim-terrorism-islam-donald-trump-prejudice-a7590336.html.

Loia, Donato. "Forms of Mediation in Ari Folman's Waltz with Bashir." *Journal of Literature and Trauma Studies,* vol. 7, no. 2, 2018, pp. 91–114.

Lund, Martin, and A. David Lewis, editors. *Muslim Superheroes: Comics, Islam, and Representation.* Harvard UP, 2017.

Malkki, Lisa H. *Purity and Exile: Violence, Memory, and National Cosmology among Hutu Refugees in Tanzania.* U of Chicago P, 1995.

Mamdani, Mahmood. *Good Muslim, Bad Muslim: America, the Cold War, and the Roots of Terror.* Harmony, 2005.

———. "Good Muslim, Bad Muslim: A Political Perspective on Culture and Terrorism." *American Anthropologist,* vol. 104, no. 3, 2002, pp. 766–75.

Mangles, Alex. "Stitching out a Life in Graphic Memoir." *Los Angeles Review of Books*, 8 June 2015, https://lareviewofbooks.org/article/stitching-out-a-life-in-graphic-memoir-baddawi/.

Margolin, Uri. "Focalization: Where Do We Go from Here?" *Point of View, Perspective, and Focalization: Modeling Mediation in Narrative*, edited by Peter Hühn et al., De Gruyter, 2009, pp. 41–58.

Markicevic, Milos. "Comic Book Author and Illustrator Shares Thoughts on Being Muslim, Arab and Artist." *Chicago Monitor*, 23 Oct. 2013, https://chicagomonitor.com/2013/10/comic-book-author-and-illustrator-shares-thoughts-on-being-muslim-arab-and-artist/.

Mbembe, Achille. "Necropolitics." *Necropolitics*, translated by Steven Corcoran, Duke UP, 2019, pp. 66–92.

McCloud, Scott. *Understanding Comics: The Invisible Art*. William Morrow Paperbacks, 1994.

McGuire, Meredith B. *Lived Religion: Faith and Practice in Everyday Life*. Oxford UP, 2008.

Mehring, Frank. "Holy Terror!: Islamophobia and Intermediality in Frank Miller's Graphic Novel." *European Journal of American Studies*, vol. 15, no. 3, 2020, pp. 1–27.

Mehta, Suhaan. "Wondrous Capers: The Graphic Novel in India." *Multicultural Comics: From Zap to Blue Beetle*, edited by Frederick Luis Aldama, U of Texas P, 2010, pp. 173–88.

Mendez, Jennifer Bickham, and Nancy A. Naples. Introduction. *Border Politics: Social Movements, Collective Identities, and Globalization*, edited by Naples and Mendez, NYU P, 2014, pp. 1–32.

Meskin, Aaron. "Comics as Literature?" *The British Journal of Aesthetics*, vol. 49, no. 3, 2009, pp. 219–39.

Messman, Terry. "Zahra's Paradise: The Fate of the Disappeared." *Street Spirit*, 19 July 2017, https://thestreetspirit.org/2017/07/19/zahras-paradise-the-fate-of-the-disappeared/.

Michaelsen, Scott, and David E. Johnson. *Border Theory: The Limits of Cultural Politics*. U of Minnesota P, 1997.

Michalak, Laurence O. *Cruel and Unusual: Negative Images of Arabs in American Popular Culture*. American Arab Anti Discrimination Committee, 1988.

Miller, Ann. *Reading Bande Dessinée: Critical Approaches to Reading French-Language Comic Strip*. Intellect, 2007.

Miller, Frank. *Holy Terror*. Legendary Comics, 2011.

Mirk, Sarah, editor. *Guantanamo Voices: True Accounts from the World's Most Infamous Prison*. Abrams, 2020.

Moosavi, Amir. "How to Write Death: Resignifying Martyrdom in Two Novels of the Iran-Iraq War." *ALIF: Journal of Comparative Poetics*, no. 35, 2015, pp. 1–23.

Morton, Stephen. "Sovereignty and Necropolitics at the Line of Control." *Journal of Postcolonial Writing*, vol. 50, no. 1, 2013, pp. 19–30.

Murray, Jessica. "A Post-Colonial and Feminist Reading of Selected Testimonies to Trauma in Post-Liberation South Africa and Zimbabwe." *Journal of African Cultural Studies*, vol. 21, no. 2, 2009, pp. 1–21.

Murray, Stuart J. "Thanatopolitics." *The Bloomsbury Handbook of Literary and Cultural Theory*, edited by Jeffrey R. Di Leo, Bloomsbury Publishing, 2018, pp. 718–19.

———. "Thanatopolitics: On the Use of Death for Mobilizing Political Life." *Polygraph: An International Journal of Politics and Culture*, vol. 18, 2006, pp. 191–215.

"Muslim Show, a French Comic Book Series Takes on the World." *OrientXXI*, 29 May 2014, https://orientxxi.info/magazine/muslim-show-a-french-comic-book-series-takes-on-the-world,0582.

Nayar, Pramod K. *The Human Rights Graphic Novel: Drawing it Just Right*. Routledge, 2021.

———. "The Human Rights Torture Novel: Unmade Subjects, Unmaking Worlds." *Orbis Litterarum*, vol. 72, no. 4, 2017, pp. 318–47.

———. "The Postcolonial Gothic: Munnu, Graphic Narrative and the Terrors of the Nation." *Rupkatha Journal on Interdisciplinary Studies in Humanities*, vol. 8, no. 1, 2016, pp. 2–12.

Ndebele, Njabulo. "Liberation and the Crisis of Culture." *Altered State? Writing and South Africa*, edited by Elleke Boehmer et al., Dangaroo Press, 1994, pp. 1–11.

Neyestani, Mana. *An Iranian Metamorphosis*. Translated by Ghazal Mosadeq, Uncivilized Books, 2014.

Ng, Andrew Hock Soon. "Nationalism and the Intangible Effects of Violence in Malik Sajad's *Munnu: A Boy from Kashmir*." *South Asian Review*, vol. 39, no. 1–2, 2018, pp. 159–74.

Nickerson, Al. "Comics versus Terrorism: Frank Miller's *Holy Terror*." *An Act of Faith*, 8 Oct. 2011, http://alnickerson.blogspot.com/2011/10/comics-versus-terrorism-frank-millers.html.

Noori, Margaret. "Native American Narratives from Early Art to Graphic Novels: How We See Stories / Ezhi-g'waabamaanaanig Aadizookaanag." *Multicultural Comix: From Zap to Blue Beetle*, edited by Frederick Luis Aldama, U of Texas P, 2021, pp. 55–72.

Nordstrom, Carolyn. *A Different Kind of War Story*. U of Pennsylvania P, 1997.

Norris, Andrew. "Giorgio Agamben and the Politics of the Living Dead." *Diacritics*, vol. 30, no. 4, 2000, pp. 38–58.

Oliver, Kelly. "Witnessing, Recognition, and Response Ethics." *Philosophy & Rhetoric*, vol. 48, no. 4, 2015, pp. 473–93.

Ortner, Sherry. "Theory in Anthropology since the Sixties." *Comparative Studies in Society and History*, vol. 26, no. 1, 1984, pp. 126–66.

Oster, Sharon B. "Impossible Holocaust Metaphors: The Muselmann." *Prooftexts*, vol. 34, no. 3, 2014, pp. 302–48.

Pamuk, Orhan. *My Name Is Red*. Translated by Erdag Goknar, Vintage, 2002.

Parsa, Misagh. "Authoritarian Survival: Iran's Republic of Repression." *Journal of Democracy*, vol. 31, no. 3, 2020, pp. 54–68.

Pedri, Nancy. "What's the Matter of Seeing in Graphic Memoir?" *South Central Review*, vol. 32, no. 3, 2015, pp. 8–29.

Perera, Anna. *Guantanamo Boy*. Penguin, 2012.

Petersen, Anne Ring, and Moritz Schramm. "(Post-)Migration in the Age of Globalization: New Challenges to Imagination and Representation." *Journal of Aesthetics & Culture*, vol. 9, no. 2, pp. 1–12.

Phelan, James. *Living to Tell about It: A Rhetoric and Ethics of Character Narration*. Cornell UP, 2005.

Pizzino, Christopher. *Arresting Development: Comics at the Boundaries of Literature.* U of Texas P, 2016.

———. "Gutter." *Keywords for Comics Studies,* edited by Ramzi Fawaz, Deborah Whaley, and Shelley Streeby, New York UP, 2021, pp. 121–26.

Polak, Kate. *In the Gutter: Empathy and Historical Fiction in Comics.* The Ohio State UP, 2017.

Ponge, Francis. *La Fabrique du Pre.* Skira, 1971.

Postema, Barbara. *Narrative Structure in Comics: Making Sense of Fragments.* Rochester Institute of Technology P, 2013.

Priyadarshini, Arya, and Suman Sigroha. "Recovering the Palestinian History of Dispossession through Graphics in Leila Abdelrazaq's Baddawi." *Eikon / Imago,* vol. 9, 2020, pp. 395–418.

Pugliese, Joseph. "Specters of the Muselmann: Guantanamo Bay Penalogical Theme Park and the Torture of Omar Khadr." *Torture: Power, Democracy, and the Human Body,* edited by Shampa Biswas and Zahi Zalloua, U of Washington P, 2011, pp. 158–87.

Raja, Masood A. "Death as a Form of Becoming: The Muslim Imagery of Death and Necropolitics." *Digest of Middle East Studies,* vol. 14, no. 2, 2005, pp. 11–26.

Rajendran, Punnya. "A Graphic Memoir from Kashmir." *Literary Journalism Studies,* vol. 8, no. 2, 2016, pp. 159–61.

Raulff, Ulrich. "An Interview with Giorgio Agamben." *German Law Journal,* vol. 5, no. 5, pp. 609–14.

Reingold, Matt. "A National Reckoning: Israeli Soldiers' Depictions of Wartime Trauma in Autobiographical Graphic Novels." *Journal of War & Culture Studies,* vol. 14, no. 3, 2019, pp. 324–44.

Rhett, Maryanne. "Orientalism and Graphic Novels: A Modern Reexamination of Popular Culture." *Graphic History: Essays on Graphic Novels and/as History,* edited by Richard Iadonisi, Cambridge Scholars Press, 2012, pp. 203–22.

Rifas, Leonard. "The Image of Arabs in U.S. Comic Books." *Itchy Planet #1,* Fantagraphics Books, 1988, pp. 11–14.

———. "Race and Comix." *Multicultural Comics: From Zap to Blue Beetle,* edited by Frederick Luis Aldama, U of Texas P, 2010, pp. 27–38.

———. "Racial Imagery, Racism, Individualism, and Underground Comix." *ImageTexT,* vol. 1, no. 1, 2004.

Rosaldo, Renato. *Culture and Truth: The Remaking of Social Analysis.* Beacon Press, 1993.

Rothberg, Michael. *Multidirectional Memory: Remembering the Holocaust in the Age of Decolonization.* Stanford UP, 2009.

Ruillier, Jerome. *The Strange.* 2016. Translated by Helge Dascher, Drawn and Quarterly, 2018.

Sabsay, Leticia. "Permeable Bodies: Vulnerability, Affective Powers, Hegemony." *Vulnerability in Resistance,* edited by Judith Butler et al., Duke UP, 2016, pp. 278–302.

Sacco, Joe. *Palestine.* Fantagraphics, 2001.

Sa'di, Ahmad H., and Lila Abu-Lughod, editors. *Nakba: Palestine, 1948, and the Claims of Memory.* Columbia UP, 2007.

Said, Edward W. *Covering Islam.* Vintage, 1997.

———. "Homage to Joe Sacco." *Palestine,* by Joe Sacco, Fantagraphics, 2001, pp. i–v.

———. "Intifada and Independence." *Social Text*, no. 22, 1989, pp. 23–39.

———. "Invention, Memory, and Place." *Critical Inquiry*, vol. 26, no. 2, 2000, pp. 175–92.

———. "Islam through Western Eyes." *The Nation*, 26 Apr. 1980.

Sajad, Malik. *Munnu: A Boy from Kashmir*. Fourth Estate, 2015.

Salaita, Steven. *Arab American Literary Fictions, Cultures, and Politics*. Palgrave Macmillan, 2007.

———. "Ethnic Identity and Imperative Patriotism: Arab Americans before and after 9/11." *College Literature*, vol. 32, no. 2, 2005, pp. 146–68.

Saldívar, José David. *The Dialectics of Our America: Genealogy, Cultural Critique, and Literary History*. Duke UP, 1991.

Salmi, Charlotta. "The Global Graphic Protest Narrative: India and Iran." *PMLA/Publications of the Modern Language Association of America*, vol. 136, no. 2, 2021, pp. 171–89.

Samanci, Özge. *Dare to Disappoint: Growing up in Turkey*. Farrar, Straus and Giroux, 2015.

Santo, Avi. "'Is It a Camel? Is It a Turban? No, It's the 99': Branding Islamic Superheroes as Authentic Cultural Commodities." *Television & New Media*, vol 15, no. 7, 2014, pp. 679–95.

Sarkar, Sreyoshi. "The Art of Postcolonial Resistance and Multispecies Storytelling in Malik Sajad's Graphic Novel *Munnu: A Boy from Kashmir*." *South Asian Review*, vol. 39, no. 1–2, 2018, pp. 104–24.

Satrapi, Marjane. *The Complete Persepolis*. Pantheon, 2007.

Sattouf, Riad. *The Arab of the Future*. John Murray Press, 2014.

Scarry, Elaine. *The Body in Pain*. Oxford UP, 1987.

Schack, Todd. "'A Failure of Language': Achieving Layers of Meaning in Graphic Journalism." *Journalism*, vol. 15, no. 1, 2014, pp. 109–27.

Schueller, Malini Johar. "Decolonizing Global Theories Today: Hardt and Negri, Agamben, Butler." *Interventions*, vol. 11, no. 2, 2009, pp. 235–54.

Schultheis Moore, Alexandra. "Teaching Mohamedou Ould Slahi's *Guantánamo Diary* in the Human Rights and Literature Classroom." *Radical Teacher: A Socialist, Feminist, and Anti-Racist Journal on the Theory and Practice of Teaching*, no. 104, 2016, pp. 27–37.

Sevcik, Stefanie. "Syrian Women's Prison Art: Toward a Poetics of Creative Insurgency." *In the Crossfire of History: Women's War Resistance Discourse in the Global South*, edited by Lava Asaad and Fayeza Hasanat, Rutgers UP, 2022, pp. 13–39.

Shaheen, Jack G. "Arab Images in American Comic Books." *Journal of Popular Culture*, vol. 28, no. 1, 1994, pp. 123–33.

———. *Arab and Muslim Stereotyping*. Center for Muslim-Christian Understanding, History and International Affairs, Edmund A. Walsh School of Foreign Service, Georgetown University, 1997.

———. "How the Media Created the Muslim Monster Myth." *The Nation* 2–9 July 2012. https://www.thenation.com/article/archive/how-media-created-muslim-monster-myth/.

Shams, Fatemeh. "Dialogues with the Dead: Necropoetics of Zahra's Paradise." *Iranian Studies*, vol. 53, no. 5–6, 2019, pp. 893–909.

Sharma, Alpana. "Paradise Lost in Mission Kashmir: Global Terrorism, Local Insurgencies, and the Question of Kashmir in Indian Cinema." *Quarterly Review of Film and Video*, vol. 25, no. 2, 2008, pp. 124–31.

Sharma, Varad, and Siddhartha Giggoo. *A Long Dream of Home: The Persecution, Exile and Exodus of Kashmiri Pandits*. Bloomsbury India, 2016.

Sinno, Nadine. "Dammit, Jim, I'm a Muslim Woman, Not a Klingon!" *MELUS: The Society for the Study of the Multi-Ethnic Literature of the United States*, vol. 42, no. 1, 2017, pp. 116–38.

Slahi, Mohamedou Ould. *Guantanamo Diary*. Back Bay Books, New York: 2015.

Slaughter, Joseph. *Enabling Fictions and Novel Subjects: The Bildungsroman and International Human Rights Law*. Routledge, 2011.

Smith, Caleb. "Detention without Subjects: Prisons and the Poetics of Living Death." *Texas Studies in Literature and Language*, vol. 50, no. 3, 2008, pp. 243–67.

Sontag, Susan. *Regarding the Pain of Others*. Farrar, Straus, and Giroux, 2003.

Spearey, Susan. "Displacement, Dispossession and Conciliation: The Politics and Poetics of Homecoming in Antjie Krog's *Country of My Skull*." *Scrutiny 2*, vol. 5, no. 1, 2000, pp. 64–77.

Steinhauer, Jillian. "The Outsider: Joe Sacco's Comic Journalism." *The Nation*, 28 Dec. 2020, pp. 36–40.

Strömberg, Fredrik. "'Yo, Rag-Head!': Arab and Muslim Superheroes in American Comic Books after 9/11." *Amerikastudien / American Studies*, vol. 56, no. 4, 2011, pp. 573–601.

Sulaiman, Hamid. *Freedom Hospital: A Syrian Story*. Interlink Books, 2018.

Tabachnick, Stephen E. Introduction. *The Cambridge Companion to the Graphic Novel*, edited by Tabachnick, Cambridge UP, 2017, pp. 1–7.

Taylor, Charles. *Sources of the Self: The Making of the Modern Identity*. Cambridge UP, 1989.

Thompson, Craig. *Habibi*. Pantheon, 2011.

Tossell, Ivor. "Cries from Paradise." *The Globe and Mail*, 5 Mar. 2010, www.theglobeandmail.com/arts/books-and-media/cries-from-paradise/article4309166/.

True Islam. "The Quranic Meaning of the Word 'Shaheed.'" http://www.quran-islam.org/main_topics/misinterpreted_verses/shaheed_(P1229).html.

Tubiana, Jérôme, and Alexandre Franc. *Guantánamo Kid: The True Story of Mohammed El-Gharani*. 2018. Translated by Tubiana and Edward Gauvin, SelfMadeHero, 2019.

Turner, Victor. *From Ritual to Theatre: The Human Seriousness of Play*. PAJ Publications, 1982.

United Nations. Article 53, "Prohibited Destruction." Geneva Convention (IV) Relative to the Protection of Civilian Persons in Time of War, 12 Aug. 1949. *International Humanitarian Law Databases*, https://ihl-databases.icrc.org/en/ihl-treaties/gciv-1949/article-53.

United Nations Relief and Works Agency for Palestine Refugees in the Near East (UNRWA). "Who We Are." https://www.unrwa.org/who-we-are.

United States, Department of Justice, Office of Legal Counsel. *Memorandum for Alberto R. Gonzales: Counsel to the President: Re Standards of Conduct for Interrogation under 18 U.S.C. §§ 2340–2340A*, 1 Aug. 2002, https://www.therenditionproject.org.uk/documents/torture-docs.html.

United States, Congress, House, Committee on Homeland Security, Subcommittee on Oversight and Management Efficiency. *Transferring Guantanamo Bay Detainees to the Homeland: Implications for States and Local Communities.* Government Publishing Office, 2016. 114th Congress, 2nd session, Serial No. 114-66. https://www.govinfo.gov/content/pkg/CHRG-114hhrg22759/html/CHRG-114hhrg22759.htm.

Vaughan-Williams, Nick. *Border Politics: The Limits of Sovereign Power.* Edinburgh UP, 2009.

Versaci, Rocco. "The 'New Journalism' Revisited: Comic Books vs. Reportage." *This Book Contains Graphic Language: Comics as Literature*, Bloomsbury, 2007, pp. 109–35.

Ware, Chris. *Dangerous Drawings: Interviews with Comix and Graphix Artists.* Juno Books, 1997.

"What's the Point of Simon Baz, Green Lantern & Car Thief? (Part 2)." *Too Busy Thinking about My Comics*, 29 Dec. 2012, http://toobusythinkingboutcomics.blogspot.com/2012/12/whats-point-of-simon-baz-green-lantern.html.

Wieviorka, Annette. *The Era of the Witness.* Cornell UP, 2006.

Wilcox, Lauren. "Dying Is Not Permitted: Sovereignty, Biopower, and Force-Feeding at Guantanamo Bay." *Torture: Power, Democracy, and the Human Body*, edited by Shampa Biswas and Zahi Zalloua, U of Washington P, 2011, pp. 101–28.

Wilson, Willow. *Cairo.* Vertigo, 2007.

Wilson, Willow, and Adrian Alphona. *Ms. Marvel: No Normal # 1.* Marvel, 2014.

Worden, Daniel. "Introduction: Drawing Conflicts." *The Comics of Joe Sacco: Journalism in a Visual World*, edited by Daniel Worden, UP of Mississippi, 2015, pp. 3–18.

Yosef, Raz. "War Fantasies: Memory, Trauma and Ethics in Ari Folman's *Waltz with Bashir.*" *Journal of Modern Jewish Studies*, vol. 9, no. 3, 2010, pp. 311–26.

Young, James E. "Interpreting Literary Testimony: A Preface to Rereading Holocaust Diaries and Memoirs." *New Literary History*, vol. 18, no. 2, 1987, pp. 403–23.

"Zahra's Paradise: An Interview with Amir and Khalil." *Jadaliyya*, 13 Sept. 2011, https://www.jadaliyya.com/Details/24389.

Zia, Ather. "'Their Wounds Are Our Wounds': A Case for Affective Solidarity between Palestine and Kashmir." *Identities*, vol. 27, no. 3, 2020, pp. 357–75.

INDEX

Aaron & Ahmed (Cantor, Romberger, Villarrubia), 20, 65, 66–67, 70n10, 71, 77–78, 84, 88
Abdelrazaq, Leila, 4. See also *Baddawi*
Abirached, Zeina, 24–25
abject: condition, 119; Easterner, 48; figure, 6, 67, 75n17, 90, 103, 121n8, 123; Muslim detainee, 20, 63–65, 68–80, 81, 85, 87, 89; refugees, 151
abstraction, 13, 18, 85–87, 89; abstract silhouettes, 166; of violence, 166
aesthetics, ix–xi, xiv, 11, 11n4, 12, 18, 22, 23, 30, 51n29, 99, 177; of violence, 165–68, 167n17; silhouette, 36
Afrofuturism, 176–77
Agamben, Giorgio, 74, 75n17, 76, 78, 85, 86, 106n19, 150, 150n7. See also *homo sacer*
Ahmed, Naseer. See *Kashmir Pending*
Al-Ali, Naji, 148, 148nn5–6
Allam, Norédine, 58
All-Negro Comics, 40n18
Al-Qaeda, 35, 36, 38, 65, 66, 79

America, x, 28n9, 38; American West, xiii, 34n12; culture of, xii, 24; democracy, 40n17; American morals, 36
American comics, 23, 25, 30
Amir, xiv, 4, 14, 15, 18, 20. See also *Zahra's Paradise*
amnesia, 16, 21, 85, 147, 157, 159
aniconism, x, xiv
Anzaldúa, Gloria, 21, 116–17, 116n1, 122, 128, 143n30
Arab, xii, xiin2, 24–28, 24n3, 28n9, 32, 50, 148n6; cartoonists, xiv; characters, 34n13, 35; culture and community, 24, 25; diaspora, 54–55; heritage, 44, 54, 139; language, 74, 123; refugee, 47; stereotypes of, 52, 62–63; studies, 24; terrorist, 49, 52n30; villain, 27; woman, 35; world, 50, 178
Arab Americans, xii, 25, 52
Arab American writing, 24
Arab in America (El Rassi), xiii, 52–56
Arab of the Future (Sattouf), xiii, 117
Arab spring, 144, 178

193

Arabia, 32, 32
Arabic, 33, 34, 44, 50, 74, 123; accent, 66; alphabet, 52; calligraphy, x, 32–34, 43, 73
Arabophobia, 52, 52n30
Arendt, Hannah, 97, 97n9
autobiography, 12, 13, 52, 55
Azadi, 118, 118n4, 124, 125, 128, 140
Azadi Square (Freedom Square), 97

Baddawi (Abdelrazaq), 9, 21, 146, 147–56, 159, 170
bare life, 68, 69, 76, 88, 106, 150
Basij, 91n2, 96, 97
Batman, xii, 27, 28, 40n17
Bayoumi, Moustafa, 35, 64, 71n11
Behesht-e Zahra, 92, 99, 100, 100n12, 107
Black Comics, 174–75
Black Panther, 40n18
border, 5, 8, 15, 21, 46, 101n15, 115–16, 119n6, 123, 124, 126, 126n16, 127n17, 138, 144, 147; borderland, 21, 118, 126, 127, 134, 137, 165; consciousness, 122, 134; crossing, 122, 127, 128, 130, 132–33, 140, 143; discourses, 116n1; existence, 19, 21, 117, 118, 133, 134; hybridity, 123; studies, 134, 137; subject, 117, 145; subjectivity, 117; tales, 134; writing, 142–43, 142n29, 143n30; zone, 115, 117, 138, 169
Botz-Bornstein, Thorsten, 176, 176n2
Boys, The, 172–73
Butler, Judith, 5, 62, 69, 71, 74n13, 94, 94n5, 98, 103
bystander, 158, 158n13, 163, 170n19

Cantor, Jay. See *Aaron & Ahmed*
Captain America, xii, 28, 35, 40n17, 174n1
Carol Danvers, 40
Charlie Hebdo, xi
Christian, 6, 17n7, 25, 49, 149; anti-, 27, 62
Chute, Hillary, 9, 11, 16, 47
citizenship, 24n3, 39; global, 134; ideal, 40n17, 46, 75n17, 97n8, 104, 106, 115; Muslim, 93; participatory, 106; submissive, 97
closure, 13–14

comics studies, 11–13, 22–23
counterarchive, 47
counternarrative, 65–67, 68, 77, 80, 81, 86, 87, 89
Covering Islam (Said), 27, 27n8, 50n28
Culture and Truth (Rosaldo), 117, 117n2

death world, 132, 133, 150, 163, 167
dehumanization, 70, 70n10, 71, 75, 80n22, 81, 85, 101, 106n19, 107, 109, 121
democracy, 15, 92; American, 40n17, 46–47, 62; Iranian, 91–93; Western, 5n3, 41n19
desubjectification, 68–69, 74, 80n22, 106
deterritorial, 138, 138n22, 142
dialogic, 107, 140n26, 146n3, 164
diaspora: Arab, 54; and belonging, 10, 150; existence in, 51n29; Iranian, 178; Palestinian, 170
Díaz, Wendy, 56
Dittmer, Jason, xii
dogs, 64n2, 71, 71n12
domestic, 3, 6, 9, 152, 174
Drowned, The (Primo Levi), 81–82, 123
Dust, 40–42, 41n19, 45

El Rassi, Toufic, xiii, 52–57, 52n30
emigration, 126, 127n18
empathy, 15, 21, 58, 78, 89, 131, 168
enemy combatant, 53, 74n13, 90
ethics, 91, 142; of seeing, 157
everyday life, 6, 97, 154; and camp, 150n8; changes in, 3–14; definition of, 7–10; erasure of, 48; and identity, 49; and mourning, 100; and Muslim experience, 49–50, 60; and religion, 95; and violence, 64; and warscape, 16, 21, 47, 74, 117, 121n9, 137, 152
Evin, 20, 92, 95, 104, 104n18, 105, 106, 109, 109n23. *See also* prison
extremism, x, 39, 122, 126–27, 126n16, 173, 174, 176
ezan, 95, 109

Fahmy, Huda, 56, 56n33
Fawaz, Ramzi, 39, 40n17, 46

Fawstin, Bosch, 37n16. See also *Infidel, The*
focalization, 77, 147, 151, 153n11, 155, 160; variable, 159
Folman, Ari, 21. See also *Waltz with Bashir*
Foucault, Michel, 69, 79n21, 96n6, 125
fragmentation, 52, 84, 117, 143n30, 158
Franc, Alexandre. See *Guantánamo Kid*
Freedom Square, 92n3, 107. *See also* Azadi Square
funeral, 8, 92, 107, 124–25, 130–32, 134, 166

Gantos, Jack, 38
gaze, 10, 22, 33, 34, 41, 41n19, 48, 75, 81, 85, 87, 104, 107, 125, 136, 157, 161, 163, 167; lingering, 153–54
graphic narrative (also graphic novel), ix, xi, xiii, xiv, 3, 4, 11–13, 18, 22, 26n4, 119n6
Green Lantern, 40, 43–44
Guadalupe, Uthman, 56
Guantánamo, 5, 19, 43, 51, 53, 64, 67, 67n6, 68, 71n11, 75, 78–79, 84, 90, 106, 112; comics, 83; counternarratives, 65–67, 80–81, 86, 87, 89, 107; "Guantánamo Limbo," 74n13; warscape, 68–70, 68n8, 75n17, 76, 76n19, 88, 105
Guantánamo Kid (Tubiana and Franc), 20, 51, 65–66, 68–70, 73–74, 76n19, 78, 80n22, 84–86, 88
Guantanamo Voices (Mirk), 20, 65, 66, 71, 71n11, 76–77, 79, 81–82, 87–88
gutters, 13–14, 170

Habibi, 32–34, 34n12
halal, 74
Halpern, Jake. See *Welcome to the New World*
Hamed, Soufeina, 58–59
Handala, 148–49, 148n5
hanguls, 1, 121, 121n8, 130, 133, 141
haram, 71, 71n12
Harari, Youval Noah, 149
Hicks, Emily, 21, 117, 142, 142n29, 143n30
hijab, 43, 172; hijabi, 56–57, 175

Hirsch, Marianne, 147, 154, 154n12, 170
Holocaust, 164, 164n16; narratives, 20; survivors, 74, 164
holography, 142
Holy Terror (Miller), 35–37, 63, 63n1, 79–81
"Homage to Sacco" (Said), ix, 22, 46–47
homo sacer, 78
horrorism, 123, 130, 132–33
human rights, ix, 61, 96n7, 114, 118n3, 121; activists, 68n7
Human Rights Watch, 76n18, 91n2, 106n20, 108n21, 109n23
hybrid token, 30, 39–49
hybridity, 52, 117, 123, 128, 133, 134, 138

iconophobia, x–xi
Infidel, The (Fawstin), 36–37
Intifada, 47, 139, 144, 145
Inzana, Ryan. See *Johnny Jihad*
Iran, ix–x, xiv, 4, 5, 14–15, 18, 28, 49, 50n28, 91, 91n2, 92–114, 96n7, 114–15, 177–78
Iranian Metamorphosis, An (Neyestani), xiv, 20, 90–91, 92–93, 101–3, 111–12, 115
Iran-Iraq War, ix, 13, 100, 101n14, 111
Iron Muslim (Johnston), 37–38
ISIS, 176, 176n2
Islam, xii, 1–3, 5, 17, 17n5, 19, 27n8, 28, 28n9, 30–34, 46, 49, 50, 60, 74, 119, 120, 128n19, 132, 140, 175; and art, x, xn1; culture of, 27; and danger, 37, 42, 50n28; Islamist militancy, 43, 104, 121n7, 122, 140, 149; Islamist state, 20, 95, 115; tenets of, x, 4, 44, 45, 48, 51, 73, 136, 151; and violence, 5n3, 63, 81, 89, 144; and warscape, 11
Islamic Revolutionary Guard Corps (IRGC), 92n3
Islamophobia, xi, 24–26, 26n5, 35–38, 39, 43, 48, 49, 52, 52n30, 54, 63, 90, 173, 174

JanMohamed, Abdul, 121n9, 122, 133
jihad, 17, 121n7, 127n18, 176
jihadi, 5n3, 17, 44, 62, 80, 89, 126n16, 172; camp, 67; characters, 35–39; politics,

43; representations of, 20, 30, 63, 79, 81, 128–30; tropes, 39
jihadism, 17, 38, 126
John Stewart, 40
Johnny Jihad (Inzana), 79, 89, 129
Johnston, Rich. See *Iron Muslim*

Kahf, Mohja, 51, 51n29
Kamala Khan, xiii, 44–46, 45nn24–25, 174, 174n1, 175
Kaplan, Amy, 65n3
Kashmir, 1–3, 5, 8, 20, 21, 117–43, 118nn3–5, 119n16, 121n7, 122n10, 124n14, 126n16, 128n19, 141nn27–28
Kashmir Pending (Ahmed and Singh), 21, 117–22, 119n6, 122n10, 124, 130–43
Kashmiriyat, 21, 119, 126n16, 138–40, 138nn23–24, 140n25
Khomeini, Ayatollah, 97, 99, 103, 107
Kismet: Man of Fate, 30–32, 32n11

Lavender, Isiah, 176–77
Levi, Primo, 74, 77, 81, 83, 86, 123; "new, harsh language," 83, 89. See also *Drowned, The*
Line of Control (LOC), 126, 127n17
liminal, 114–15, 137–38, 147

Mamdani, Mahmood, 39, 49
martyr, ix, 6, 17, 17nn6–7, 21, 83, 99, 100, 100n11, 100n13, 110, 111, 118, 123, 123n12, 124, 132–34, 136
Maus (Spiegelman), 121, 167
Mbembe, Achille, 96, 96n6, 117, 123, 123n13, 127, 132, 150
McKean, Dave, 38
memory, 22, 144, 146–51, 146n3, 160, 168–70; collective, 9; crisis of, 158; defective, 154n12; Holocaust, 164n16; laws, 169; public, 92, 157; and recollection, 84; sensory, 9; traumatic, 164
Middle East, xiin2, xiii, xiv, 9, 11, 25, 26nn4–5, 27, 28n9, 34, 46, 50n28, 65, 176
Miller, Frank. See *Holy Terror*
miniature, x
Mirk, Sarah. See *Guantanamo Voices*
Mohammad, Prophet, x, 5n3, 17, 35, 37, 130

Moloch, 104
morgue, 98, 98n10, 132, 133, 134
mosque, 1, 21, 44, 45, 54, 66, 128n19
Munnu (Sajad), 1–3, 8, 21, 117–22, 122n11, 127n17, 130–43, 147, 165
Muselmann, 6, 20, 67n6, 68–69, 74–89, 90, 105, 112, 123
Muslim binary, "good" vs. "bad," 39–40, 41n19, 43–44, 46, 49, 56, 80n22, 95
Muslim Americans, 35n14, 43–44, 45–46
Muslim American writing, 24, 51n29
multidirectional memory, 146, 146n3

nafs, 136
Nakba, 145, 145n1, 146, 154
namaz, 73, 125
nation, x, 2, 4, 8, 9, 21, 25, 26, 27, 37, 46, 55, 60, 65n3, 93, 106, 115, 127, 128, 134, 138, 157, 170, 177, 178; building, 14, 40n17, 139, 141n28; Muslim, 3, 99; national security, 92; national trauma, 63n1
nationalism, 40n17, 95, 100, 122
nationalist, 100n11, 115, 126, 128n19, 138, 169
native, 1, 23, 40, 43, 90, 121, 121n9, 170
Nayar, Pramod K., 3, 67, 70, 124, 133, 135
necropolitics, 139; aesthetics of, 99; conditions of, 107, 123–25, 132, 144, 148, 150, 152, 154, 161, 165; logic of, 124n14; mechanisms of, 104; necropolitical power of the state, 96–98, 110, 124, 136; and theocracy, 99, 103, 111, 125; necropolitical trap, 163; and warscape, 118, 141
new journalism, 48, 48n26
Neyestani, Mana, xiii, 20, 21, 90–92. See also *Iranian Metamorphosis, An*
9/11, xii, 24, 26n5, 27, 32, 35, 35n14, 36, 38, 40, 43, 52, 63, 66; post-9/11, 42
99, The (Al-Mutawa), 175
Nordstrom, Carol, 3, 61

Oliver, Kelly, 16
Orientalism, 41, 42n20, 49, 55, 175
Osama bin Laden, 37, 52, 55, 67
otherness, 26–27, 75; Orientalized, 26n4, 30–34, 34n12

INDEX • 197

Palestine (Sacco), ix, 22, 46, 48, 139
Pamuk, Orhan, x
Pandits, 8, 138, 138nn23–24
perpetrator, 5, 16, 39, 63, 142, 158, 158n13, 161, 166, 167, 170n19, 173
Persepolis (Satrapi), ix–xi, xiv–xv, 8–9, 13, 93
photograph, 1, 64, 66, 71, 93, 98, 163, 165, 167, 168
photorealism, 47, 103
Platt Agreement, 65n3
point of view, 153, 173
Polak, Kate, 13
postcolonial, 52, 60, 124n14, 137
Postema, Barbara, 13
posthumanism, 46
postmemory, 18, 21–22, 146–48, 151, 154–56, 163–64, 169
prison, 20, 43, 53, 57, 62–89, 68n8, 70n10, 71n11, 74n13, 75–76nn16–19, 79n21. See also Evin
propaganda, 100, 110, 128n19, 133, 134, 146, 157, 171

Qur'an, x, 17, 17nn5–6, 32, 33, 35, 35n15, 37, 71, 73, 80, 81, 95

race, xii, 4, 24–26, 49, 52, 54, 63, 71, 71n11, 116, 138, 176
racialization, xiin3, 3, 24, 54, 71n11
racism, xii, 24, 26, 26n7, 30, 43, 55, 71n11
Rafsanjani, Ali Akbar, 97
recognition (politics of), 11, 14, 16, 78, 80n22, 135, 146, 146n3, 165, 169; misrecognition, 53
refugee, 20, 113, 147, 150, 151, 154, 161, 163, 170; Arab, 47; camp, 21, 41, 145–46, 148n5, 149, 157, 161, 166, 170; Muslim, 156; Palestinian, 4, 22, 55, 148–49; Syrian, xiii, 57
regime, 18, 91–93, 91n1, 92n3, 111, 113
regional belonging, 21
regional identity, 114, 138–40
regionalism, 123, 139, 143
regional rituals, 49, 170
regional struggle, 135
resistance, 6, 58, 90–98, 124, 134, 174; artistic, 101; collective, 16, 103; emblem of, 18; Islamist, 140; limited, 80n22, 113; movements, 144; political, 94n5, 104n18, 115, 118, 137, 139; and speaking, 173; and witnessing, 110–13. See also vulnerability
revolution, ix, 8, 65n3, 91n1, 93, 113
Rifas, Leonard, xii, 11, 24, 26, 26n7, 27
ritual, 1, 4, 6, 8, 11, 44, 49, 71, 73, 124, 125, 127, 132, 150
Romberger, James. See *Aaron & Ahmed*
Rosaldo, Renato. See *Culture and Truth*
Rothberg, Michael, 146, 146n3, 164, 171

Sabra and Shatila massacre, 22, 157, 163, 168
Sacco, Joe, 48n27, 57, 148, 148n6. See also *Palestine*
Said, Edward, ix, 22, 26n4, 27, 27n8, 34n12, 46–50, 60, 165. See also *Covering Islam*; "Homage to Sacco"
Sajad, Malik, xiii, 121n9, 122, 122n10, 144, 169, 178. See also *Munnu*
Satrapi, Marjane. See *Persepolis*
Scarry, Elaine, 79
Secret of My Hijab, The, (Díaz and Guadalupe), 56
secular, 4n2, 15, 16, 17, 45, 49, 54, 60, 91, 115, 118n5, 126n16, 138, 140n25, 173; postsecular, 4
self-sacrifice, 17, 123, 123n13, 126, 130. See also martyr
sequential art, xiii, 11n4, 23, 26n4
shaheed, 6, 17, 17n6, 21, 80, 100, 110, 111, 123–26, 123nn12–13, 132–39, 140, 142, 143
Shaheen, Jack G., xii, 24, 27–28, 62
silence, 16, 57, 60, 89, 97, 107, 109, 128, 137, 155, 159, 165, 167, 169
Singh, Saurabh. See *Kashmir Pending*
Slaughter, Joseph, 61
Sloan, Michael. See *Welcome to the New World*
society, xiii
Sontag, Susan, 167, 168
Sooraya Qadir. See *Dust*
space of appearance, 97, 97n9
Spiegelman, Art. See *Maus*
spiritual, 3, 4n2, 37, 44, 54, 74, 119, 120, 127
state of exception, 68, 76, 124, 150, 150n7

stateless, 19, 21, 46, 145, 147, 148, 170
stereotype, 28, 71n11, 176
stone pelting, 137
Suicide Bomber Sits in the Library, A, 38
suicide-bombing, 38, 67, 140
Superman, 25, 40n17
superhero, 26n5, 32, 35, 36, 37, 39, 40–46, 40nn17–18, 45n24, 54, 57, 89, 172–73, 175, 176
supervillain, 28, 35, 62

Taliban, 41, 41n19
tatreez, 170
territorial, 115, 138, 138n22, 143
terror, 70n10, 78, 80, 108, 127
terrorism, 5, 39, 48, 52n30, 81, 104, 123, 125n15, 126, 126n16, 130, 132–33, 144
terrorist, xii, xiin2, 10, 25, 27, 28, 35–39, 35n14, 43, 44, 49, 52, 54, 62, 63, 64, 66, 74n13, 79n21, 104n16, 119, 160; post-terrorist, 119n16
testimony, 128, 148, 151, 151n10, 152; of border witness, 144; embodied, 84; false, 91, 111, 113; and fiction, 18, 154n12; of others, 169; personal, 46; political, 18; power of, 87; and propaganda, 21; religious, 17; as resistance, 173; value of, 83, 154n12; witness, 16, 18, 22, 83, 92, 110, 159, 167
theocratic state, 4, 92, 93, 95, 104, 111
Thompson, Craig. See *Habibi*
token, xiv; hybrid, 30, 39–44
tombstone, 97, 118, 133–34, 165
torture, 14, 20, 27, 57, 63, 74–80, 76n18, 78n20, 79n21, 84–88, 93, 104n16, 108, 108n21, 109n22, 111; waterboarding, 77, 81; white, 108
trauma, xiv, 83, 86, 89, 104, 114, 141n28, 151, 151n10, 154n12, 158, 159, 163–64, 170, 178; and amnesia, 85, 147, 157; and border existence, 134; collective, 122, 134, 135, 140n26; and comics, 16; cultural, 155; effects of, 16; experts, 159; and guilt, 103; historical, 146; national, 36, 63n1; and postmemory, 18; representations of, 10; traumatized Muslim, 42, 65; and war, 9; and warscape, 61, 142, 173; and witnessing, 117, 158, 165
trauma aesthetic, 167
traumatic, 150; effects of torture, 108n21; events, 147, 151, 158n13, 166; experience, 149, 168; memory, 164; reality, 10, 61; silence, 107; stories, 136; violence, 131
tribalism, 138
Tubiana, Jérôme. See *Guantánamo Kid*

ummah, 4, 25, 44n23, 50, 54, 95, 128n19, 177

veil, x, 8–9, 10, 41, 56, 93, 174. See also hijab
Villarrubia, Jose. See *Aaron & Ahmed*
vulnerability, 6, 16, 20, 61, 93–95, 93n4, 94n5, 97, 99, 105–9; vulnerability-resistance dialectic, 90–91, 95, 103, 110–14

Waltz with Bashir (Folman), 146–47, 156–68, 169, 170, 170n19
War on Terror, 43, 49, 63
Welcome to the New World (Halpern and Sloan), 57–58, 58n35
witness: border, 117, 118, 123, 133–40, 141–43, 144, 169, 170; complete, 82–83; eye-, 16, 18, 135, 147, 149, 166; false, 18, 20–21, 90, 91, 109–13, 115; flesh, 149–53, 159, 160, 166; immediate, 148; recollecting, 150–52; reluctant, 20, 86, 88–90, 107; surrogate, 21, 83, 147–48, 151–52, 156, 159–66, 168–70; true, 81, 82, 83, 123

za'atar, 9–10, 150
Zahra's Paradise (Amir and Khalil), xiv, 4, 14, 18, 20–21, 90–91, 97–101, 98n10, 100n12, 104n17, 106–14, 115, 177–78
zombie, 20, 37, 69, 75, 95, 106, 133

STUDIES IN COMICS AND CARTOONS
Jared Gardner, Charles Hatfield, and Rebecca Wanzo, Series Editors
Lucy Shelton Caswell, Founding Editor Emerita

Books published in Studies in Comics and Cartoons focus exclusively on comics and graphic literature, highlighting their relation to literary studies. The series includes monographs and edited collections that cover the history of comics and cartoons from the editorial cartoon and early sequential comics of the nineteenth century through webcomics of the twenty-first. Studies that focus on international comics are also considered.

Muslim Comics and Warscape Witnessing
  ESRA MIRZE SANTESSO

Beyond the Icon: Asian American Graphic Narratives
  EDITED BY ELEANOR TY

Comics and Nation: Power, Pop Culture, and Political Transformation in Poland
  EWA STAŃCZYK

How Comics Travel: Publication, Translation, Radical Literacies
  KATHERINE KELP-STEBBINS

Resurrection: Comics in Post-Soviet Russia
  JOSÉ ALANIZ

Authorizing Superhero Comics: On the Evolution of a Popular Serial Genre
  DANIEL STEIN

Typical Girls: The Rhetoric of Womanhood in Comic Strips
  SUSAN E. KIRTLEY

Comics and the Body: Drawing, Reading, and Vulnerability
  ESZTER SZÉP

Producing Mass Entertainment: The Serial Life of the Yellow Kid
  CHRISTINA MEYER

The Goat-Getters: Jack Johnson, the Fight of the Century, and How a Bunch of Raucous Cartoonists Reinvented Comics
  EDDIE CAMPBELL

Between Pen and Pixel: Comics, Materiality, and the Book of the Future
  AARON KASHTAN

Ethics in the Gutter: Empathy and Historical Fiction in Comics
  KATE POLAK

Drawing the Line: Comics Studies and INKS, 1994–1997
  EDITED BY LUCY SHELTON CASWELL AND JARED GARDNER

The Humours of Parliament: Harry Furniss's View of Late-Victorian Political Culture
  EDITED AND WITH AN INTRODUCTION BY GARETH CORDERY AND JOSEPH S. MEISEL

Redrawing French Empire in Comics
  MARK McKINNEY

www.ingramcontent.com/pod-product-compliance
Lightning Source LLC
Chambersburg PA
CBHW020332240426
43665CB00043B/444